Recreation and Leisure for Persons with Emotional Problems and Challenging Behaviors

Carol Ann Baglin
M. E. B. Lewis
Buzz Williams

Cover Design: Janet Wahlfeldt
Interior Design: Janet Wahlfeldt

Library of Congress Catalog Card Number: 2003112438
ISBN: 1-57167-521-3

Printed in the United States

10 9 8 7 6 5 4 3 2 1

Contents

Acknowledgments

The twenty-fifth anniversary of the Individuals with Disabilities Education Act (IDEA) was celebrated this past year. It is sometimes difficult to predict the profound impact of a single act, yet because of this important piece of legislation, all children with disabilities have access to education and full inclusion opportunities. There are additional landmark pieces of legislation which have had similar impact on community and employment, including the Rehabilitation Act of 1973, section 504, and the Americans with Disabilities Act.

Each of the individuals who contributed to this book have a deep commitment and extensive professional history working in the fields of special education and recreation. This unique blending of these fields has provided us an exceptional professional opportunity at this point in our lives. The long-term commitment and investment of our energies over these two decades have contributed to us personally and professionally. This kind of commitment over the long haul cannot be measured in years, only through the individual gains of children and their families.

An Overview

Carol Ann Baglin

For many families, the concepts of mental illness and mental health problems are incompatible with their daily expectations and perceptions of family life. The symptoms are not obvious, such as a fever or blood. Mental health issues can be overwhelming for families and community systems, and affect children of all ages, creating a nationwide crisis for families (Surgeon General, 2001). Children demonstrating behaviors that do not respond to typical disciplinary interventions and children who are assaultive and aggressive stress the resources of the family, the school, and the community. It is of little comfort to most families that many of the problems associated with mental illness are not the result of parenting or an identified precipitating event and that, in fact, there may be biological or other environmental causes, which are external to the family.

The early recognition of emotional and behavioral problems can prevent the development of long-term associated issues. However, the causes of many of these problems are not easily determined. The literature suggests the importance of focusing on prevention and early intervention services to help the children and to assist families to cope with the emotional challenges (Kutash, Duchnowski, Sumi, Rudo, & Harris, 2002; National Center for Children in Poverty, 2002; Walbrath, Nickerson, Crowel, & Leaf, 1998) and to prevent the onset of more serious problems (Schoenholtz, 2000).

Who are the Children?

While estimates vary, in 2001 Surgeon General David Satcher (Surgeon General, 2001) reported that from 16 to 22 percent of children had mental health problems. Many of these children are referred to as emotionally disturbed, socially maladjusted, behaviorally challenged, conduct disordered, or anti-social oppositional. The disorders may be designated by a variety of terms in the mental health system and community; however, the Individuals with Disabilities Education Act (IDEA), reauthorized in 1997, defines emotional disturbance as follows:

(i)   The term means a condition exhibiting one or more of the following characteristics over a long period of time and to a marked degree that adversely affects a child's educational performance:
  (A)   An inability to learn that cannot be explained by intellectual, sensory, or health factors.
  (B)   An inability to build or maintain satisfactory interpersonal relationships with peers and teachers.
  (C)   Inappropriate types of behavior or feelings under normal circumstances.
  (D)   A general pervasive mood of unhappiness or depression.
  (E)   A tendency to develop physical symptoms or fears associated with personal or school problems.
(ii)   The term includes schizophrenia. The term does not apply to children who are socially maladjusted, unless it is determined that they have an emotional disturbance (Assistance to States for the Education of Children with Disabilities).

For the school year 1999-2000, 469,907 children were identified as students with emotional disturbance in the public schools (U.S. Department of Education, 2001). Prevalence rates within school age children for mental, emotional, and behavior disorders are estimated to range between 14% to 20% (Walbrath, Nickerson, Crowel, & Leaf, 1998).

Schools are now educating increasing numbers of students who are more different from than similar to each other. These challenges confront a school environment ill equipped to effectively manage behaviors when teachers are focusing on student achievement and learning. Yet every student and parent longs for the teacher who will make a difference in their lives, who will care in and out of school. The teacher who makes a call with good news, who dares to make a home visit just to establish contact, and the conference rooted in the caring school/parent relationship are the exceptions to today's school experience.

Schools focus on implementing classroom management strategies to influence behavior to focus on instruction and curriculum. Through example, teachers can use direct teaching of social problem solving within the classroom setting to model and resolve the more management behaviors manifest in the classroom. Schoolwide programs involving the student body and staff in identifying goals and addressing training reduce office referrals and vandalism. One of the most effective interventions targets parent involvement and counseling through a system of rewards and contingency contracting (NICHCY, 1999).

As more students with severe and increasingly complex problem behaviors are being identified, teachers and administrators are overwhelmed. For these students, suspension is the commonly used strategy, yet it is one of the most frequent reasons students drop out of school. The use of punishment is among the least effective responses to violent behavior in schools, yet there are so few effective behavioral strategies available within the schools and the community.

Recreation and Leisure Interventions

Recreation and leisure provide expanded opportunities for children with emotional and behavior problems to participate successfully within in-school programs as well as family- and community-based experiences. The importance of leisure activities in the development of positive social skills is recognized across all segments of our communities, our states, and this nation (Hibben, 1984; Thompson & Wade, 1974). Outdoor education offers benefits with a full range of programs in the school and the community (Lappin, 1997) free of classroom limitations. Outdoor education offers a broad range of benefits to children with behavior disorders, from simple, school activities to wilderness and camping experiences. In a study of 16 students with emotional problems in a public high school, students participated in a holistic approach incorporating academics, art, parents, and a humanistic philosophy (Schoenholtz, 2000) to address psychological problems. Recreation therapy consists of more than just the hands-on application of knowledge, requiring a broader approach impacting health care and education (Brasile, Skalko, & Burlingame, 1998).

Recreational theory embraces the natural interwoven nature of joy, discovery, and the positive impact on mental health. The word "recreation" comes from the Latin "recreare" which means to restore or renew. Each of us finds opportunities through many varieties of sports and leisure activities to express our individuality and refresh our spirits. James (1998) describes ancient teachings from the times of Plato extolling the benefits of recreation experiences. Both Florence Nightingale and physician Benjamin Rush in the 19th century integrated recreation as an important component in the recovery of patients. In the 1890s, following a period of intense immigration and urbanization, reformers expanded recreation opportunities in an effort to improve society. In 1907, the first issue of *Playgrounds* (renamed *Recreation*) was published and 'play' became the focus of recreation specialists. During this same period, social worker Neva Boyd identified the useful contribution of recreation experiences to the social and behavioral development of youth (James, 1998).

The World Wars precipitated the ongoing application of physical rehabilitation through recreation workers in varied hospital settings. In the early 1900s Karl Menninger (Menninger Clinic, 1995) facilitated the integration of recreation therapy techniques as a component of the team to address the mental health problems of patients and improve their overall functioning.

Throughout the 1900s recreational therapy was introduced into a variety of settings to improve self-control and self-confidence and include the development of the public recreation movement in community and school settings. In 1929, Johan Huizinga asserted that play was an end unto itself and helped to establish recreation experiences as beneficial in themselves. In 1945 G. Ott Romney moved the field of recreation into the mainstream, seeking to enhance recreation opportunities and facilities as an individual right and a public obligation (James, 1998). The professional tensions between recreation as leisure or as recreational therapy continued throughout the late 1990s, with growth in both the business of recreation and the practice of recreation therapy directed to specific treatment outcomes.

Recreation continues as an important outlet for the disabled in their everyday life and to their self-esteem. In fact, for many disabled, the opportunity for participation in sports is a key to their social and emotional well-being. Like everyone else today, individuals with disabilities have more time to pursue leisure and to socialize with friends.

The importance of leisure and recreation opportunities is well known by professionals and others who work with children who have special needs and disabilities. For example, in the area of rehabilitation, the teaching of leisure skills is critical, as free time often increases during the rehabilitation process. In a similar manner, young children who are in special education need to learn how to utilize leisure activities and experiences as a prelude to maximizing their non-school hours. Outdoor recreation and sports programs in the community are just beginning to acknowledge the existence of populations of children with disabilities. The integration of these children into these community experiences has been slow in coming but appears to be moving in a positive direction. Barriers do exist in accessing and participating in leisure and recreational opportunities, particularly for the very youngest of our children and their families. While physical barriers predominate, expectations and opportunity are just opening for all persons with disabilities. For children with behavior disorders, gains have been noted in self-concept, social adjustment, academic achievement, and group relationships (Lappin, 1997) in addition to improved relationships with peers, parents, and teachers.

Recreation for everyone is accessed through public and private organizations and represents a range of activities from arts and crafts, book clubs, sports, competitive games, and professional teams. This diversity of opportunities presents challenges for change. These goals can be reached through a broad array of programs, including long-and short-term residential programs and camping experiences. Camping, hiking, rock climbing, repelling, canoeing, rafting and backpacking are activities which can be implemented with children with novice abilities and limited exceptional abilities (Lappin, 1997).

Helping the Family, Schools, and Communities

Families need help in understanding their children's behaviors and how to seek assistance from mental health professionals. The complex nature of mental health problems pervades these children's lives and impacts their families. Parents may first encounter the call from school because of behavioral problems. Many students experience a wide range of school problems but unfortunately many experience external and internal barriers that all too often also interfere with learning (Adelman & Taylor, 2002). Increasingly these teachers and students are expected to achieve and be accountable for their performance.

One of the key components within this framework is early and effective intervention for behaviors that impact learning. This reflects an increasing shift from the pathology of mental illness to the strengths-based approach of mental health (Koller & Svoda, 2002). Behavioral expectations and patterns can be taught like academic skills. Any discussion of intervention must address the educational implications of emotional problems and related challenging behaviors that impact academics, peer interactions, and discipline problems. Understanding behaviors and developing practical approaches to oppositional and challenging problems require the use of positive behavioral interventions within this comprehensive framework.

Increasingly, schools and communities are confronting the real challenges of children whose behaviors are so difficult and whose emotional problems are so severe that the everyday solutions are not effective. These are children who are not just defiant or acting out. These are children with behaviors which exceed the capacity of schools and communities to address in the context of the regular school day or the typical community setting. Some of these are students with disabilities receiving special education, some of these are students with antisocial and acting-out behaviors, and some are involved with the juvenile justice system. There is a heightened awareness of the importance of antisocial behavior and the negative outcomes for schools and society. Many of these children are threatening their peers or staff. Children are attacking school personnel causing serious injury. Parents lock their doors at night so that they can feel safe from their own children. Schools have metal detectors and juvenile/probation officers on site. Police patrol the halls and supervise the parking lots.

Preventing the onset of the more complex aspects of school failure necessitates integrated and effective strategies. Outdoor education is an innovative curriculum approach that provides unique benefits to students with behavior and emotional problems (Lappin, 1997).

Addressing the Issues

The Individuals with Disabilities Education Act (IDEA) requires that positive behavioral interventions and supports be developed by the Individualized Education Program (IEP) team to address problem behaviors that impede learning. Chronic behavior problems impact significantly on the school environment and require organized and systematic interventions. Promising interventions for students with challenging behaviors are increasingly the focus of research. Application of behavioral analysis through the use of positive behavioral supports can be effective with a wide range of social and academic problems (Sugai & Horner, 2002). This focus broadened interventions beyond individual students to a more systemic approach that supports the achievement of students while at the same time preventing problem behaviors for all students. There is a long-term outcome for society if all students have improved behavior and achievement. The post-school outcomes of graduates with behavioral disorders are below their peers, with few successfully completing any form of postsecondary education programs (Malmgren, Edgar, & Neel, 1998).

Interventions for students with challenging behaviors include a wide range of educational and behavioral strategies that are addressed throughout these chapters. Chapter 2, ***Characteristics and Needs of Students with Emotional Problems and Challenging Behaviors,*** provides an overview of issues related to students with emotional problems and challenging behaviors. Specific references are made to types of eligibility, services, and the national and state perspectives. Behavioral interventions and strategies provided to encourage inclusion in general education and the curriculum. General principles of supporting emotional development and applicable strategies for intervention are reviewed, using opportunities in recreation and leisure. A review of primary and adolescence causation and manifestations are provided to assist in diagnosis and specific points of interventions. Suggestions for using family recreational activities to facilitate mental health are provided. This chapter also includes the distinctive needs of children with emotional disorders with and without accompanying behavioral problems and the individuals who are primarily behaviorally disordered. A checklist for behavioral interventions is included.

Functional Assessments of Problem Behaviors, Chapter 3, defines the requirements for a functional behavior assessment and the behavioral intervention plan. Major components of this chapter are the descriptions of current policies and practices, the articulation of the need for early recognition, and the management of problem behaviors in school, community, and leisure settings.

Chapter 4, ***Recreation and Leisure Strategies,*** addresses recreational and leisure activities for families and children with emotional problems and behavioral issues, in addition to their family members. Recommended modifications and accommodations are given to assist in providing community and school opportunities. Also, options available to families, including appropriate settings suggestions are provided. Families are encouraged to take advantage of recreational, social, and leisure opportunities within their communities. A major component of this chapter is focused on providing practical recreation and leisure information and options to enable participation with peers and to allow the family to enjoy recreation and leisure activities while including children with emotional and behavioral problems.

In Chapter 5, ***Development of Recreation and Leisure Skills Through Art Interventions,*** a therapeutic art intervention approach to implementing special education services with specific considerations for students with challenging behaviors is described. Utilization of art therapy and related interventions and play therapy models with children can be an effective strategy for providing recreation and leisure and special education services.

An overview of collaborative teaming and the utilization of interagency services are provided in Chapter 6, ***Collaborative Intervention: Creating Interagency Partnerships.*** The capacity-building process will address academic, social, affective, and community strategies, including accessing alternative programming and funding options. A discussion of the opportunities for settings for implementation will be provided, including the school, residential treatment center, nonpublic schools, home, and the community

Chapter 7, ***Treatment Models with Recreation and Leisure Components,*** examines the unique needs of children and adolescents with emotional problems and challenging behaviors. Also included in this chapter are curricular implications, strategies and techniques related to developing recreational and leisure skills, use of community facilities and programs, sample activities, and ideas to promote sibling play. Homemade equipment design, thematic units, checklists, and resources are provided as curricula ideas for professionals and parents, including selecting toys for quality play and activities for infants and toddlers that address their unique needs.

A hands-on approach to implementing management strategies for students with emotional problems and challenging behaviors is presented in Chapter 8, ***Implications for Education and Community Providers***. Discussions specific to the full range of options for the provision of intervention through identified services are provided.

Chapter 9, ***Resources***, presents a comprehensive list of curriculum ideas, books, activities, Internet resources, parent support organizations and programs. Additional information will be presented in a usable format related to the use of medications for treatment, state level organizations, and useful contacts.

A variety of useful appendices are included for support and application within the community.

References

Assistance to States for the Education of Children with Disabilities, 34 CFR § 300.7(4), (1999).

Adelman, H. S., & Taylor, L. (2002). Building comprehensive, multifaceted, and integrated approaches to address barriers to student learning. *Childhood Education Infancy Through Early Adolescence Annual Theme, Association for Childhood Educational International, 78*(5), 261-268.

Brasile, F., Skalko, T. K., & Burlingame, J. (1998). *Perspectives in Recreational Therapy: Issues of a Dynamic Profession.* Ravansdale, WA: Idyll Arbor, Inc.

Hibben, J. (1984). Movement as musical expression in a music therapy setting. *The Journal of Music Therapy Perspectives, 4*(1), 91-97.

Koller, J. R., & Svoboda, S. K. (2002). The application of a strengths-based mental health approach in schools. *Childhood Education Infancy Through Early Adolescence Annual Theme, Association for Childhood Educational International, 78*(5), 291-294.

Kutash, K., Duchnowski, A. J., Sumi, W. C., Rudo, A., & Harris, K. M. (2002). A school, family, and community collaborative program for children who have emotional disturbances. *Journal of Emotional and Behavioral Disorders, 10*(2), 99-107.

Lappin, E. (1997). Outdoor education for behavior disordered students. ERIC Digest. Retrieved June 7, 2002, from Kid Source OnLine. Web site: http://www.kidsource.com/kidsource/content2/Outdoor.Education.ld.k12.3.html

Malmgren, K., Edgar, E., & Neel, R. S. (1998). Postschool status of youths with behavioral disorders. *Behavioral Disorders, 23*(4), 257-263.

Menninger Clinic. (1995). A national resource. Topeka, KS: Menninger Clinic.

National Center for Children in Poverty. 2002). Promoting the emotional well-being of children and families, Policy paper #4, New York, NY: Author.

Robbins, J., (1998). How to calm a child. *Parade Magazine.* June 28, 1998, 10-11.

Schoenholtz, S. W. (2000). Teaching as treatment: A holistic approach for adolescents with psychological problems. *Preventing School Failure, 45*(1), 25-30.

Sugai, G., & Horner, R. H. (2002). Introduction to the special series on positive behavior support in schools. *Journal of Emotional and Behavioral Disorders, 10*(3), 130-135.

Surgeon General of the United States. (2001). *Report of the Surgeon General's conference on children's mental health: A national action agenda.* Available online at: *www.surgeongeneral.gov/topics/cmh/defaut.htm.*

Thompson, A. R., & Wade, M. G. (1974). Real play and fantasy play as modified by social and environmental complexity in normal and hyperactive children. *Therapeutic Recreation Journal, 8*(4), 160-167.

U.S. Department of Education. (2001). Twenty-third Annual Report to Congress on the Implementation of the Individuals with Disabilities Education Act.

Walrath, C. M., Nickerson, K. J., Crowel, R. L., & Leaf, P. J. (1998). Serving children with serious emotional disturbance in a system of care: Do mental health and non-mental health agency referrals look the same? *Journal of Emotional and Behavioral Disorders, 6*(4), 205-213.

Characteristics and Needs of Students with Emotional Problems and Challenging Behaviors

M. E. B. Lewis

Buzz Williams

Emotional and Behavioral Aspects in School

Everything is behavior. Behavior is our response to our environment. Choosing to interact with someone or something, or choosing to ignore someone or something, is a matter of choice, and our response is a behavior. *All humans behave -* children, adolescents, and adults.

With the recent review and reauthorization of the Individuals with Disabilities Education Act, known as IDEA '97, the structure for delivering services to students who may have special needs in these behavioral aspects of school performance and participation, has been clarified and expanded. Students with special needs are often included in the general educational environment, using the general education curriculum of their peers. Accommodations or adjustments may be provided in the classroom, including special instructional techniques, specific materials, assistive technology or specialized behavior management programs.

In addition, related services, such as counseling or therapeutic interventions such as individual or group therapy, play therapy, art, music or movement therapies, or family counseling might be part of the educational plan for the student. In classrooms throughout the country, students display their emotions and act on them. Usually, the combination of effective behavioral systems used by teachers, clearly defined limits and rules for being a member of the learning community that is the class, work for most students. There are some students, however, who do not express their emotions or display behaviors that are more challenging for the teacher to manage. These can be non-compliant behaviors, such as refusing to participate in activities, openly defying the teacher's authority, or disrupting the classroom with physical or verbal aggression.

Not all of these behaviors may intrude or disrupt the progress of other students, but they do require the attention of educators and others who have responsibility for assisting children in their development—academically and socially. Some children are not very social or friendly, and need encouragement to join in activities and share their insights and act as a member of the class. From the earliest childhood education settings, such as preschools or nursery schools, the behaviors of the children require assessment and management. This organization, structure, and reinforcement of the social behaviors of the children can impact on them as they go through the rest of their school career.

As children become adolescents, emotions and behaviors grow and change. If the student has distorted perceptions about himself or herself, or misperceives the actions of others, the resulting acts on their part can range from isolated to dangerous. Again, the educational program of such students must be supported with activities out of school that provide social growth, appropriate formation of relationships, and opportunities for students to learn to make reasonable choices.

Defining Emotional Problems and Challenging Behaviors

In school settings it is necessary to distinguish between behaviors that respond to efficient management systems and those that go beyond the scope of such systems. It is also necessary for teachers to recognize when students have emotional problems that go beyond the scope of temporary frustration or loss, and are actually manifestations of severe distress requiring the attention of a mental health professional or behavior specialist.

Since the mid-70s, federal and state laws have provided for the special educational needs of students with disabilities. The concept of inclusion, which maintains students who might otherwise be excluded from general curriculum settings because of learning or behavioral problems, demands greater vigilance on the part of teachers, counselors, administrators and parents to provide meaningful instructional and social opportunities.

With inclusion has come greater variability of temperament and ability in classrooms, and as a result, a new social order has emerged. Additionally, there is a greater demand for teachers and others in the school to know what their challenges are in managing the learning and social behaviors of students.

Here is a list of disorders and challenging behaviors that may be manifested as emotional, social or behavioral problems:

- *Pervasive Developmental Disorders*, including autism and Asperger's Disorder
- *Attention Deficit Disorder and Attention Deficit Disorder with Hyperactivity* (ADD and ADHD)
- *Conduct Disorder* (CD) and *Oppositional/Defiant Disorder* (ODD)
- *Anxiety Disorders,* including Obsessive-Compulsive Disorder (OCD) and Post-Traumatic Stress Disorder (PTSD)
- *Eating Disorders,* such as Anorexia Nervosa, Bulimia Nervosa, and Obesity
- *Mood Disorders,* such as Depression or Bipolar Disorder
- *Other challenging disorders,* such as Tourette's syndrome, Motor Tic Disorder, Selective Mutism, Attachment Disorder, and Separation Anxiety Disorder
- *Self-injurious, suicidal and homicidal behaviors*
- *Delinquency*

A more comprehensive look at these disorders from the diagnostic perspective is found in Chart 2-1.

Let us look at these disorders and the challenges they present, in school, at home and in the community. Keep in mind that some children and adolescents have more than one disorder at the same time.

Pervasive Developmental Disorders (PDDs)

This group of disorders is characterized by social and language deficits that may range from mild to severe. Included in this spectrum of disorders is *autism*, a severe impairment of social and communication skills affecting an individual's ability to learn. Another condition is *Asperger's Disorder*, in which the individual shows many features of autism in social interactions and behavior, but with little to no impairment in language, communication and cognitive skills. *Pervasive Developmental Disorder—Not Otherwise Specified (NOS)*, denotes individuals who have many of the features of autism as children, but with a later onset (autism's onset is prior to

Chart 2.1

Components of a Comprehensive Assessment of the Behaviors of Children and Adolescents (from Achenbach) (Derived From The CBCL)

Category	Diagnoses & Brief Clinical Definitions
Mental Retardation	• Mild—IQ 50-70 with limitations in adaptive functioning • Moderate—IQ 35-50 with limitations in adaptive functioning • Severe—IQ 20-35 with limitations in adaptive functioning • Profound—IQ below 20 with limitations in adaptive functioning
Learning Disorders	• Reading—Standardized Reading test scores significantly below peers of the same age • Math— Standardized Math test scores significantly below peers of the same age • Written Expression-- Standardized Writing test scores significantly below peers of the same age
Motor Skills Disorder	• Developmental Coordination Disorder—Marked impairment of motor coordination such that performance (crawling, walking etc.) is significantly below peers of the same age
Communication Disorders	• Expressive Language—Limited vocabulary, errors in tense, difficulty recalling words • Phonological Disorder—Incorrect pronunciation considering age and dialect • Stuttering—Disturbance in fluency and time patterning of speech, (i.e. repetition of syllables, silent pauses)
Pervasive Developmental Disorders	• Autism—Abnormal social interaction & communication, restricted repertoire of interests and activities • Rett's—Impairment shows between 5 and 48 months of age, associated with severe or profound mental retardation, decreased social interests and motor impairment. • Asperger's Disorder—social impairment with repetitive patterns of behavior, activities, and interests, no clinically significant delays in language, cognitive development, adaptive functioning
Attention Deficit and Disruptive Behavior Disorders	• Attention Deficit/Hyperactivity Disorder—difficulty maintaining attention with a persistent pattern of hyperactivity and impulsivity • Conduct Disorder—behavior which violates the basic rights of others i.e. bullying, threatening, assault • Oppositional Defiant Disorder—pattern of defiant and hostile behavior toward authority
Feeding and Eating Disorders of Infancy or Early Childhood	• Pica—persistent eating of non-nutritive substances i.e. paint, cloth, insects, pebbles etc. • Rumination Disorder—repeated regurgitation and re-chewing and swallowing of food

Continued

Chart 2-1 DSM IV Definitions Continued

Category	Diagnoses & Brief Clinical Definitions
Tic Disorders	• Tourette's Disorder—repetitive movements (motor tics) with one or more vocal tics (sounds or words which are repeated without conscious effort Note: Coprolalia is a complex vocal tic involving the uttering of obscenities and is present in less than 10% of individuals with Tourette's
Elimination Disorders	• Encopresis—involuntary or intentional passage of feces into inappropriate places i.e clothing, floor • Enuresis—involuntary or intentional urination into bed or clothes
Other Disorders of Infancy, Childhood or Early Adolescence	• Separation Anxiety—developmentally inappropriate anxiety concerning separation from home or from those to whom the individual is attached • Selective Mutism—the persistent failure to speak in specific social situations
Delerium, Dementia, and Amnestic Disorders	• Delerium—disturbance of consciousness with change in cognition, i.e. lack of awareness • Dementia—multiple cognitive deficits including memory impairment • Amnestic Disorder—disturbance of memory from a medical condition or effects of a substance
Substance Related Disorders and Intoxication	• Alcohol-Induced • Amphetamine-Induced • Caffeine-Induced • Cannabis-Induced • Cocaine-Induced • Hallucinogen-Induced • Inhalant-Induced • Nicotine-Induced • Opioid-Induced • Phencyclidine-Induced • Sedative-Induced
Psychotic Disorders	• Schizophrenia—marked social and occupational dysfunction associated with one or more of the following: delusions, hallucinations, disorganized speech, catatonic behavior
Mood Disorders	• Depressive Disorder—depressed mood and loss of interest and pleasure in nearly all activities • Bipolar Disorder—cyclical pattern of manic episodes and depressive episodes
Anxiety Disorders	• Panic Disorder—recurring unexpected panic attacks and worry about future attacks • Agoraphobia—anxiety associated with experiencing publicly embarrassing symptoms, usually associated with Panic Disorder • Obsessive Compulsive Disorder—recurrent obsessions or compulsions such that the time-consuming nature causes significant impairment • Post Traumatic Stress Disorder (PTSD)—psychological distress associated with actual or threatened death

Continued

Chart 2-1 DSM IV Definitions Continued

Category	Diagnoses & Brief Clinical Definitions
Somatoform Disorders	• Hypochondriasis—preoccupation with fears of having an illness or disease • Body Dysmorphic Disorder—preoccupation with a defect in appearance
Factitious Disorders	• Factitious Disorder—faking physical or psychological symptoms, motivated by assuming the "sick" role
Dissociative Disorder	• Dissociative Disorder—disruptions to memory, consciousness, and or identity
Paraphilias	• Exhibitionism—exposure of one's genitals to strangers • Fetishism—sexual preoccupation with non-living objects i.e. shoes • Frotteurism—touching and or rubbing against a non-consenting person • Pedophilia—adult sexual activity with a prepubescent child • Voyeurism—observing unsuspecting people who are naked, disrobing, or engaging in sexual activity
Eating Disorders	• Anorexia Nervosa—intense anxiety associated with gaining weight, refusal to maintain a minimally normal body weight, and a misperception of the shape and or size of one's body • Bulimia Nervosa—binge eating and purging through vomiting or diahhrea
Sleep Disorders	• Insomnia—difficulty initiating or maintaining sleep • Hypersomnia—excessive sleepiness
Impulse Control Disorders	• Explosive Disorder—failure to resist aggressive impulses resulting in serious assaults or destruction of property • Kleptomania—failure to resist impulses to steal items not needed for personal use • Pyromania—deliberate and purposeful fire setting
Personality Disorders	• Paranoid Personality—pattern of distrust and suspiciousness • Schizoid Personality—detachment from social relationships • Antisocial Personality—pattern of disregard for and violation of others' rights • Borderline Personality—pattern of instability in interpersonal relationships and self image • Histrionic Personality—pattern of excessive emotionality and attention-seeking • Narcissistic Personality—need for admiration and a lack of empathy • Avoidant Personality—pattern of social inhibition, feelings of inadequacy, hypersensitive to negative feedback • Dependent Personality—pattern of submissive and clinging behavior, excessive need to be taken care of • Obsessive Compulsive—pattern of preoccupation with orderliness, perfection, and control

age three), and briefer duration. A diagnosis of PDD-NOS may occur when a child is young, but may not be accurate to describe them when they are adolescents or adults.

Individuals diagnosed as having PDD may engage in ritualistic or obsessive behaviors, such as rocking or shaking their fingers in space. This self-stimulatory behavior is representative of their inability to act outside of defined and closed social structures or to recognize social situations when they are included in them. These children do not readily engage in representational play, nor do they "pretend" in their play. Social relationships are impaired and communication is affected as well, because these children often engage in perseveration or echolalia, repeating songs, commercials, or words or phrases which may have no apparent meaning to others. Young children with PDD may engage with objects in the way other young children play with soft toys—carrying around string or a block of wood, or engaging with pieces of a game or toy instead of the whole object (Mauk, Reber & Batshaw, 1997).

Individuals with PDD may be hypersensitive to the proximity of others, and hence, will remove themselves physically, seating themselves at a distance, not making eye contact, and not responding to the presence of others, or responding by panicking or becoming anxious.

In school settings or social activities in the community, these individuals are hard to draw into group activities, which limits their ability to benefit from social modeling, pragmatic language development, fine and gross motor skill refinement, or social leadership. They may be easily targeted by others' bullying and intimidation because of their eccentric mannerisms or speech patterns. In the home and community, these individuals may be isolated and change the activity pattern of their whole family, causing parents and siblings to have to change their own social life.

Attentional Disorders (ADD and ADHD)

According to the American Psychiatric Association (1994), attention-deficit hyperactivity disorder is the most common neurodevelopmental disorder of childhood, with a prevalence of 3-5%. Although called by many names over the years, this condition can be severe enough to interfere with a child's ability to progress in school and to participate in social and recreational activities. Attention-deficit disorder is characterized by inattentiveness and distractibility, and may lead to problems completing assignments in school in the time provided. As these students get older, their inability to focus their attention and process information can lead to defiance of authority, social difficulties in unstructured situations, and problems with organization and self-management (Wender, 1995; Blum & Mercugliano, 1997).

When attention deficits are complicated by hyperactivity, these children and adolescents may demonstrate impulsive reactions, a low tolerance for frustration, and an inability to predict consequences of their behavior. Children with ADHD are often motivated only by the most stimulating activities, becoming bored easily.

In school, it is often difficult to place students with ADD or ADHD in groups, as their processing of information may be delayed and their performance on tasks may require accommodation of scheduling or format. As these students become adolescents and adults, problems may occur for them because they have difficulty completing long-term projects, or juggling the demands of college or a job without accommodation from instructors or employers.

At home and in the community, these children can be hard to manage physically, sometimes running away from those directing their actions. They may start activities before directions are given, or take risks or otherwise engage in unsafe behavior because they do not perceive or anticipate any danger in what they are doing. As adolescents, they may be led into criminal or other anti-social behaviors because of the stimulation they get from such things, and as adults they may have trouble meeting the demands of long-term relationships, ongoing employment, or parenting.

Conduct Disorder (CD) and Oppositional/Defiant Disorder (ODD)

Patterns of aggression, destruction of property, and deliberate disregard for rules or expected behavior characterize the individual with a *Conduct Disorder*. An important distinguishing factor in this diagnosis is that it is applied to individuals who *comprehend what they are doing*, and are not cognitively limited in their ability to understand rules and limits (Lovell & Reiss,1997). Children and adolescents with conduct disorder may have been exposed to inappropriate models of behavior in their homes or communities. They demonstrate such behaviors as bullying, taunting, stealing, vandalism, and fire setting (Reber & Bocherding, 1997).

In school, these students present a real threat to the security and instructional continuity of other students. Because another factor involved with conduct disordered students is truancy, they are difficult to assist. Their disregard for social conventions of behavior (turn taking, sharing, listening to others) limit the activities they can participate in at school, including sports teams or student government. Although these individuals are often quite verbal and intelligent, they are likely to distance themselves from appropriate models of behavior and seek others like themselves with whom to engage in dangerous or destructive conduct.

In the community, children and adolescents with conduct disorders can cause problems that range from relatively mild (verbal threats and taunting) to serious (robbery, arson, assault). Community standards generally do not tolerate the participation of such individuals in community-sponsored recreation activities, and so the assistance of professionals in channeling the energies and emotions of these individuals is important.

Children and adolescents with *Oppositional/Defiant Disorder* also demonstrate non-compliant behaviors and defiance of authority, but their behaviors are generally less serious or antisocial than those with CD. In school, students with ODD may defy teachers or administrators, but they may also respond to consistent behavior management techniques. It is important to address the needs of students with ODD as soon as possible, so that potentially more serious behaviors may be averted as they progress through grades into middle and high school.

At home and in the community, children with ODD pose behavior problems which require consistency and agreement about management of behavior on the part of the adults in their lives. If adults are not clear and consistent in establishing limits, rewards and consequences, children may learn to manipulate the adults and remain non-compliant or they may escalate their non-compliance to more difficult-to-control behaviors. Parents (and grandparents) need assistance in understanding how to set limits and make demands of children, as well as understanding how behaviors come and go with development. Tantrums, for example, are not uncommon in very young children, but usually disappear by the end of preschool age.

In the community, providing opportunities for children to participate in play groups, or other social groups, offers a way for them to learn the boundaries of behavior, how to comply with rules, and how to practice language, motor and social skills with peers. Children with ODD may demonstrate non-compliance in situations requiring sportsmanship, sharing, turn taking, choosing sides on a team, or other situations where they are made to comply with an established order or procedure of a game or task. In trying to reduce or eliminate oppositional or defiant behavior, these individuals may respond to behavior systems (points, token economies, verbal warnings, time out) when they are applied fairly within groups. Otherwise, individual behavioral contracts or protocols may be required.

Anxiety Disorders

These are psychiatric disorders in which the individual experiences feelings of anxiety or uneasiness that affect their ability to carry out normal life functions or behaviors (Batshaw, 1997; Kauffman, 1997). Unlike CD and ODD, which are known as *externalizing* disorders, *Anxiety Disorders* are considered *internalizing* disorders, and the components of anxiety, social withdrawal and behaviors such as eating problems and obsessive rituals may appear as part of this disorder as well.

Anxiety is connected to fear and worry (Stevenson-Hinde & Shouldice, 1995). Certain fears are normal in child development (falling, strangers, some objects), and as long as a fear doesn't interfere with normal activities it is not considered maladaptive. Children with anxiety disorders, however, are very affected by their fears to the extent that the fear keeps them from attending school, sleeping, eating, exploring new environments, touching objects, etc. When these irrational fears persist and interfere with the child's perception of reality, intervention is needed, as these fears amount to *phobias*. Some fears are learned from watching the non-verbal responses of others to objects or individuals. When children see significant people in their lives react fearfully, they may internalize that fear themselves. Also, when adults react to situations with constant verbal warnings to children to be cautious or fearful (around dogs, for example), an over-reaction may result (Kauffman, 1997).

Obsessive/Compulsive Disorder (OCD), is characterized by two elements—obsessions (persistent thoughts or images) and compulsions (repetitive, stereotyped actions taken to delay or ward off dreaded events). The American Psychiatric Association (1994) notes that children with OCD often do not realize that their behaviors are excessive or unusual. OCD connects to anxiety by its manifestation. Individuals with the disorder are often deliberately slow in taking actions for fear that they will miss a step in a routine, or miss a word in a statement, causing them to become fearful that they have not completed a task accurately or efficiently, resulting in a dreaded rebuke or less than perfect grade (Campbell & Cueva, 1995).

Stereotypic movements are also part of this constellation of disorders. *Tic disorders*, manifested by jerky movements of the facial muscles, head, neck, arms or legs, may be part of this group. The greatest amount of research has been done on *Tourette Disorder* or *Tourette Syndrome*, (TS), in which motor and verbal tics are presented by the individual. The onset of TS is prior to age 18, so its manifestation is often seen in school. Individuals with TS may have clustering of such tics as twitching, grunting, shouting obscenities, or making sounds such as barking. The disorder, which can be manifested mildly to severely, is neurologically based, but has definite social and emotional aspects.

In school, individuals with TS may be ridiculed or otherwise treated with hostility by others. Teachers and administrators, trying to establish a systematic behavior management program, may find it difficult to accommodate the impulsive movements and sounds that come from the student with TS. Ignoring or otherwise handling these behaviors may result in confusion for other children. Sometimes triggered by stress, the management of TS must reflect a willingness on the part of all in the social setting to accept the individual as he or she is, and continue normal social activities and recreational and leisure opportunities as much as possible. Cognitive-behavioral therapies are often effective in handling TS and these, combined with medications, have been successful in maintaining individuals with TS in school and community social settings (Kane, 1994).

The same need for tolerance and acceptance recommended in the school setting is needed in the community. Focusing on the strengths and contributions of the individual with TS is vital for their effective social and emotional development (Riddle, 1988).

Another related disorder is *Post Traumatic Stress Disorder (PTSD)*. This disorder is found among individuals who have experienced an extremely traumatic event, and as a result, are left with feelings of fear, horror, or helplessness (Kauffman, 1997). As a result, the individual has problems sustaining concentration, paying attention to events going on around him or her, or may experience problems sleeping. Often, the emotional reaction occurs a considerable period of time after the actual traumatizing event (Terr, 1995; Yule, 1994). Symptoms may include persistent revisualizing of the trauma, repetitive behaviors similar to obsessions or compulsions, fears, or altered attitudes toward people or the future. Individuals with PTSD are quite vulnerable, and require support and encouragement from those in their social groups, in school and in the community.

Children and adolescents who grow up in settings in which they may be repeatedly exposed to violence, physical or sexual abuse, or who witness such events in the lives of others, are vulnerable to PTSD. Intervention with such individuals is affected by how much they are continually exposed to re-experiencing the traumatic events (Arroyo & Eth, 1995; Horowitz, Weine & Jekel, 1995; Shaw, Applegate & Schorr, 1996). Providing healthy recreational activities to individuals whose homes are not in safe or stable settings can be problematic, and so the efforts of teachers, parents and recreation professionals is vital.

Eating Disorders

Eating disorders, such as *Anorexia Nervosa* and *Bulimia,* are also related to anxiety and obsession. They can be easily masked by the individual with the disorder until the problem is acute (Boodman, 1995; Mizes, 1995). Anorexia is manifested by severely reduced intake of food due to the misperception of the individual, usually an adolescent female, that she is fat, and with an obsession with slenderness. Bulimia, also related to an obsession about appearance, is manifested in binge-eating. The depression that the individual, once again usually an adolescent female, over their lack of control about eating, causes them to resort to extreme measures to remove the effects of food—induced vomiting, excessive use of laxatives, over-exercising.

Anorexics and bulimics often engage in their behaviors in secret, and it is hard for educators (and parents) to note their emotional and behavioral problems early, especially in light of the fact that they are often very good students, as a result of their personal obsession with perfection in all things. They may seem to be socially accepted, particularly since other students in high school and college may have the same ideals of body image and school performance. Parents and other significant adults in their lives may also be encouraging them with compliments and urging to keep up such behavior. It is dangerous, however, to ignore such problems, because these individuals are engaging in self-destructive behavior.

There are other eating disorders. *Pica* is the eating of inedible substances (dirt, cloth, hair, etc.). *Rumination* is self-induced vomiting, (a behavior established in early childhood or even infancy). Children with eating disorders often set a pattern that follows them into adulthood, including highly selective eating habits (certain foods, ritually selected and/or prepared), or obesity, a disorder that places the obese individual at great risk for social rejection (Boodman, 1995; Johnson & Hinkle, 1993), not to mention the health risks associated with such over-eating.

Social Isolation and Related Disorders

There is a certain amount of social isolation that occurs naturally in all school settings. As children emerge socially, experiencing their social skill development through imitation and trial and error encounters, they may periodically withdraw. When the withdrawal becomes a consistent behavior and the child becomes a loner or is isolated within the social group, a problem exists.

Some social isolation occurs as a result of the rejection of others in the class due to excessive behaviors, such as hyperactivity or aggression (Wentzel & Asher, 1995; Kauffman, 1997). Because others do not want ongoing daily contact with these individuals, normal development of friendships and inclusion in play does not occur, with the result being few if any social skills. The rejection fosters continued isolation, and a cycle is formed.

Other forms of social isolation may come from low self-esteem and inappropriate reinforcement for prior attempts to form social alliances. Parental restrictiveness of early social learning opportunities may contribute to social ineptness on the part of a child as they enter school, and the social overtures of the child may be rebuffed by other children, causing more withdrawal on the part of the child. Without an opportunity to interact with others socially early in life, self-concept and self-confidence are affected (Campbell, 1995).

Disorders such as *Separation Anxiety* or *Attachment Disorder* may also be shown by children of school age. Children with separation anxiety disorder have problems leaving the company of parents or caretakers, seeing them as the only ones they can trust for their safety and security. Screaming and tantruming when made to leave the physical presence of these individuals may result as children enter their first social encounters alone. Consultation with counselors or other child development experts in determining how to separate the child from the significant other person may be needed.

Children with attachment disorder overly identify with objects or toys, and cannot function during daily tasks without the presence of the object or toy. In school, this presents a challenge, but management of the amount of time and circumstances when the child can interact with the object can be made, decreasing the child's dependence on the contact throughout the day.

Selective Mutism is a related disorder that is puzzling as well as frustrating. These children, whose communication skills and cognitive abilities are normal, are sometimes the victims of PTSD, but they may not be. These children choose to speak to some individuals, but will not speak to others at all. This may be related to fears of certain people or with social withdrawal in general (Jacobsen, 1995). Specific therapeutic interventions are used with these children to alter and shape the demands and conditions of speech, and to reinforce the child's eventual speaking to previously excluded individuals. Teachers have a real challenge with these students, and consultation with speech/language pathologists is important. Interventions with selective mutes must be non-punitive, and may be very long-term in their implementation (Harris, 1996).

In school, the problems of children and adolescents with anxiety and related disorders present diverse challenges to teachers and administrators. Careful observation on the part of staff is required to determine exactly what the nature of the student's problem may be. Because these are internalized disorders, they are not obvious. The services of specialists within the school or school district can often prove essential, and therefore, knowing what to describe to them from classroom and other school social encounters is important.

Mood Disorders

Depression and *depressive mood disorders* are controversial issues in child psychology and psychiatry. This is because there is not agreement on whether or not children actually show the symptoms of depression, or mask them with other behaviors, such as bed-wetting, tantruming, hyperactivity or learning disabilities. Most researchers agree that childhood depression does exist, and parallels adult depression in many ways (Kauffman, 1997).

Mood disorders include a range of emotional responses, including the inability to express pleasure at all, irritability, disturbed appetite, disturbed sleep patterns, psychomotor agitation, loss of energy, feelings of worthlessness or inappropriate guilt, diminished ability to concentrate, and recurrent thoughts of death (including suicide) (Stark *et al,* 1995). Children with serious mood disorders experience these feelings episodically and for long periods. This disorder can be *endogenous* (responding to genetic, biochemical or biological factors), or *reactive* (a response to environmental influences such as a death, or academic failure). Some research indicates that depression in children may relate to depression in their parents (Reynolds, 1992; Stark et al., 1995).

Children and adolescents with *bipolar disorder* (sometimes called *manic-depressive disorder*) demonstrate mood swings, often unpredictable, which can be extreme. A close partnership with the parents and others in the child's home and medical treatment can be helpful in working with the child in school and in the community.

In school, depressed or otherwise mood-disordered students may have trouble becoming motivated to perform, or to focus their attention on assignments or relationships within the class. Failure to see themselves as worthy can be reinforced in their own mind by failure on assignments or in physical activities. Maag and Forness (1991) note that cognitive-behavioral therapy highlighting social skills, productive and pleasurable activities, causal attribution, cognitive assertions and self-control, may be a successful intervention strategy used in school.

At home and in the community, those who are depressed or otherwise mood-disordered may isolate themselves, not joining in any community activities and remaining at home. The individual does not know where to turn or which direction to take. This places the child or adolescent at risk, because intervention opportunities are limited. Anti-depressant medication has been used successfully with individuals with depression and mood disorders, but some side effects have been noted as problematic (Quintanna & Birmaher, 1995).

Self-injurious, Suicidal and Homicidal Behaviors

There is not a clear-cut distinction between attempted suicide and suicidal gestures, that is, an active attempt to end one's life versus a threat, half-hearted self-injury, or thought of suicide. Nevertheless, the most recent decade has shown an increase in such attempts and related suicidal behaviors among adolescents and to some extent, younger children (Shaffer & Hicks, 1994). Although males actually commit suicide more often than females, attempts are made more frequently by females. Commonly, those who actually commit suicide and who attempt suicide, feel that they have nothing to contribute to the world around them (Kauffman, 1997).

School performance among these adolescents and children is almost uniformly poor, and as the school year comes to an end, these individuals often see their situations as hopeless, and act on this hopelessness. Other influences on these decisions are social and personal issues with family members, friends, and difficulties with their emerging sexuality (Wagner, Cole & Schwartzman, 1995).

Individuals who are impulsive due to co-morbidity with other disorders may act on an impulse, only to regret their actions later. Substance abuse may play a role in this emotional pattern, because the individual is depressed and seeks to "medicate" his or her own "illness" with anything that will, even temporarily, make them forget their problems and feel better.

Eisenberg (1984) identifies three potential causes and preventive measures related to this problem: (1) easy access to devices which can be used for self-destruction (guns, other weapons), (2) too much publicity and imagery available to young people about suicide and premature death, and (3) relatively little assessment for the detection of depression in young children. Little has changed since Eisenberg's findings were published.

Access to weapons continues to be an issue debated in American society, and its political importance is likely to keep the topic open for discussion. The growing availability of multimedia images of violence, death, murder, suicide, emotional upheaval, sexual permissiveness, and substance abuse is alarming and has also become a political topic in the wake of recent acts of violence in schools and communities throughout the United States.

Families may find the idea of their child having serious emotional or psychological problems stigmatizing as well as expensive to access mental health evaluation services. Most communities, however, have mental health services available on a sliding scale, and schools are good sources for assistance in determining the needs of students in the area of emotional development and its impact on their overall social and academic growth.

In all settings, school, home or community, when children and adolescents talk about their feelings of pain and worthlessness, their anger about their problems with friends, school and family, their confusion and fear about the future, these comments should be taken *very* seriously. More direct or serious comments about a desire to die or to be gone from the pressures of life should be immediately referred to a mental health professional who can assess the likelihood of the individual's acting on the feelings expressed. The individual should not be turned away or sent home without some action. Continued communication should be established as much as possible (Kauffman, 1997).

Acts of aggression toward others, especially when a child or adolescent expresses a desire to kill, should be taken seriously as well. This can be a manifestation of mental illness, or can be part of a constellation of impulsive acts and rage on the part of the individual. Whatever the cause, expressed desire to kill, play that continually imitates or supports killing as a goal, and aggression toward others that is overly menacing or dangerous (especially when objects are used as weapons), should be reported for immediate action on the part of mental health professionals.

Behaviors Resulting from Abuse and Neglect

Children with problems in social settings, both at school and in the community, may be exhibiting their reactions to abuse (physical, verbal and/or sexual) or neglect. Abused children and adolescents may be hiding their reactions and substituting other behaviors to express their anxiety, fear or anger. Because child abuse is symbolic of the unequal relationship of abuser and abused, the abused individual grows up having been given a message of inequality of worth in the family or other social groups, and may as a result have a distorted ability to seek his or her place in social groupings in school, the community and in recreation or leisure activities (Heineman, 1998). Without proper therapeutic and behavioral assistance, these individuals may grow into adolescence and adulthood without controls on their reactions, and may engage in aggression toward others or even engage in a continuation of the cycle of their own abuse. It is important, therefore, for these children to be given recreational and social opportunities to learn how to establish themselves among groups of peers and how to form relationships with boundaries of privacy and respect, both physically and socially.

Imitative play in children can be indicative of actions they are seeing in their home or community environment. Children who hit others, pull hair, scream at others, threaten violence to others or who manipulate others with threats of self injury may be "crying out" for help by their own inappropriate behaviors for assistance in seeking structure, limit-setting, and self-control. The adults around them, teachers, counselors, recreational staff, community leaders and other adults, should seek help for these individuals so that the cycle of abuse may be broken (Chesney-Lind & Brown, 1999).

A history of abuse and victimization can contribute to later delinquency, incarceration, promiscuity, drug use, early pregnancy and gang affiliation. It is noted that high numbers of mentally ill adults were sexually and physically abused children and adolescents.

Delinquency

Not all "delinquent" behavior is illegal. *Juvenile delinquency* is actually a legal denotation involving illegal acts. Delinquent behavior may be part of an array of deviant behaviors that children and adolescents have demonstrated over a long period of time (Siegel & Senna, 1994). A disproportionate amount of children who live in poverty are counted as engaging in delinquent behaviors (Leone, Walter & Wolford, 1990; Kazdin, 1994). The older the child is when the delinquent behavior is discovered and addressed, the more likely he is to continue such behavior (Kazdin, 1994). Additionally, the younger the individual is when she starts the delinquent behavior, the greater the likelihood that she will not respond as well to intervention (Bryant, et al, 1995).

Delinquents fall into three categories, according to Achenbach (1982):

- *Socialized-subcultural*—those who maintain their social relationships with equally delinquent peers by membership in gangs, forming relationships with unsavory companions, and who do not experience parental rejection for their acts.
- *Unsocialized psychopathics*—aggressive persons who feel persecuted. These individuals display rage, insensitivity, explosive anger, and do not respond to interventions that offer praise or positive reinforcement.
- *Disturbed neurotics*—overly sensitive, anxious, fragile and unhappy with their acts.

Because there is a spectrum of personality types among those called delinquent, the interventions used with them vary. What is agreed upon by experts is the fact that interventions must include agencies that can assist the individual in family relationships, education, career pathways, court and corrections systems, and management of substance abuse or hazardous sexual activity (Kauffman, 1997). Educators can assess learning needs and how those needs may be helped in school placement, including connecting the student with appropriate recreational programs.

Family mental health professionals can provide counseling for the individual and his family to identify the source of trouble in the family structure and how reasonable progress can be made in communication among the members of the family. Vocational specialists can assess career pathways that are reasonable for the individual and how to gain access to skills for lifelong independence. Officers of the court can work with the individual on avoiding situations that can lead back into criminal activities and monitor the individual as he reintegrates into the community. Referrals should be made to substance abuse counselors or other mental health professionals who can discuss and assist the individual in effective decision making about social connections, substance use and abuse, and inappropriate or dangerous sexual activity.

Sexual Behaviors

As mentioned above, sexual activity may be related to delinquent activity. Sexual behavior that involves violence or force can be, in fact, illegal. But beyond the illegal aspects of sexually delinquent behavior, there are unsafe, irrational and impulsive behaviors engaged in by children and adolescents.

Children who engage in provocative imitation of behaviors they have witnessed among adults may be improperly supervised outside of school hours, and need appropriate leisure or recreational activities. Additionally, children with PTSD may have experienced sexual trauma, and act out in an overt sexual manner as a result. Consultation with mental health professionals is recommended.

Young teens and adolescents are experiencing changes that may cause them to focus their attention on their sexual needs. When these individuals are unsupervised, or not given accurate and complete information about sex, they may engage in dangerous behaviors resulting in disease or teen pregnancy. The addition of these stressful aspects to an already turbulent period of a student's life may result in several of the disorders of anxiety or conduct outlined above. Support is vital for these individuals, so that they can learn to make choices and explore options independently and fully.

Sexual activity can also indicate an individual's feelings of low self-esteem, and a desire for emotional closeness, even temporarily. Such behavior may also be in reaction to earlier sexual abuse, or carried out during periods of alcohol or substance abuse. The connection of sexual behavior to other maladaptive behaviors makes intervention complicated.

The Role of Medication

No school can operate and serve students without some knowledge of the role that medication is currently taking in the development of children at all grade levels. The disorders mentioned above are often treated with medications that range from stimulant medications, to antidepressants and neuroleptics.

Stimulant medication is often used to treat deficits of attention and learning. Among the best known of these medications is Ritalin, or methylphenidate. Neuroleptics are used with individuals with aggressive or self-injurious behaviors. These medications reduce agitation, stereotypic behaviors and social withdrawal behaviors. Lithium is used to treat individuals with bipolar disorder and some autistic clients. It is intended to inhibit extreme aggression and self-injury.

Some children are treated with megavitamins. Vitamins such as B6 have been considered in the treatment of individuals with autism, and research continues into efficacy of mega-doses of vitamins for individuals with certain disorders (Walker & Roberts, 1992).

The danger inherent in medication protocols is that side effects may occur. Stimulants may produce weight changes, sleep interruption, and tics. Neuroleptics may produce lethargy and related changes in cognitive behaviors. Antidepressants may produce physical discomfort such as constipation or dry mouth, and occasionally cardiac concerns. Lithium may produce gastrointestinal and/or cardiac symptoms. Megavitamin regimens may produce no results whatever, or harmful imbalances of body chemistry (Gualteri, Evans & Patterson, 1987). There is a thin margin of error between a helpful or therapeutic dose of medication and a toxic level that can cause more problems that it cures.

Medication is best used when it supports other interventions. This is the value of teamwork, uniting the home, school, and community health resources. The effects of medication need to be monitored by all those concerned with the child so that changes in dosage, or eventual elimination of medication, may occur.

Schools are social communities, and while some members are developing learning and social skills at a normal pace and with no apparent problems, other members may be evidencing the start of later serious problems. Externalized disorders, such as conduct disorder, PDD, autism, ADD and ADHD may gain the attention of teachers and other adults in the school setting, resulting in interventions that help these children, but others are experiencing internalized disorders of anxiety, withdrawal and mood that are subtle and require extra effort on the part of these adults in order to gain help.

Middle schools and high schools are often the places where specialized social groups, or cliques, are established, and ongoing patterns of acceptance or rejection may be set before the adults in the school setting are aware of them. Awareness and observation of students with withdrawn, obsessive, compulsive, stereotypic or worry-induced behaviors must be the role of teachers and administrators. Sharing and discussing those observations with other educators and mental health professionals can be helpful, both in the professional growth of the school staff, but certainly in the development of the students.

A Word About Learning Disabilities

Learning disabilities is a broadly used term that describes a wide scope of difficulties in learning. Often quite intelligent, these individuals find themselves unable to process information in the same way as others. Neurologically, they may not perceive written symbols consistently, affecting their ability to learn to read. They may not conceptualize numbers and numeric symbols in a way that allows for facile mathematical skill. Although verbal and full of ideas demonstrating their comprehension of subjects under study, these individuals may not be able to get their thoughts onto paper in a legible or comprehensible manner when writing is demanded (Church, Lewis & Batshaw, 1996).

Students identified as having learning disabilities may evidence some of the disorders mentioned above. One should not infer, however, that emotional and behavioral problems are necessarily a part of the diagnosis of learning disabilities. Just as a psychologist or psychiatrist identifies the specific aspect of an emotional or psychiatric disorder in order to assist in the process of treating an emotional or behavioral problem, a specialist would also define a student's needs in learning more specifically than to say, "This student has a learning disability." Learning disabilities can prove frustrating and frightening to children and adolescents when they are students. Many students are not identified as having a learning disability until quite late in their school career, after years of thinking themselves "incapable of learning," "retarded," "crazy," or other inaccuracies.

It is not hard to understand, therefore, how these individuals might experience lowered self-esteem, anxiety in school, lack of motivation, non-compliant behaviors in response to teacher demands and peer teasing or intimidation, or even self-injurious thoughts. It is important for teachers and parents to realize that students with learning disabilities may have emotional reactions to their limitations, but they are not *disturbed*.

Behavior and Misbehavior

In settings such as school, where the behaviors of adults and children are organized into a routine, diversion from the routine, or expected behavior, may be interpreted as "misbehavior."

Adults often place their own values on the behavior of others, labeling some behaviors as "inappropriate" and others "compliant" or "appropriate." When a systematic approach to the management of behavior is in place, members of the group understand just what the perimeters of "appropriate" behavior are. When the members of the group not only understand, but help to form the rules of behavior for the group, they are more likely to comply with the expectations of the group, and therefore, display appropriate behavior.

As children develop, their social perspective about what is expected of them emerges along with their physical growth, and they learn how reinforcement works. When they do something that pleases others, they are "rewarded" with something significant to them. When they do something that does not please others, they experience the removal or withholding of the reward, or they experience a consequence, or negative response. The association of the reward with the appropriate behavior hopefully promotes the increase of that behavior. The desire to avoid the consequence is intended to reduce or eliminate the inappropriate behavior. Scientific study has shown that positive reinforcement has a longer lasting effect than negative reinforcement.

Knowledge of the development of the brain's executive function system, however, can be helpful. As we mature, our system of self-control, centered in the frontal lobe, develops as well, and any disorder involving impulsivity or perceptual difficulty, may influence how we organize ourselves, our time, our belongings, and our responses. This system is known as *executive function*, and its development continues into our young adulthood (Denckla, 1994; 1996). Individuals with ADHD, learning disorders, or other perceptual disorders, may have executive function problems as well.

In school, teachers and administrators are sometimes accused of using the word "behavior" when they mean "misbehavior." When a teacher calls a parent to discuss a student's *behavior*, it is usually to discuss a student's *misbehavior*, or lack of compliance with expected behaviors in the school or classroom setting. When schools are designed around the concept of positive reinforcement, or the recognition and reward of positive behaviors, those behaviors often emerge as the constant for daily activity in the school, and diversion from this constant stands out as an example of unacceptable behavior (Hinshaw, 1994).

At home, parents shape their children's behaviors from birth. Children learn early how to gain a response from the adults in their lives—by crying, smiling, cooing, babbling, tantruming, screaming, clinging, and many more displays. Adults give children more power than they sometimes know in increasing or decreasing certain behaviors. A child who is always picked up or fed upon their screaming or crying demand, soon learns that screaming or crying will get the attention they crave. The child who is reinforced positively for using language to identify what they want and ask appropriately soon develops more mature and appropriate social behaviors. Learning early to use language, demonstrate patience, share objects, and play with others is a good start to later social growth, both in school and other social settings.

Consistency is the key to shaping appropriate behaviors in children. A systematic way of defining what is expected, rewarding the expected behavior appropriately, and ignoring or decreasing behaviors that are not appropriate, generates lifelong behaviors and an understanding of what is expected in a variety of settings.

In the community, there are a variety of experiences that demand social skills and compliant behavior. Social settings such as going to church or synagogue, joining a swim club, shopping at the mall, participating in scouting, special interest clubs, or sports teams, demand a level of expected compliance. This compliance takes the form of appropriate language, exchange of ideas, the use of humor and other higher order language and cognitive skills, the ability to pay attention and stay in a physical location, the ability to share, the ability to wait for the attention of others, and the ability to control impulses.

These environments—home, school and the community—demand a level of ability from all members in forming social relationships. When an individual has problems that are manifested as emotional disorders, or whose behaviors present challenges to others in the social group, they risk being eliminated from opportunities to play, use leisure time effectively or to engage in recreational activities.

Assistance and Services

Children who are experiencing problems such as those outlined in this chapter need help, coordinated among parents, educators and professionals who can address the specific area of need. Services can be coordinated between home and school. Parents or teachers with concerns should do the following to get assistance for the child or adolescent:
- ask for a conference or team meeting to discuss the exact areas of concern
- identify the professionals who should be called for an opinion—physician, counselor, psychologist, recreational staff member, etc.
- request an evaluation to determine the extent of any problems
- become comfortable with the meaning of the assessment results—ask questions until you are certain you understand the meaning of results
- share the results of assessment with all those who contact the child or adolescent
- consider all options for assistance—counseling, recreation programs, therapy
- request periodic updates on progress and future team meetings as needed

Services are available in schools and through community mental health and recreational agencies. Camps, sports teams, arts programs and drama groups are ways that individuals can develop social skills and more stable relationships with the supervision of trained adults.

Services may involve extensive treatment, such as hospitalization, or ongoing therapy for months. Parents need to get support for their own concerns about their child's special needs. There are parent support groups and the professionals who assist children and adolescents can recommend support for the families of those in treatment.

Instruments for Identifying Children and Adolescents with Needs

Behavior Checklists

There are several checklists used by pediatricians, educators and others to accurately note the patterns of behavior seen in school-aged children and adolescents. One of the most reliable and often used is the Child Behavior Checklist, developed by Dr. Thomas Achenbach of the University of Vermont. Pediatricians, psychologists, and psychiatrists often ask teachers and parents to use their respective forms of the checklist to characterize the behaviors they see in an individual child.

The assessment of behaviors is sometimes quite different between the teacher, who sees the child in a systematically designed learning environment, and the parent, who sees the child in the home and community. It is very important that the interpretation of the meaning of the results be done by a trained professional.

If the adults who are using the checklist see the same behaviors as being of concern, it gives the behavioral specialist, pediatrician or psychologist a stable idea of what to target as a behavior to change. Once a behavior has been identified for change, it is very important that the process of change be the center of activity, not the labeling of the child as having a specific type of problem.

Here is some helpful summary information about the Child Behavior Checklist:

Development & Background

A. *Title:* **The Teacher's Report Form** (adapted from the Child Behavior Checklist).

B. *Author:* Thomas M. Achenbach & Craig Edelbrock, University of Vermont.

C. *History:*

The original Child Behavior Checklist (CBCL) was first published in 1980. Achenbach, a psychiatrist at the University of Vermont, conducted research beginning in 1966 which identified traits common to children with reported behavior problems. These traits (i.e., steals, argues, talks out) make up 113 test items, and are grouped under eight different behavioral "syndromes." Since 1980, Achenbach has developed adaptations of his CBCL to include reported data from the child, school staff, classroom teachers, and even the clinician. The research validating the correlation between the problem items and reported behavior problems was replicated in 1989. The CBCL and its related forms are among the most widely used instruments in measuring child behavior.

D. *Forms:* See diagram 1.

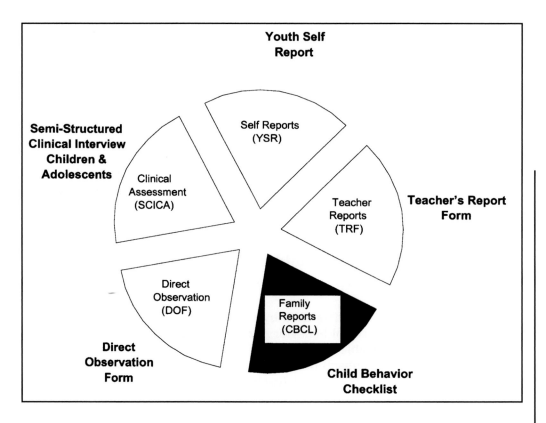

E. *Population:* Boys ages 5-11 & 12-18 and Girls ages 5-11 & 12-18.
F. *Acronym:* TRF.
G. *TRF Publisher & Dates:* Thomas M. Achenbach, 1982-1991.
H. *Time To Complete:* Achenbach reports 15 minutes, up to 45.
I. *Scoring:* Criterion Referenced, Manual scoring @ 30 minutes, Software available.
J. *Price:* $10 per 25 test forms, $10 per profile, $25 per test manual (subject to change).
K. *Availability:* 33 languages.

Intended Uses

A. *Purpose:* To obtain teachers' reports of their pupils' problems and adaptive functioning in a standardized format.
B. *Uses:*
   1. To provide a standardized DESCRIPTION of behavior, not intended for classification or diagnosis, independently.
   2. To be an "assessment-to-intervention" link, facilitating selection of appropriate behavioral interventions.
   3. To provide a brief description of the child's academic performance and socioemotional well-being.
C. *Instructions:*
   1. TRF is to be completed by a classroom teacher in the academic (math, science, reading...) areas only. Teachers in "related areas" (Physical Education, Foreign Language, Music, Art...) should use the "Direct Observation Form" (DOF).
   2. Teachers should compare the student with "normal" peers of his/her age. Reports should be based on observations made during the preceding two months.
   3. Scores should be interpreted by a mental health professional with a Master's level degree and/or training in educational research.

Field Experiences: Appropriate Uses and Cautions

I. Appropriate uses for the TRF instrument include:
   1. Preliminary assessment of a new student.
   2. Assessment for purposes of seeking appropriate mental health referral (Dr. Brady reports using the TRF 3-5 times weekly for this).
   3. Tracking progress during treatment.
   4. Describing a student's behavior when making a case for an SED disability to get a placement or special education services.
   5. Assessing in order to provide an appropriate behavioral intervention—the "assessment-to-intervention" link.
II. The cautions which need to be recognized include:
   1. Not using the TRF as a diagnostic tool (description only).
   2. Not to classify students into any "category" or with any "label."
   3. Not to confuse "adaptive functioning" with assessment of mental retardation, as it is commonly referred to in psychiatric literature.
   4. Not to place heavy significance on the adaptive scale, since it is secondary to the behavior problem component.
   5. Not to allow untrained people to interpret the scores and miscommunicate their meaning.

Summary

Who: A mental health professional with a Master's degree and above can order, issue, and interpret report scores. Only classroom teachers of academic subjects may complete the form.

What: The TRF is a 118-item assessment to obtain teachers' reports of their students' problem behaviors and adaptive functioning in a standardized format.

When: Teachers should have worked with the student for at least two full months. It takes between 15 and 30 minutes to complete, and about 30 minutes to score manually. Software is available.

Where: Teachers should complete the form when uninterrupted to facilitate concentration and focus.

Why: The TRF is used to describe student behavior. It is one tool that may be used in gaining a better understanding of the student's performance and appropriateness during academic class time.

How: Assessment forms must be purchased from Dr. Achenbach at the University of Vermont at a cost of $10 per 25 forms. Profile sheets for communicating and graphing scores are also $10 per 25. Once forms are issued to a teacher, he/she returns the form to the mental health professional for scoring. Then results may be interpreted and communicated by the mental health professional.

References

Achenbach, T.M. (1982). *Developmental psychopathology* (2nd ed.). New York, NY: Ronald Press.

American Psychiatric Association. (1994). *Diagnostic and statistical manual of mental disorders* (4th ed.). Washington, D.C.: author.

Arroyo, W., & Eth, S. (1996). Assessment following violence-witnessing trauma. In E. Peled, P.G. Jjaffe, & J.L. Edelson (Eds.), *Ending the cycle of violence: Community responses to children of battered women.* (pp. 27-42). Thousand Oaks, CA: Sage.

Barkley, R.A. (1997). *ADHD and the nature of self-control.* New York, NY: The Guilford Press.

Batshaw, M. (ed.). (1997). *Children with disabilities* (4th ed.). Baltimore, MD: Paul H. Brookes Publishing Company.

Blum, N., & Mercugliano, M. (1997). Attention-Deficit/Hyperactivity Disorder. In *Children with disabilities* (4th ed.). (pp. 449-470). Baltimore, MD: Paul H. Brookes Publishing Company.

Boodman, S.G. (1995a). Researchers study obesity in children. *The Washington Post Health.* 6/13/95, pp. 10, 13, 15.

Boodman, S.G. (1995b). Stressed for success: Youths face enormous pressures, yet most are happy. *The Washington Post,* 12/11/95, pp. A1, A16-A17.

Bryant, E.S., Rivard, J.C., Addy, C.L., Hinkle, K.T., Cowan, T.M., & Wright, T. (1995). Correlates of major and minor offending youth with severe emotional disturbance. *Journal of Emotional and Behavioral Disorders, 3,* 76-84.

Campbell, S.B. (1995). Behavior problems in preschool children: A review of recent research. *Journal of Child Psychology and Psychiatry, 36,* 113-149.

Campbell, M., & Cueva, J.E. (1995). Psychopharmacology in child and adolescent psychiatry: A review of the past seven years. *Journal of the American Academy of Child and Adolescent Psychiatry, 34,* 1124-1132.

Church, R., Lewis, M.E.B., & Batshaw, M. (1996). Learning disabilities. In M. Batshaw (Ed.), *Children with disabilities* (4th ed.). (pp. 471-498). Baltimore, MD: Paul H. Brookes Publishing Company.

Denckla, M.B. (1994). Measurement of executive function. In G.R. Lyon (Ed.), *Frames of reference for the assessment of learning disabilities: New views on measurement issues* (pp. 117-142). Baltimore, MD: Paul H. Brookes Publishing Company.

Denckla, M.B. (1996). A theory and model of executive function: A neuropsychological perspective. In G.R. Lyon, & N.A. Krasnegor (Eds.), *Attention, memory and executive function* (pp. 263-277) Baltimore, MD: Paul H. Brookes Publishing Company.

Eisenberg, l. (1984). The epidemiology of suicide in adolescents. *Pediatric Annals (13)*, 47-54.

Hamburg, B.A. (1997). Education for healthy futures: Health promotion and life skills training. In Takanishi, R., & Hamburg, D.A. (Eds.), *Preparing adolescents for the twenty-first century-challenges facing Europe and the United States.* Cambridge, UK: Cambridge University Press.

Harris, H.F. (1996). Elective mutism: A tutorial. *Language, Speech and Hearing Services in Schools, 27*, 10-15.

Hindshaw, S.P. (1994). *Attention deficits and hyperactivity in children.* Thousand Oaks, CA: SAGE Publications.

Horowitz, K., Weine, S., & Jekel, J. (1995). PTSD symptoms in urban adolescent girls. *Journal of the Academy of Child and Adolescent Psychiatry, 34*, 1353-1361.

Jacobsen, T. (1995). Case study: Is selective mutism a manifestation of identity disorder? *Journal of Child and Adolescent Psychiatry, 34*, 863-866.

Johnson, W.G., & Hinkle, L.K. (1993). Obesity. In T.H. Ollendick, & M. Hersen, (Eds.), *Handbook of child and adolescent assessment* (pp.364-383). New York, NY: Pergamon.

Kane, M.J. (1994). Premonitory urges as "attentional tics" in Tourette's syndrome. *Journal of the Academy of Child and Adolescent Psychiatry, 33*, 805-808.

Kaslow, N.J., & Rhem, L.P. (1991). Childhood depression. In T.R. Kratochwill, & R.J. Morris, (Eds.), *The practice of child therapy* (2nd ed.) (pp. 43-75). New York, NY: Pergamon.

Kauffman, J. M. (1997). *Characteristics of emotional and behavioral disorders in children and youth.* Upper Saddle River, NJ: Merrill.

Kazdin, A. E. (1994). Interventions for aggressive and antisocial children. In L.D. Eron, J.H. Gentry, & P. Schlegel (Eds.), *Reason to hope: A psychosocial perspective on violence and youth* (pp. 341-382). Washington, D.C.: American Psychological Association.

Leone, P.E., Walter, M.B., & Wolford, B.I. (1990). Toward integrated responses to troubling behavior. In P.E. Leone (Ed.), *Understanding troubling and troubled youth* (pp. 290-298). Newbury Park, CA: Sage.

Levin, D. (1998). Play with violence: Understanding and responding effectively. In Fromberg, D.P., & Bergen, D. (Eds).

Lovell, R.W., & Reiss, A.L. (1993). Dual diagnoses: Psychiatric disorders in developmental disabilities. *Pediatric Clinics of North America, 40*, 579-592.

Maag, J.W., & Forness, S.R. (1991). Depression in children and adolescents–identification, assessment, and treatment. *Focus on Exceptional Children, 24*(1), 1-19.

Mauk, J.E., Reber, M., & Batshaw, M. (1997). Autism and other pervasive developmental disorders. In M. Batshaw (Ed.), *Children with disabilities* (4th ed.). (pp. 425-448). Baltimore, MD: Paul H. Brookes Publishing Company.

Mindes, G. (1998). Can I play too? Reflections on the issues for children with disabilities. In Fromberg, D.P., & Bergen, D. (Eds.), *Play from birth to twelve and beyond*. New York, NY: Garland Publishing, Inc.

Mizes, J.S. (1995). Eating disorders. In M. Hersen, & R.T. Ammerman (Eds.), *Advanced abnormal child psychology* (pp. 375-391). Hillsdale, NJ: Erlbaum.

Pellegrini, A.D. (1998). Rough-and-tumble play from childhood through adolescence: Differing perspectives. In Fromberg. D.P., & Bergen, D. (Eds.),

Quintanna, H., & Birmaher, B. (1995). Pharmacological treatment. In M. Hersen, & R.T. Ammerman, (Eds.), *Advanced abnormal child psychology* (pp. 189-212). Hillsdale, NJ: Erlbaum.

Reber, M., & Borcherding, B.G. (1997). Dual diagnosis. In M. Batshaw (Ed.), *Children with disabilities* (4th ed.). (pp.405-424). Baltimore, MD: Paul H. Brookes Publishing Company.

Reynolds, W.M. (1992). Depression in children and adolescents. In W.R. Reynolds (Ed.), *Internalizing disorders in children and adolescents* (pp. 149-253). New York, NY: Wiley.

Riddle, M.A., Hardin, M.T., Ort, S.I., Leckman, J.F., & Cohen, D.J. (1988). Behavioral symptoms in Tourette's syndrome. In D.J. Cohen, R.D. Brunn, & J.F. Leckman (Eds.), *Tourette's syndrome and disorders* (pp.151-162). New York, NY: Wiley.

Shaffer, D., & Hicks, D. (1994). Suicide. In I.B. Pless (Ed.), *The epidemiology of childhood disorders* (pp. 339-365). New York, NY: Oxford University Press.

Siegel, L.J., & Senna, J.J. (1994). *Juvenile delinquency: Theory, practice and law*. (5th ed.). St. Paul, MN: West.

Shaw, J.A., Applegate, B., & Schorr, C. (1996). Twenty-month follow-up study of school-age children exposed to Hurricane Andrew. *Journal of the American Academy of Child and Adolescent Psychiatry, 35*, 39-364.

Silvern, S. (1998). Educational implications of play with computers. In Fromberg, D.P., & Bergen, D. (Eds.).

Stark, K.D., Ostrander, R., Kurowski, C.A., Swearer, S., & Bowen, B. (1995). Affective and mood disorders. In M. Hersen, & R.T. Ammerman (Eds.), *Advanced abnormal child psychology* (pp. 253-282). Hillsdale, NJ: Erlbaum.

Stevenson-Hinde, J., & Shouldice, A. (1995). 4.5 to 7 years: Fearful behavior, fears and worries. *Journal of Child Psychology and Psychiatry, 36,* 1027-1038.

Wagner, B.M., Cole, R.E., & Schwartzman, P. (1995). Prosocial correlates of suicide attempts among junior and senior high school youth. *Suicide and Life Threatening Behavior, 25,* 358-372.

Wentzel, K.R., & Asher, S.R. (1995). The academic lives of neglected, rejected, and controversial children. *Child Development, 66,* 754-763.

Functional Assessments of Problem Behaviors

Carol Ann Baglin

with Donna Riley and Timothy McCormick

Over the past decade, a major concern in both schools and community settings has been the issue of student behavior and the formidable task of designing effective behavior interventions. The process of identifying and analyzing behaviors that create challenges for the student, teacher, and the parent is an important component in structuring the intervention process. The accelerated movement in the past decade implementing comprehensive school reform and accountability has increased the pressures for a safe and orderly school environment. With this popular outcry for improvement and change and the restructuring of current efforts for educational reform, the impact on students with disabilities, many with behavioral concerns, remains uncertain. As students with disabilities are integrated into the general classroom, consistent with inclusion and improving access to the content curriculum, many of these students are encountering academic and social pressures that exacerbate the impact of their disability and create issues related to discipline.

Many schools are also facing the impact of increasing diversity both in the racial and economic arenas. Violence in the community, reflecting increased crime rates and the inevitable problems of substance abuse, spills into the schools. Everywhere teachers, community members, and parents cite assaultive student behaviors and aggression as major factors disrupting the educational environment. The management of behavior and consistent discipline of students, both general and special education, is becoming a major policy concern at the national, state and local levels. Low community tolerance for discipline and behavior problems has pressured the schools into implementing zero-tolerance policies in the school building.

The readings suggest a number of approaches designed to facilitate improvement of discipline. The constructivistic approach (Fields & Tarlow, 1966) promotes recognition of the integrity of the entire child, not just the "disability" aspect of the child. Through honoring and respecting the child, implementing related consequences and effective communication, negotiated solutions can be reached through structured problem solving. The behavior-analytic approach (Haring & Kennedy, 1996) identifies fundamental principles related to behavior, which if systematically studied as part of a larger environment and paired with designing these interventions in school settings, the role of teachers would result in functional changes in behavior. School-wide discipline models (Colvin, Sugai, & Kameenui, 1993; Luiselli, Putnam, Sunderland, 2002; Nelson, Martella, & Galand, 1998; Sugai & Horner, 2002) promote the usefulness of proactive instructional approaches to problem behavior that utilize staff development and team-building strategies. The number of student detentions decreased progressively and student attendance increased (Luiselli, Putnam, & Sunderland, 2002). The role of teachers in managing problem behaviors is crucial to student success. The reconceptualization of the role of schools (Walker, Horner, Sugai, Bullis, Sprague, Bricker, & Kauffman, 1996) in the prevention of antisocial behavior through a primary, secondary, and tertiary prevention model identifies the central role of schools in coordinating services, and references the "hub model" for delivery of social and mental health services in school and community settings.

These models, although consistently identifying schools in the prevention and remediation of behavior, may overlook the main purpose of school—student achievement—particularly in this era of school reform. Superintendents, administrators, teachers, and parents throughout this nation are demanding safe and orderly schools and the flexibility to deal with students without regard to disability status. No one disputes the importance and clear role of schools and teachers with the student in facilitating active learning and meaningful content. However, the role of teachers in discipline can be overemphasized and requires further support through research and practical application. Certainly the special education teacher has long been seen as a consultant to the general education teacher for behavior and discipline issues but is also frequently called on to assist in leisure and work settings within the community to assist these children.

The trend to make the school and teacher the centerpiece for change in the behavior of students, while at the same time ensuring accountability for all students, diminishes the recognition of parents and community impact on behavior and discipline outcomes. In addition, the lack of resources for support services in the schools for students adds an increased burden to teachers to both educate and to create a discipline structure which may not be consistent with the demands of the community. Protections are available to require that students with disabilities who behave inappropriately remain in school. It is believed by many that these students are less capable of conforming in demanding and traditional school environments because of their disabilities, yet they are entitled to a free, appropriate public education.

The relationship between problem behaviors and academic failure has been the subject of substantial research (McEvoy & Welker, 2000). Consistently, there are references to the onset of delinquent behaviors and poor school achievement independent of socioeconomic status (Maguin & Loeber, 1996). In addition, deficits in cognition and attention problems are linked to poor academic performance and delinquency. Disruptive behaviors interfere with learning, compete with classroom instructive, and stress the resources of the school, demanding significant resources from personnel (Luiselli, Putnam, & Sunderland, 2002).

The many dramatic incidents of school violence have created an environment of zero tolerance and increased procedures for student discipline. Despite this increase in the use of stringent controls on school behavior there is little evidence that these methods have improved student behavior or deterred student violence (Skiba & Peterson, 2000). Frequently, the initial response of the school to problem behaviors which interfere with the safety of the school process or impact on staff and other students is to discipline the student through suspension and/or expulsion. While these procedures are applicable to all students within the school, students with disabilities are subject to the specific protections of IDEA. These protections may result in the continuation of services for the student, while dealing with serious behavior problems within an educational setting.

Disciplining Students with Disabilities

While discipline problems are common in public schools, intervention is dependent upon effective preventative interventions. When these fail, the system is subject to specific policies and procedures. Many of the procedures regarding discipline of students with disabilities are dependent on the length of a disciplinary removal. Schools have more flexibility when a student with a disability is removed for less than ten days. On the other hand, there are a number of requirements a school must follow when a student is removed for more than ten days (see Appendix A).

The procedures for removing students with disabilities for less than ten days are consistent with the procedures for all students. Schools may remove a student with a disability to the same extent they remove students without disabilities. Schools do not have to provide services to students with disabilities during the removal if services are not provided to students without disabilities. No matter how long a student is removed or whether a student's placement is changed, the principal must notify the parents of a disciplinary action on the date a decision is made and provide the parents with a procedural safeguards notice.

Schools need to be knowledgeable of the potential impact of multiple removals of students with disabilities. Requirements for removals greater than ten days apply if the total days of removals exceed ten days and form a pattern. In order to determine whether the removals form a pattern, the Individualized Education Program, (IEP), team must consider three factors:

1. length of each removal,
2. total amount of time the student is removed and
3. amount of time between removals.

Multiple removals for a total of ten days in one school year are also considered a pattern and a change in placement. In order to ensure that a decision may be made concerning the issue of a pattern of removals, schools must record all removals in the student's record.

When a student is removed from school for more than ten days, the IEP team must make a manifestation determination within ten days of the disciplinary removal. In other words, the team must determine if there is a connection between the student's disability and the behavior that led to the disciplinary action. During this process, the IEP team is to consider all relevant information including evaluations, observations, information supplied by parents, the student's IEP and the student's current educational setting.

In order to determine that the behavior is not a manifestation of the disability, an IEP team must consider and determine that:

1. The IEP and the current placement appropriately meet the student's needs.
2. The special education services, the supplementary services and the behavior intervention strategies that were provided were consistent with the IEP and the placement.
3. The student's disability did not impair his/her ability to understand the impact and consequences of the behavior.
4. The student's disability did not impair the student's ability to control the behavior.

If the IEP team finds that one or more of these requirements is not met, they must determine that the behavior that led to the removal is a manifestation of the student's disability.

The results of a manifestation determination have a major impact on the student and the school. When an IEP team determines that the behavior that led to the removal is a manifestation of the student's disability, the IEP team must:

1. Revise the student's IEP to address needed services in light of the problem behavior.
2. Revise the student's behavioral intervention plan to address the behavior.
3. Review the student's placement and implement services as soon as possible.

When an IEP team determines that the behavior was not a manifestation of the student's disability, the school may discipline the student in the same manner the school disciplines a student without disabilities, except for the requirement for services described in the next paragraph. No matter what the decision is concerning the manifestation determination, the school system must provide services to the student to progress in the general curriculum and advance toward achieving the goals of the IEP.

The IEP is the main vehicle for effective behavior management for children with significant behavior challenges. It is through this process that comprehensive and varied interventions and strategies can be effectively integrated. Another requirement is that the school's IEP team meets within ten days of the disciplinary action to develop a functional behavioral assessment plan or to review the behavioral intervention plan. The school must create an assessment plan if:

1. There is no behavioral intervention plan in place, or
2. The behavioral intervention plan does not address the behavior that led to the disciplinary action.

Once the assessment is completed, the IEP team is to meet again to develop appropriate interventions to address the behavior and implement the behavioral intervention plan.

If there is a behavioral intervention plan for the student, the school is to *review* the behavioral intervention plan to determine if:

1. The plan addresses the behavior that led to the disciplinary action, and
2. The plan was in place prior to that behavior.

When reviewing the plan, the IEP team is to decide if the plan needs to be revised or if the implementation of the plan needs to be modified in some manner. If the IEP team finds that one or more of these requirements is not met, they must determine that the behavior that led to the removal is a manifestation of the student's disability.

The IEP team must meet within ten days of the disciplinary removal and address the issue of the behavioral intervention plan. The IEP team may find that there is either no behavioral intervention plan in place or that the plan in place does not address the behavior that led to the disciplinary action. In that case, the IEP team is to develop a behavioral assessment plan. Once the assessment is completed, the IEP team is to develop behavioral interventions that address the behavior that led to the disciplinary action and implement a behavioral intervention plan that includes these interventions. Conversely, the IEP team may find that a behavioral intervention plan is already in place prior to the problem behavior and the plan addresses the behavior at issue in the disciplinary action. If a plan that addresses these issues is in place, then the IEP team is to review that plan to determine if:

1. The plan needs to be modified or
2. The implementation of the plan needs to be modified in order to better address the problem of striking/harming other students.

The IEP team may find it useful to make modifications that take into account the latest incident.

In certain special circumstances the school has the option of removing a student and placing that student in an Interim Alternative Educational Setting, (IAES), for up to 45 days. The special circumstances are:

1. When a student carries a weapon to school or a school-sponsored event.
2. When a student knowingly possesses or uses illegal drugs at school or a school-sponsored event.
3. When a student sells or solicits the sale of a controlled dangerous substance at school or a school-sponsored event.

The IEP team decides which IAES is appropriate. The IAES must allow the student to:

1. Progress in the general curriculum.
2. Receive the services and modifications included in the IEP.
3. Meet the goals of the IEP.
4. Receive the services and modifications designed to address the behavior that led to the IAES placement.

The school may keep the student in the IAES regardless of the IEP team's findings in the manifestation determination.

There is a two-step process for removal when the issue is causing harm. The first step is the school may request a due process hearing to seek an order to remove a student to an IAES, if the school believes the behavior of the student is likely to cause harm to the student or others. In this situation, the school may not place the student directly into the IAES until the school obtains an order. The second step is the due process hearing may order the removal of a student to an IAES if remaining in the current placement is likely to result in injury to the student or to others (Maryland State Department of Education, 2002).

Implementing a System of Support

Positive behavior support is a non-aversive strategy designed to reduce behavior problems and to intervene to improve the quality of family and community life. While all children with challenging behaviors can benefit from focused behavioral interventions and positive support, children identified as eligible for special education have specific requirements. The implementation of these requirements for functional behavioral assessments as required by the reauthorization of the Individuals with Disabilities Education Act (IDEA) in 1997 has been presented as a unique issue for school-based personnel. The IDEA required that functional behavioral assessments and behavioral intervention plans be included as part of the individualized education program. There has been an expansion of efforts to both implement behavior supports and to analyze their success (Clarke, Worcester, Dunlap, Murray, & Bradley-Klug, 2002; Smith, 2000). In addition there has been an expansion to a focus on an improvement in the overall quality of lifestyle for the family within the community setting. The optimum approach to these students is to identify the challenging behaviors at earlier points of the process and develop appropriate positive behavior interventions through a functional behavioral assessment.

What is a Functional Behavioral Assessment?

Functional Behavioral Assessment (FBA) is an individualized approach to examining the specific variables that influence behaviors. In this case it is the undesirable behavior that is targeted. The purpose is to relate the behavior to an observable environmental event and differentiate the origins by the uniqueness of these events for each student in facilitating the behavior. Once these events are isolated, intervention can be logically related to the specific needs of the individual. The specific process of gathering information will reliably predict the conditions and/or circumstances surrounding a student's behavior that is considered inappropriate.

Proactive positive interventions/strategies are used to prevent rather than suppress undesirable behaviors. Before personnel are able to redirect instructional interventions and supports or teach an appropriate replacement behavior, the targeted behavior must be identified across settings and described in accurate, objective, observable terms.

A functional behavioral assessment is an assessment of a student's behavior to determine its function. Assessment skills include the expectations of an adequate functional behavioral assessment conducted through the IEP process (Smith, 2000); however, this is not defined in law. All behaviors serve a function for individuals, to either get something or avoid something. When students exhibit behaviors considered troublesome, a behavioral assessment is needed to accurately describe and ascertain how the behavior functions for the students. A replacement behavior or strategy for the targeted behavior must satisfy the same function as the targeted behavior. The terminology of behavioral assessment can be confusing and requires accurate use in the implementation of intervention strategies.

Identifying the functions of behavior for a student provides individuals with a direct explanation of how a particular behavior "works" for an individual student in a given context. Behaviors serve a function:

- To get something (positive reinforcement) such as social attention, sensory stimulation, peer status and peer attention, tangible rewards;
- To escape or avoid something (negative reinforcement). This function typically results in a behavior that enables the student to terminate or postpone an event. Students may tantrum, display physical or verbal aggression; or engage in other activities to control antecedent stimuli such as instructional activities.

The functions of behavior may be different depending upon the context in which the behavior occurs. Also, multiple behaviors may serve similar functions or different functions in different contexts. As humans we do not engage in isolated behaviors or display single behaviors, but rather a string of behaviors that are connected to the ongoing interactions that we have with others (Maryland State Department of Education, 2002).

The Process of the Functional Behavioral Assessment

Functional behavioral assessment is a collaborative, student-centered process for gathering information that reliably predicts the conditions and/or circumstances around why a student is exhibiting an inappropriate behavior. A functional assessment is an assessment of a student's behavior of concern to determine the function

Table 3.1
Frequently Used Terminology

A-B-C Analysis	ABC analysis is a problem-solving process in which the antecedents and consequences currently operating for both the problem and the correct behavior are identified.
Accuracy	Describes whether or not a student uses a behavior or similar behavior the same way in response to the same antecedent.
Antecedents	An antecedent is a person, place, thing or event coming before a behavior that encourages an individual to perform that behavior.
BIP	Behavioral Intervention Plan
Consequence	An action in response to a behavior that maintains the behavior.
Duration	Describes how long the behavior lasts within a set period of time (e.g., 30 seconds, 1 minute, 10 minutes, etc.).
FBA	Functional Behavioral Assessment
Frequency	Describes how often the behavior occurs within a set period of time (e.g., 1-3 times per day).
Intensity	Describes whether the target behavior is becoming more pronounced.
Setting Event	Environmental, social, physical, events or actions that occur at some time prior to the antecedent or behavior that is influencing the behavior.
Topography	The appearance of the behavior (e.g., screams, yells, strikes others, etc.).

of that behavior for the student. Teams design and implement behavioral intervention plans for students subject to disciplinary consequences (Smith, 2000).

When a student displays inappropriate behavior, an assessment of that behavior should involve the collection of objective, observable data and information concerning that behavior across settings from a variety of individuals, including educators, parents, and the student (Smith, 2000). It is most critical that the problem behavior is described in objective terms. The data obtained should clearly and objectively describe the events leading to the behavior, the behavior itself, and the consequences in response to the behavior. In order to change the problem behavior, supports and intervention strategies used to teach the student an appropriate replacement behavior must satisfy the same function for the student.

The intent of the behavioral assessment process is to attribute responsibility for behaviors primarily to the student (Smith, 2000). Since all behaviors serve a function, such as the need to get something, avoid something, or control events, the problem behaviors students engage in are typically attributable to:

- Skill deficits;
- Performance deficits;
- Environmental factors;
- Interpersonal factors;
- A failure to self-regulate; and/or an instructional "mismatch" (Maryland State Department of Education, 2002).

Basic Assumptions of Intervention

Most referrals for intervention are due to inappropriately arranged antecedents rather than inappropriately arranged consequences. A systematic process to identify factors that contribute to the maintenance of problem behaviors can function as the basis (Smith, 2000). Intervention directed only to challenging behaviors without recognizing environmental antecedents may not lead to a decrease in problem behavior or teacher complaints.

Some behaviors are intractable and may not respond to interventions or experience only marginal change. Standard intervention procedures do not work adequately when procedures have not addressed the functions of the behavior or the context of the behavior. A student may display the problem behavior because they have not learned appropriate function. It may be more efficient and effective to engage in the problem behavior.

A functional behavioral assessment is a problem-solving approach to assist in predicting the conditions and circumstances as to:

- Why is the student misbehaving
- What strategies might be used to replace inappropriate behaviors with appropriate behaviors
- Develop an effective behavior intervention plan
- Identification of specific target behaviors—observable, measurable, operationally defined
- Identification of antecedent behaviors that logically serve as a stimulus for the current behavior
- Establish a baseline of behavior to identify patterns
- A description and the identification of consequences that follow specific target behaviors
- The analysis of purpose and the effect of behavior by evaluating function and intent

The Functional Behavior Assessment identifies behavior that is interfering with the student's instructional program and the instruction of others. It can assist in identifying behavior that is not responding to typical management or intervention strategies used within the classroom or instructional setting. The assessment is most appropriately completed by a collaborative team approach, which will include:

- IEP team members
- Support services personnel
- Parents
- Student

The team must share in problem identification and development of an action plan that includes mutual responsibility for implementation, evaluation, modification, and accountability for outcomes of the interventions. See Appendix B.

The FBA and BIP should be positive and proactive for the purpose of replacing challenging behaviors with appropriate behaviors that serve a function for the student. The intervention, while initiated at first signs of challenging behaviors, is intended to create long-term and effective instructional strategies and supports.

Contents of Intervention Plans

The positive behavioral intervention plan targets behaviors which impede the student's learning or the behaviors of others. The IEP team needs to consider what types of behavioral interventions would be appropriate as strategies to improve behaviors. The use of positive reinforcement is integrated into inservice and parent training courses to assist in teaching appropriate behavior. Deescalating behaviors depends on effective use of direct and indirect behavior management strategies. Positive reinforcement and rewards provide immediate praise within behavioral change programs. The use of leaving notes, whispering, and offering choices are examples of indirect strategies (Knowlton, 1995).

The process needs to include the regular education teacher, as well as other personnel who may be included in the consideration of positive behavioral strategies. The process should include:

- Operational description of the target behavior to be reduced or eliminated
- The function (cause) of the behavior
- Operational description of the behavior that will replace the target behavior

In addition, the process needs to address actions to be taken:

- to prevent the occurrence of the target behavior
- when the correct replacement behavior occurs
- when the target behavior occurs
- to model and practice the correct replacement behavior

Summary

The functional assessment of behavior assumes that behavior does not occur randomly (Mueller, Jenson, Reaves, & Andrews, 2002). The collaborative team approach (Skiba & Peterson, 2000; Colvin, Kameenui & Sugai, 1993) integrates the expertise of the professionals and the family to target the behaviors that can be most effectively addressed. The main focus is a systemic and clear description of problem behaviors, patterns, and consequences that occur together. The identification of behavior antecedents, including the identification of events, times, and situations that predict when behaviors will and will not occur across the full range of a typical day will assist in the development of the plan. The identification of consequences that maintain problem behaviors will focus the strategies for intervention.

References

Clarke, S., Worcester, J., Dunlap, G., Murray, M., & Bradley-Klug, K. (2002). Using multiple measures to evaluate positive behavior support: A case example. *Journal of Positive Behavior Interventions, 4*(3), 131-145.

Colvin, G., Sugai, G., & Kameenui, E. (1993). Reconceptualizing behavior management and school-wide discipline in general education. *Education and Treatment of Children, 16,* 361-381.

Fields, M. V., & Tarlow, M. C. (1996). Constructivistic approaches to classroom management for students with disabilities. In W. Stainback, & S. Stainback (Eds.), *Controversial issues confronting special education.* Boston: Allyn and Bacon.

Haring, T. G., & Kennedy, C. H. (1996). Behavior-analytic foundations of classroom management. Stainback, W., & Stainback, S. (Eds.), Controversial issues confronting special education. Boston: Allyn and Bacon.

Knowlton, D. (1995). Managing children with oppositional behavior. *Beyond Behavior, 6*(3), 5-10.

Luiselli, J. K., Putnam, R. F., & Sunderland, M. (2002). Longitudinal evaluation of behavior support intervention in a public middle school. *Journal of Positive Behavior Interventions, 4*(3), 182-188.

Maguin, E., & Loeber, R. (1996). Academic performance and delinquency. In M. Tonry (Ed.), *Crime and justice: A review of research* (Vol. 20, pp. 145-264). Chicago: University of Chicago Press.

Maryland State Department of Education & Maryland Coalition for Inclusive Education. (1999). *Functional behavior analysis & positive behavior support: A resource for school-based teams.* Baltimore, MD.

Maryland State Department of Education (2002). *Procedures related to disciplinary removal of students with disabilities.* Baltimore, MD.

Maryland State Department of Education (2002). *Behavioral assessment and intervention.* Baltimore, MD.

McEvoy, A., & Welker, R. (2000). Antisocial behavior, academic failure, and school climate: A critical review. *Journal of Emotional and Behavioral Disorders, 8*(3), 130-140.

Mueller, F. M., Jenson, W. R., Reaves, K., & Andrews, D. (2002). Functional assessment of behavior can be as easy as A-B-C. *Beyond Behavior, 11*(3), 23-27.

Nelson, J. R., Martella, R., & Galand, B. (1998). The effects of teaching school expectations and establishing a consistent consequence on formal office disciplinary actions. *Journal of Emotional and Behavioral Disorders, 6* (3), 153-161.

Smith, C. R. (2000). Behavioral and discipline provisions of IDEA '97: Implicit competencies yet to be confirmed. *Exceptional Children, 66*(3), 403-412.

Skiba, R. J., & Peterson, R. L. (2000). School discipline at a crossroads: From zero tolerance to early response. *Exceptional Children, 66*(3), 335-346.

Sugai, G., & Horner, R. H. (2002). Introduction to the special series on positive behavior support in schools. *Journal of Emotional and Behavioral Disorders, 10*(3), 130-135.

Walker, H., Horner, R., Sugai, G., Bullis, M., Sprague, J., Bricker, D., & Kauffman, M. (1996). Integrated approaches to preventing antisocial behavior patterns among school-age children and youth. *Journal of Emotional and Behavioral Disorders, 4,* 194-209.

Behavioral Assessment and Intervention

Maryland State Department of Education
Division of Special Education/Early Intervention Services
July 2002

Introduction

Behavior is purposeful and cannot be understood outside of the context within which it occurs. Often behaviors interfere with learning. When these behaviors are repetitive and resistant to behavioral interventions, a functional assessment of behavior should be conducted to understand the function of the behavior for the student and to plan effective interventions. Assessing and intervening on the problem behaviors of students early has the potential of reducing the incidences of school failure and facilitating positive social behavioral development of students.

A functional assessment and positive interventions on problem behaviors should be considered as soon as a student exhibits behaviors that significantly interfere with their own learning or the learning of others. Positive early intervention upon behaviors should be integrated into all aspects of the school community. Each local school system is encouraged to examine standards and practices and adopt a comprehensive school-wide approach of proactive positive interventions and standards of behavioral assessment and intervention practices for all students. Standards should be congruent with research-based best practices and sensitive to the experience, culture, and ethnic diversity of the students and families.

Purpose

The purpose of this document is to provide administrators, educators, parents, and community members with a better understanding of the behavioral assessment and intervention process. The disciplinary requirements of the Individuals with Disabilities Education Act (IDEA) have provided school systems with an opportunity to examine their practices for assessing behaviors, implementing appropriate interventions for all students, not only for students with disabilities. This document is intended to be a user-friendly resource document on current research-based best practices. The concept of intervening upon inappropriate behaviors early with the use of positive supports and strategies is incorporated within the behavioral assessment process.

Whenever a student's behavior that is interfering with his or her learning or the learning of others comes to the attention of individuals involved with a student, it is recommended that the IEP team convene to plan for the functional assessment of the student's behavior. This assessment of the student's behavior is used to develop a behavioral intervention plan (BIP). The functional behavioral assessment (FBA) of the student's behavior increases our understanding of that behavior and its function for the student.

Terminology

A-B-C Analysis	ABC analysis is a problem-solving process in which the antecedents and consequences currently operating for both the problem and the correct behavior are identified.
Accuracy	Describes whether or not a student uses a behavior or similar behavior the same way in response to the same antecedent.
Antecedents	An antecedent is a person, place, thing or event coming before a behavior that encourages an individual to perform that behavior.
BIP	Behavioral Intervention Plan
Consequence	An action in response to a behavior that maintains the behavior.
Duration	Describes how long the behavior lasts within a set period of time (e.g. 30 seconds, 1 minute, 10 minutes, etc.).
FBA	Functional Behavioral Assessment
Frequency	Describes how often the behavior occurs within a set period of time (e.g., 1-3 times per day).
Intensity	Describes whether the target behavior is becoming more pronounced.
Latency	Immediately
Setting Event	Environmental, social, physical, events or actions that occur at some time prior to the antecedent or behavior that is influencing the behavior.
Topography	The appearance of the behavior (e.g., screams, yells, strikes others, etc.).

Positive Behavioral Supports and Intervention Strategies

Positive behavioral supports and intervention strategies represent a comprehensive system of behavior management that uses multiple approaches that include changing school-wide systems, classroom management techniques, altering environments, and overtly recognizing appropriate behavior, positively, rather than simply using one intervention in an attempt to eliminate a problem behavior. Positive behavioral supports and strategies can be described as actions and beliefs that reflect respectful interpersonal relationships, choice, communication, inclusive communities and self-determination to assist a student to become a more interdependent, contributing member of the school community. The purpose of positive behavioral supports and strategies is to develop new skills and competencies to enable a student to achieve better control over his or her behavior.

Too often the term "discipline" has been used to describe punitive actions in response to inappropriate behaviors. Positive behavioral supports and interventions represent a shift in thinking from traditional behavior management.

Traditional Behavior Management	Positive Behavioral Support
1. Views individual as "the problem."	1. Views systems, settings, and skill deficiencies as "the problem."
2. Attempts to "fix" individual.	2. Attempts to "fix" systems, settings and skills.
3. Extinguishes behavior.	3. Creates new contacts, experiences, relationships and skills.
4. Sanctions - aversives.	4. Sanctions positive approaches.
5. Takes days or weeks to "fix" a single behavior.	5. Takes years to create responsive systems personalized settings, and appropriate empowering skills.
6. Implemented by a behavioral specialist often in atypical settings.	6. Implemented by a dynamic and collaborative team using person-centered planning in typical settings.
7. Often resorted to when systems are inflexible.	7. Flourishes when systems are flexible.

Source: Functional Assessment: Putting Research on Methods of Behavior Management to Practical Use in the Classroom.

Behavioral supports and interventions should begin with early interventions in an effort to proactively alter current troublesome behaviors before the behavior becomes a larger problem. Early interventions include the building of a positive school and peer culture. The school's leadership establishes the positive school and peer culture also known as the school's climate. The development of effective school-wide, setting specific, classroom, and individual student procedures are necessary for the creation of a positive school climate.

The following are various positive support strategies that may be considered effective for a student. The emphasis of these strategies is for adults within schools to direct attention, time, and resources on the positive rather than to continually define behavior management in terms of negative, aversive, or punitive conditions. Students will perform to the level of our expectations. Since all behaviors occur for a reason, a student's challenging or problem behavior is usually the result of a skill or performance deficit. Before we can directly address the specific skill or performance deficits, students first need an increased opportunity for:

• Individual control and choice;
• Positive attention; and
• Adult and Peer Status.

Teachers also need to examine:

• Teaching Strategies;
• Environmental Arrangements;
• Instructional Activities and Materials;
• Expected Responses; and

- Assessment Methods in order to provide explicit instruction to individual students that are aligned with the student's strengths.

Systemic Positive Intervention Strategies and Supports

It is important that existing school structures and processes include universal interventions where positive reinforcement is dominant and all students are provided explicit instruction on the expected behavior to ensure every student understands the limits and expectations. Positive interventions need to occur as early as possible after the undesired behavior occurs. Universal interventions are those strategies or supports that are:

- Applied to all students;
- Proactive;
- Based on clear and predictable limits and expectations;
- Positive reinforcement dominant; and
- Linked to the school's organizational goals.

The leadership of a school is the most significant indicator of successful behavior management that leads to the performance of desired behaviors by the members of the school community. Personnel must continually monitor interventions to ensure that the consequences of behavior are such as to increase the frequency of desired behavior and decrease the frequency of undesired behaviors. To be most effective, informal frequent positive acknowledgement of desired behaviors are needed to support behavior that leads to the attainment of organizational goals. Individuals respond to many kinds of rewards, tangible and intangible. Consequently, school personnel need to carefully review the behavioral systems being employed at all levels within the school. To institute a comprehensive school-wide approach to positive behavioral interventions, the following actions need to occur:

Define Parameters and Mechanisms

Once the decision is made to approach school-wide discipline from the position of meaningful positive recognition of appropriate behavior, rather than aversive punishment, the specific parameters and mechanics for implementation must be defined. The rules must be clear, understood by all, and implemented uniformly across all settings. This feature is what will make a positive behavioral support system powerful and can make a clear connection between the level of performance and the appropriate consequences.

Obtain Commitment and Support

Once the procedures and mechanics of a positive behavioral support system are clear, the purpose and objectives for the program must be clearly communicated to all members of the school community. All staff members and students must be provided the skills for effective implementation and planned opportunities for practice. For staff and parents this is usually accomplished most effectively through interactive professional development that employs adult learning styles to provide the adults an opportunity to practice these skills in a comfortable and supportive environment. This practice for both staff and students should be presented in such a manner as to benefit everyone. School administrators may consider eliciting the help of school staff, students, and parents in both planning and implementing the parent, student, and professional instructional activities.

Monitor Effectiveness

Any program is only as good as its implementation. Positive interventions and supports, including universal supports must be monitored to see if they are being used as intended and to measure whether the desired results are being obtained. Even the best system of universal positive behavioral supports will be apt to lose its effectiveness over time because one of the defining characteristics may not be consistently implemented across school environments.

Linkage to Improved Student Results

Administrators and teachers must ensure that a system of universally designed positive behavioral supports is in line with the school's plan for improved student results. This outcome can most easily be achieved by making informal strategies, supports and rewards a subset of a larger, more formal recognition/reward program. For example, a school or class award (a formal reward) could be given to the student who receives the greatest number of recognition points (an informal reward) for assisting peers in academic skill development that resulted in improved academic performance during a specified timeframe.

Reinforcement

When tailoring a student's behavior intervention plan, the team should consider the student's strengths and utilize strategies and supports previously used as reinforcers for the student that have proved effective for that particular student in the past. Choosing the best reinforcer for an individual student is not an easy task. To make it easier, here are some critical components that needs to be explored.

- **Personal**   Strategies used by the persons responsible for implementing the supports must consider that those supports and "reinforcers" are delivered in a personal way. Calling the student by his or her name is one important criterion.

- **Sincere**   It is important that you mean what you say.

- **Specific**   The student must know exactly why he received a particular reinforcer. He or she has to know why he's being praised. Behavior is clearly a complex, ongoing stream of events. The contingency between a behavior and the consequence may not be clear. Pinpoint exactly the behavior you liked.

- **Immediate**   Try to catch the student in the act of being good. Reinforce the student while the student is doing what you want. Do not wait until the end of class, the activity, or the end of the day to give specific objective recognition to the student for his or her actions. The longer the time between the completion of a behavior and the delivery of a reinforcing consequence, the less effective the reinforcer will be.

- **Frequently**   This means that at first, the student's desired replacement behavior needs to reinforced first by approximations, if needed, until the student is able to consistently demonstrate the expected results.

School may wish to consider incorporating some or all of the following positive reinforcement strategies within the school's comprehensive plan:

- Administrators, teachers, staff members, and students personally congratulate peers who do a good job;
- Administrators, teachers, staff members, and students write personal notes to peers for good performance;
- Administrators, teachers, and staff members publicly recognize students for good performance;
- Administrators, teachers, and staff members directly teach appropriate social and affective skills through modeling, guided practice; and
- Administrators, teachers, staff members, and students celebrate successes.

Positive reinforcement is effective for several reasons. First, under conditions of positive reinforcement, the response produces a consequence that results in an increase in the frequency of the response. Second, the adverse emotional responses associated with punishment and extinction are apt to be reduced and, in fact, favorable emotions may be elicited. By understanding what drives human behavior, we can create the conditions necessary to encourage desired behaviors.

The following conditions should be addressed when developing a behavior intervention plan. The challenge will be to create those conditions that encourage students and staff to collaborate because they want to, not because they have to.

Effective support systems are **SMART**:

Specific   Focuses on the desired behaviors and provides the performer with clear 'line of sight' between action and the result.

Meaningful   The interventions and supports need to be personalized for the student taking into consideration the student's strengths, needs, and a replacement behavior that serve the same function and is considered "worth the effort" to the student.

Achievable   The replacement behavior must be viewed as achievable, though not easy.

Reliable   The rewards are provided 'contingent' on taking an action or achieving a result.

Timely   Interventions and supports are provided consistently and as timely as necessary to reinforce the desired behaviors to achieve desired result.

Functional Behavioral Assessment

Functions of Behavior

Identifying the functions of behavior for a student provides individuals with a direct explanations of how a particular behavior "works" for an individual student in a given context. Behaviors serve a function to:

- Get something (positive reinforcement) such as social attention, sensory stimulation, peer status and peer attention, tangible rewards;
- Escape or avoid something (negative reinforcement) such as someone. This function typically results in a behavior that allows the student to terminate or postpone an event. As examples, students may tantrum, display physical or verbal aggression; or
- Engage in other activities to control events such as instructional activities.

The functions of behavior may be different depending upon the context in which the behavior occurs. Also, multiple behaviors may accomplish similar functions or different functions in different contexts. Of course, the positive interventions that are appropriate for one student will differ for another student depending upon the function of the specific problem behavior for the student.

All behaviors are purposeful and serve to meet a need. Behaviors change from environment to environment and are maintained by consequences that reinforce the behavior. When a student is exhibiting a behavior that is considered challenging, troublesome or inappropriate, this behavior may be inadvertently maintained because the interventions being used are not addressing the root cause or function of that particular behavior for the student. In addition, individuals who work with a student may have different levels of behavioral tolerance. One person may perceive a behavior as troublesome, while another may not.

Behavioral Assessment

Functional behavioral assessment is a collaborative, student-centered process for gathering information that reliably predicts the conditions and/or circumstances around why a student is exhibiting an inappropriate behavior. A functional assessment is an assessment of a student's behavior of concern to determine the function of that behavior for the student.

When a student displays inappropriate behavior, an assessment of that behavior should involve the collection of objective, observable data and information concerning that behavior across settings from a variety of individuals, including educators, parents, and the student. It is most critical that the problem behavior is described in objective terms. The data obtained should clearly and objectively describe the events leading to the behavior, the behavior itself, and the consequences in response to the behavior. In order to change the problem behavior, supports and intervention strategies used to teach the student an appropriate replacement behavior must satisfy the same function for the student.

Since all behaviors serve a function, such as the need to get something, avoid something, or control events, the problem behaviors students engage in are typically attributable to:

- Skill deficits;
- Performance deficits;
- Environmental factors;
- Interpersonal factors;
- A failure to self-regulate; and/or
- An instructional "mismatch."

Although, under the IDEA, a functional behavioral assessment is not required until a student with a disability has been removed for 10 school days or its cumulative equivalent in a school year, it is recommended that school personnel engage in the FBA process whenever a problem behavior is first observed to enable professionals to develop and implement appropriate supports and services in a behavioral intervention plan (BIP).

The FBA is to describe the behavior and the context in which it is observed. This information is used to guide the development of a behavior intervention plan. As such, FBA should be conducted whenever a student's behavior is difficult to understand and/or a student's BIP needs to developed or revised.

An FBA should include the following three steps: a collection of data, a proposed hypothesis, and an assessment of hypothesis validity.

- **Step 1: Collect Information**

The collection of data is needed to:

- Identify the specific problem behavior; and
- Define that behavior in specific and objective terms.

This is accomplished through indirect observations and direct observations. Indirect observations, such as informal conversations, questionnaires, checklists, and structured interviews with key persons who have contact and experiences with the individual student and can offer insights into the contexts or conditions under which the behavior occurs. Direct observations are the most reliable and valid procedures for collecting information because observers watch the behaviors as they are occurring and note the environmental events (environmental factors, antecedent and consequence events) that are associated with the behaviors. The collection of data should include specific information regarding the environment, events, activities immediately prior to the behavior, as well as following the behavior.

- **Step 2: Propose a hypothesis of the student's behavior**

The hypothesis should explain the relationship between a target behavior and general conditions that appear to predict and maintain that behavior. The hypothesis focuses on the relationship between an observable and measurable antecedent, the target behavior, and consequence variables.

Most importantly, the statement indicates the possible function of that behavior for the student. A complete hypothesis includes:

- An objective description of the target behavior;
- Possible setting events and antecedents that trigger the target behavior; and
- Possible consequences that maintain the target behavior.

- **Step 3: Assess the validity of the hypothesis**

This is to collect additional information about the conditions under which the problem behavior occurs and does not occur, and demonstrate that occurrences of the behavior and the presence of these conditions are related and predictable. Typically this entails systematic observations of a student to identify and confirm patterns of predictable behaviors in order to create an effective intervention plan for changing the behavior. If during the validation phase, the hypothesis cannot be confirmed, the hypothesis would need to be reformulated and revalidated.

There are a variety of formats and instruments public agency personnel may use to conduct an FBA. Please refer to Appendix A for a variety of instruments that personnel may wish to use.

Behavioral Intervention Plans

Effective behavior interventions are planned, data-driven, and based on an assessment of the problem behavior. Undertaking an "intervention" without an assessment or a plan can lead to increased misbehavior. A BIP is individualized for the student, designed for the settings where the behavior occurs, and implemented consistently across those settings. Follow-up, monitoring and revision of the intervention plan are essential as the problem behavior is replaced by an acceptable behavior.

An FBA is the basis for developing an effective BIP. A student's BIP is designed to positively address the specific individual needs, not aversive interventions. The components of the BIP should address:

- Procedures to teach the student an appropriate replacement behavior;
- How to alter or neutralize any known setting events;
- How to alter or manipulate the events that typically occur before the problem behavior (antecedents);
- How to alter or manipulate the events that typically occur after the problem behavior (consequences) to positively reinforce the appropriate replacement behavior; and
- How personnel are to consistently respond to occurrences across settings.

Depending upon the problem behavior, it may be necessary to begin with a series of approximations that will serve the same function for the student while more extensive modifications are developed. For example, if the function of a behavior is to escape or avoid an academic task, we may have to teach a replacement behavior that temporarily will serve this function (e.g., raise hand and ask to be excused as opposed to creating a disturbance in the classroom). With the temporary replacement behavior established, we can begin modifying instructional tasks to make them less difficult and provide reinforcement to the student for each successive approximation toward the longer-term objective. The selection of replacement behaviors that require less effort to display than the problem behavior is important. A replacement behavior which takes more effort to display than the problem behavior is unlikely to occur. For example, if a student historically has screamed to get the teacher's attention, the student can be taught to raise his or her hand. However, because screaming is easy, immediate, and historically effective, it is not likely to be automatically abandoned in favor of hand raising. Thus, the goal is to carefully select and directly teach replacement responses that are easier to do than the problem behavior (screaming) and serves the same function (attention from the teacher). It is important to remember that if a replacement behavior does not meet the student's need, the replacement behavior will not persist.

Even after appropriate replacement behaviors are identified and instruction has facilitated the student's success in using an appropriate replacement behavior, events will occur that may hasten the return of the problem behavior. To increase the likelihood of a student exhibiting the desired replacement behavior in settings formerly associated with the problem behavior, various modifications to these settings may be needed to minimize the risk of the problem behavior recurring.

Functional Behavioral Assessment

Definitions	Source
Functional behavioral assessment (FBA) is generally considered to be a problem-solving process for addressing student problem behavior.	Center for Effective Collaboration and Practice http://cecp.air.org/
Functional behavioral assessment is an approach that incorporates a variety of techniques and strategies to diagnose the causes and to identify likely interventions intended to address problem behaviors.	Center for Effective Collaboration and Practice http://cecp.air.org/
Indirect or *informant assessment* relies heavily upon the use of structured interviews with students, teachers, and other adults who have direct responsibility for the students concerned.	Center for Effective Collaboration and Practice http://cecp.air.org/
Direct assessment involves observing and recording situational factors surrounding a problem behavior (e.g., *antecedent* and *consequent* events). An evaluator may observe the behavior in the setting that it is likely to occur, and record data using an Antecedent-Behavior-Consequence (ABC) approach.	Center for Effective Collaboration and Practice http://cecp.air.org/
Data analysis. Once the team is satisfied that enough data have been collected, the next step is to compare and analyze the information. This analysis will help the team to determine whether or not there are any patterns associated with the behavior.	Center for Effective Collaboration and Practice http://cecp.air.org/
Hypothesis statement. Drawing upon information that emerges from the analysis, school personnel can establish a hypothesis regarding the function of the behaviors in question. This hypothesis predicts the general conditions under which the behavior is most and least likely to occur (antecedents), as well as the probable consequences that serve to maintain it.	Center for Effective Collaboration and Practice http://cecp.air.org/
FBA Steps: Collect information regarding conditions under which problem behavior is & is not observed & more appropriate behavior is required. Develop testable (manipulatable) hypotheses. Collect direct observation information. 4. Design behavior support plans. 5. Develop implementation scripts. Collect information on effectiveness & efficiency of behavior support plan & redesign based on evaluation information	OSEP Center on Positive Behavioral Interventions and Support http://pbis.org
Functional behavioral assessment (FBA) is a process for collecting information. The data the team collects is used to help determine why problem behaviors occur. The data will help identify ways to address the behaviors. FBA data are used to develop a positive behavioral intervention plan.	Families and Advocates Partnership for Education (FAPE) PACER Web: *http://www.fape.org*

Continued

Functional Behavioral Assessment Continued

Definitions	Source
Steps in conducting a functional behavior assessment: Identify and agree on the behavior(s)that most need to change. Determine where the behaviors occur and where they do not. Identify what may contribute to the behaviors. Collect data on the child's performance from as many sources as possible. Develop a hypothesis about why problem behaviors occur (the function of the behaviors). Identify other behaviors that can be taught that will serve the same function for the child. Test the hypothesis. The team develops and uses positive behavioral interventions that are written into the child's IEP or behavior intervention plan. Evaluate the success of the interventions. Change or fine-tune as needed.	Families and Advocates Partnership for Education (FAPE) PACER Web: *http://www.fape.org*

Positive Interventions and Supports

Definitions	Source
Positive: characterized by or displaying approval, acceptance, or affirmation *Behavior:* what we do *Intervention:* an action that a changes a course of events	Families and Advocates Partnership for Education (FAPE) PACER Web: *http://www.fape.org*
Positive behavioral support is a general term that refers to the application of positive behavioral interventions and systems to achieve socially important behavior change.	OSEP Center on Positive Behavioral Interventions and Support *http://pbis.org*
Practical Interventions - Functional behavioral assessments are used to develop behavior support plans. Interventions emphasize environmental redesign, curriculum redesign, & removing rewards that inadvertently maintain problem behavior. Teaching is a central behavior change tool. Research-validated practices are emphasized. Intervention decisions are data-based.	OSEP Center on Positive Behavioral Interventions and Support *http://pbis.org*
Positive behavioral support (PBS) is an approach that emphasizes teaching as a central behavior change tool, and focuses on replacing coercion with environmental redesign to achieve durable and meaningful change in the behavior of students.	OSEP Center on Positive Behavioral Interventions and Support *http://pbis.org*
PBS interventions have common features. Foremost among these features is the application of FBA, but equally important are emphases on: environmental redesign (changing aspects of the setting), curriculum redesign (teaching new skills), modification of behavior (teaching and changing student and adult behavior), and removing rewards that maintain problem behaviors (Carr et al., 1994; Luiselli & Cameron, 1998; O'Neill et al., 1997).	OSEP Center on Positive Behavioral Interventions and Support *http://pbis.org*
A central PBS tenet is that behavior change needs to be socially significant. Behavior change should be: (a) *comprehensive* in that all relevant parts of a student's day (before, during, and after school) and important social contexts (home, school, neighborhood, and community) are affected; (b) *durable* in that the change lasts for long time periods, and (c) *relevant* in that the reduction of problem behaviors and increases in prosocial behaviors affect living and learning opportunities (academic, family, social, work).	OSEP Center on Positive Behavioral Interventions and Support *http://pbis.org*
The PBS approach emphasizes the use of data collection and analysis to inform decision-making (e.g., direct behavioral observations, curriculum-based measurement). A variety of data sources (e.g., office discipline referrals, attendance and	OSEP Center on Positive Behavioral Interventions and Support *http://pbis.org*

Continued

Positive Interventions and Supports Continued

Definitions	Source
tardy reports, and academic progress) are collected through a range of methods (e.g., archival review, interviews, direct observations) and from multiple sources (i.e., students, family members, educators, community members).	
Examples of behavioral intervention strategies: *Stop, Relax, and Think* *Planned Ignoring* *Preventive Cueing* *Proximity Control* *Touch Control* *Humor* *Nonverbal Warnings* *Discipline Privately* *Positive Phrasing* *I-messages* *Behavior Shaping* *Clear routines and expectations*	Families and Advocates Partnership for Education (FAPE) PACER Web: *http://www.fape.org*

Behavior Intervention Plan

Definitions	Source
Behavior Intervention Plan - An effective behavior intervention plan (often called a behavior support plan or positive intervention plan) is used to teach or reinforce positive behaviors. Typically a child's team develops the plan. It usually includes: skill training to increase appropriate behavior changes that will be made in classroom or other environments to reduce or eliminate problem behaviors strategies to replace problem behaviors with appropriate behaviors that serve the same function for the child supports for the child to use the appropriate behaviors A positive behavior intervention plan is <u>NOT</u> a plan to determine what happens to a student who violates a rule or code of conduct. That would be more appropriately called a discipline plan or a punishment plan.	Families and Advocates Partnership for Education (FAPE) PACER Web: *http://www.fape.org*
Behavior Intervention Plan (BIP) The behavioral intervention plan will include, when appropriate: (1) strategies, including positive behavioral interventions, strategies, and supports; (2) program modifications; and (3) supplementary aids and services that may be required to address the problem behavior. After collecting and analyzing enough information to identify the likely function of the student's behavior, the IEP team must develop (or revise) the student's positive behavioral intervention plan. This process should be integrated, as appropriate, throughout the process of developing, reviewing, and, if necessary, revising a student's IEP.	Center for Effective Collaboration and Practice *http://cecp.air.org/*
Elements of a BIP - The IEP team should include strategies to: (a) teach the student more acceptable ways to get what he or she wants; (b) decrease future occurrences of the misbehavior; and (c) address any repeated episodes of the misbehavior. The resulting behavioral intervention plan generally will not consist then of simply one intervention; it will be a plan with a number of interventions designed to address these three aspects of addressing a student's problem behavior.	Center for Effective Collaboration and Practice *http://cecp.air.org/*
This step in the process of creating positive behavioral intervention plans and supports includes discussion of information on strategies	Center for Effective Collaboration and Practice *http://cecp.air.org/*

Continued

Behavior Intervention Plan Continued

Definitions	Source
to address different functions of a student's behavior and how to select the appropriate interventions; skill deficits and performance deficits; student supports; and reinforcement considerations and procedures. It also addresses special considerations, such as the use of punishment and emergency/crisis plans. The IEP team should know about and consider all of these elements as it develops and implements the behavioral intervention plan.	
Evaluate Effectiveness of the Behavioral Intervention Plan - The team should then continue to measure the behavior (e.g., direct classroom observation of Charles' disruptive acts) once the intervention has been implemented. These progress checks need not be as detailed as the initial functional behavioral assessment observations, but should be detailed enough to yield information that the IEP team can then use to begin to evaluate the impact of the intervention plan. The team does this by using the baseline information as a standard against which to judge subsequent changes in student behavior, measured through progress checks. Team members may see positive changes, negative changes, or no changes at all. Data on student behavior should be collected and analyzed about every two to three days; more complex or intrusive intervention plans may necessitate more frequent measurement.	Center for Effective Collaboration and Practice *http://cecp.air.org/*
Throughout this series on functional behavioral assessment and positive behavior intervention plans, we have emphasized that IEP teams should develop multi-step programs that capitalize on existing skills and the idea that knowledge of the functions causing the original misbehavior can shape more appropriate, alternative behavior. In that way, emphasis is on building new skills rather than on simply eliminating student misbehavior. Again, it is important to understand that the problem behavior may have "worked" very well for the student for some time. For this reason, IEP team members must exercise patience in implementing behavioral intervention plans and supports.	Center for Effective Collaboration and Practice *http://cecp.air.org/*

Non-Exclusionary Time-Out

Definitions	Source
The removal of reinforcers (e.g. preferred activity, teacher attention) from the child or youth. There are two levels of this type of time-out. **Planned Ignoring** – Removal of reinforcement such as teacher or peer attention for a short amount of time. **Removal Reinforcement** – The removal of materials that a student is working with for a given amount of time.	Colorado Department of Education, Guidelines for the Use of Time-Out, 2000 *http://www.cde.state.co.us/cdesped/download/pdf/spTimeOut.pdf*
Time-out is a procedure that involves denying the student access to all sources of reinforcement (e.g. teacher and peer attention, participation in on-going activities) as a consequence of undesired behavior. There are three levels of time-out: (a) *contingent observation* – The student remains in a position to observe the group without participating or receiving reinforcement for a given amount of time. (b) *exclusionary* – The student is completely removed from the on-going activity, but remains in the educational setting. (c) *seclusionary* – The student is completely removed from the educational setting.	Kentucky Department of Education 2000 *http://www.state.ky.us/agencies/behave/homepage.html*
Time-out is defined as removing a child from a reinforcing and placing them in a non-reinforcing environment contingent on a specific misbehavior. • It is not limited to a specific place or location. • Time-out must be less reinforcing than the situation in which the misbehavior occurs. • Although there are similarities, time-out is NOT the same as punishment; technically, time-out involves removal of reinforcement, whereas punishment involves presentation of adverse stimuli.	Effective Use of Time-Out Procedures To Reduce Child Misbehavior Ken Merrell PH.D. University of Iowa 2000 *http://www.uiowa.edu/~schpsych/handouts/time-out.pdf*
Time-out involves removing a student from all sources of positive reinforcement, as a consequence of a specified undesired behavior. Time-out may be implemented on many levels ranging from a student taking a time-out at their desk to removing a student to a separate area.	Effective Use of Time-Out *http://www.tces.fcps.net*

Exclusionary Time-Out	
Definitions	**Source**
Exclusionary Time-out - The student is completely removed from the on-going activity, but remains in the educational setting.	Kentucky Department of Education 2000 *http://www.state.ky.us/agencies/behave/home page.html*
Exclusionary time-out is defined as the removal of the child from the reinforcing conditions. Exclusionary time-out has three levels: • *Contingent Observation* – The removal of the child from the current environment to another location within the educational setting. The student may not participate, but still observes the class. • *Exclusion* – The removal of the child from the reinforcing conditions to another location where the student cannot observe the on-going activities. • *Isolation* – The student is removed from the setting and placed in a separate room under constant supervision of qualified staff.	Colorado Department of Education, Guidelines for the Use of Time-Out, 2000 *http://www.cde.state.co.us/cdesped/download/ pdf/spTimeOut.pdf*

Seclusion

Definitions	Source
Seclusion – A behavior management technique that involves locked isolation. Seclusion is the removal of an offender from the general population by placing them in a secure room designed for the purpose of resolving destructive behavior that threatens the safety of others.	Restraint and Seclusion:What You Need to Know 2001 *http://www.thomas.loc.gov* Oregon State Archives Oregon Youth Authority *http://arcweb.sos.state.or.us/rules/OARS_400/OAR_416/416_490.html*
Seclusion- The involuntary separation of a youth from others with the use of a locked door.	Subtitle 04 Office for the Children, Youth, and Families
Seclusion means the involuntary confinement of a child/youth in a room in a covered facility, whether alone or with staff supervision, in a manner that prevents the child/youth from leaving.	Rhode Island Public Law
Seclusion means the involuntary confinement of a patient under the direction of a physician or registered nurse alone in a room which a patient is physically prevented for leaving.	DHMH Memorandum Friday, May 3, 2002

Physical Restraints

Definitions	Source
Any employee may, within the scope of the employee's duties, use and apply physical restraint to a student if the employee reasonably believes restraint is necessary in order to: 1. Protect a person, including the person using physical restraint, from personal injury. 2. Obtain possession of a weapon or dangerous object. 3. Remove a student refusing a lawful command of a school employee from a specific location, including classroom or other school property, in order to restore order or to impose disciplinary measures. 4. Restrain an irrational student. 5. Protect property from serious damage.	*Http://www.tasb.org/policy* Lamesa Independent School District Texas
Therapeutic Physical Restraint means the acceptable use of a staff member's body to immobilize or reduce the free movement of a child/youth arms, legs, torso, or head, in order to ensure the physical safety of a child/youth or other individual in the facility.	*Http://www.rilin.state.ri.us* Rhode Island Public Law
Physical restraint should only be used to protect children when they are in danger to themselves or to others or to keep them from damaging property. The purpose of restraint is to help out of control students regain appropriate control. • Never use as a punishment Does not involve the reinforcement of an alternative behavior and therefore should be used with caution.	Amarillo Independent School District Amarillo Texas *http:www.amarillo.isd.tenet.edu*

Continued

Physical Restraints Continued

Definitions	Source
Restraints – *Category I* means a device identified by the facility which limits a patient's mobility to the extent that the patient would not be able to independently reposition himself/herself or would otherwise be rendered helpless in an emergency. Category I includes but is not limited to, four point restraints and safety suits. *Category II* means any device which is not considered by the facility as a category I restraint and includes, but not limited to, mittens and camisoles. A restraint does not include a helmet when used as a sole form of restraint, chemotherapy, protective devices, or cold wet sheet packs used as a treatment procedure ordered by a physician.	DHMH Memorandum Friday, May 3, 2002
Restraints must be used for the minimal amount of time necessary and only to ensure the physical safety of the individual, other patients or staff members and when less restrictive measures have proven ineffective.	American Psychiatric Nurses Association(APNA) *Http://www.apna.org*
Use of Physical Restraints – Restraints should only be administered by personnel trained in the use of restraints. Personnel should check restrained subject at least every two hours.	COMAR 10.07.09.14
Restraints may not be used for staff convenience. Restraints are to be used as a last resort to protect the safety of the patient and others.	HCFA *http://www.hcfa.gov/pubforms*
The use of involuntary mechanical or human restraints or involuntary seclusion is only justified as an emergency safety measure in response to imminent danger to a patient or others. These extreme measures can be justified only so long as, and to the extent that an individual cannot commit to the safety of him or herself and others.	NAMI The Nation's Voice on Mental Illness *http://www.nami.org*
Physical restraints may be used under the following circumstances: 1. non-physical interventions would not be effective; and 2. The student's behavior poses a threat of imminent, physical harm to self and/or others.	Massachusetts Department of Education *www.doe.mass.edu*

Continued

Physical Restraints Continued

Definitions	Source
Physical restraint is prohibited in the following circumstances; 1. As a means of punishment; or 2. As a response to property destruction, disruption of school order, a student's refusal to comply with a school rule or staff directive, or verbal threats that do not constitute a threat of imminent, serious, physical harm.	Massachusetts Department of Education *www.doe.mass.edu*
No restraint shall be administered in such a way that the student is prevented from breathing or speaking. During the administration of a restraint, a staff member shall continuously monitor the physical status of the student, including skin color and respiration.	Massachusetts Department of Education *www.doe.mass.edu*
Any person in a restraint should be monitored for circulatory problems every fifteen minutes. The restraint should be loosened every sixty minutes to allow for change of position.	Minnesota State Legislature *http://www.revisor.leg.state.mn.us*

Reporting Use of Restraints

Definitions	Source
Use of a physical restraint must be reported: 1. If a student or staff member are injured. 2. Any time a restraint is in place for greater than five minutes.	Massachusetts Department of Education *www.doe.mass.edu*
Administration should be informed: Verbally notified by the staff member who administered the restraint as soon as possible, and in writing no more than twenty-four hours after the restraint was administered.	Massachusetts Department of Education *www.doe.mass.edu*
Parents should be notified: Verbally by the principal or director as soon as possible, and no later than three school days in writing.	Massachusetts Department of Education *www.doe.mass.edu*

Time-Out Room

Definitions	Source
When using an "isolation" or time-out room: 1. It must not be locked. 2. The period of time needs to be kept to a minimum. 3. At least every ten minutes, checks are made on the child's emotional and physical state and a decision is made by the designated staff member on whether the child should be retained in isolation.	COMAR 01.04.04.21
Once a student is placed in a time-out room, staff needs to monitor the student every fifteen minutes. The door to the room **may** be locked.	Oregon Youth Authority
When using an isolation time-out the following cautions should be used: 1. Isolation time-out should not be accomplished by forced or physical coercion of a student into the time-out area. 2. A student should not be placed in a time-out area where they cannot be observed by trained staff members.	Colorado Department of Education 2000
The room used for an isolation time-out should meet the following criteria: • An adequate opening to view the student. • Adequate lighting. • Adequate size, no smaller than 6x6 with normal ceiling height. • A non-injurious environment, which may include carpeting or padded surface and no loose furniture. • An _unlocked_ door.	Colorado Department of Education 2000

Time-Out Length

Definitions	Source
A few minutes of time out should be the norm, and excessive time-out periods (e.g., more than about 10 or 12 minutes) should be avoided-they quickly become isolation punishments rather than time-outs.	Effective Use of Time-Out Procedures To Reduce Child Misbehavior Ken Merrell PH.D. University of Iowa 2000 *http://www.uiowa.edu/~schpsych/handouts/time-out.pdf*
It is appropriate to tell the student that the time-out will end once the pre-specified time period has ended and the child's behavior is appropriate.	Effective Use of Time-Out Procedures To Reduce Child Misbehavior Ken Merrell PH.D. University of Iowa 2000 *http://www.uiowa.edu/~schpsych/handouts/time-out.pdf*
The frequency and duration of time-out should be closely reviewed and monitored to ensure no individual student is chronically in time-out. Excessive time-out length can be counter-productive in reducing challenging behaviors.	Colorado Department of Education 2000
Time-out should be brief (e.g. 1-5 minutes).Time-outs are effective as longer time-outs if the student hasn't been exposed to longer time-outs first. Time-out duration should be no longer than fifteen minutes. If it is necessary for a longer period, alternate interventions should be used.	Effective Use of Time-Out *http://www.tces.fcps.net*
Children should not be secluded in a time-out setting for more than 5-10 minutes at a time, depending on the age of the child, and never more than 15 minutes at a time.	Kentucky Department of Education 2000 *http://www.state.ky.us/agencies/behave/homepage.html*

65

Recreation and Leisure Strategies

Buzz Williams

Introduction

This chapter provides a practical methodology for planning developmentally appropriate sport, leisure, and recreation activities for people with emotional and behavioral disabilities. Operational definitions are provided for sport, recreation, and leisure that facilitate understanding the context in which activities are discussed. The selection of appropriate activities will depend initially on the outcomes, or goals, that are desired as a result of participation. Goals are discussed in terms of the physical, cognitive, and social-emotional domains. Coinciding with the goals are the unique traits of each activity that we refer to as "dynamics." Each activity discussed in this chapter embodies specific social, emotional, motor-skill, and cognitive dynamics. A basic understanding of these dynamics is critical in adapting and modifying activities to be developmentally appropriate. Practical strategies for adapting and modifying activities are then presented. The chapter concludes with a framework for planning developmentally appropriate activities.

Operational Definitions

It is a cumbersome task to define sport, recreation, and leisure. It is not the intent of this chapter to stimulate philosophical debate; however, clarification of these terms is a prerequisite for consistent and reliable communication of the material in this chapter. Basketball, for example, may be discussed as a sport emphasizing teamwork and competition. It may also be explored recreationally with a group of friends playing for fun. Still yet, it may be viewed as a leisurely endeavor, whereby one shoots foul shots in the driveway.

Sport

Sport, for our purposes, is defined as an activity that requires physical skills, compliance with rules, includes score, and incorporates a competitive spirit with the goal of winning. Sports include participation as an individual, a partner, or as a member of a team.

Recreation

Recreation is defined as an activity that requires physical skills, rules, and either a score or an end result. The major difference is that recreation is played with a cooperative spirit with the goal of having fun. All sports may be played in a recreational capacity; however, not all recreation is considered sport. Consider basketball as an example. In the same physical education class one group of students may choose to participate in a competitive sport-game of five-on-five basketball, while another group may choose to play a turn-taking-type recreational shooting game, H.O.R.S.E. Golf as a sport may be played competitively for nine holes, while recreationally as Putt-Putt. Baseball may be played competitively in traditional terms, or recreationally as home-run derby.

Leisure

Leisure encompasses activities that include physical and/or cognitive participation. Walking is a physical leisure activity, while chess is a cognitive one. Leisurely activities usually do not include score, and typically involve "standards of practice" instead of rules. For example, while leisure rock climbers do not keep score, they adhere to a variety of ethical and safety standards established by the climbing industry. Leisurely activities share the goals of relaxation and exercise. Any recreational activity may be participated in a leisurely capacity, but not all leisure is recreation.

If by now one is curious about the significance of defining the previous terms, consider the following vignette of how terminology impacts our discussion of adapting strategies.

Vignette: Jason at Day Camp

The setting is summer day camp. Jason is an adolescent who is emotionally disabled. He has low self-esteem, little self-confidence, and is awkward in social situations. Jason has not had positive experiences in school physical education classes. He does not possess mature physical skills or age-appropriate hand-eye coordination. The activity for the afternoon involves basketball. If the Activity Director can distinguish between sport, recreation, and leisure, then developmentally appropriate activities may be created to meet Jason's needs. While some students may be ready for basketball as a sport, Jason certainly is not. Yet some camps only offer activities such as basketball in the "sport" context. In addition to basketball sport activities, there need to be recreational and leisurely options. The recreational option includes a small group of people who mutually "choose" to be together. The counselor explains the rules of a game called "Around The World," and then allows the students to play at their own pace. Supervision is provided to keep students on task and socially appropriate. The leisurely option includes individuals and/or partners who take turns shooting. No score is kept, and rules are limited to those necessary for safety and cooperation.

It would be ideal if all people with emotional disabilities were afforded a flexible and therapeutic environment such as Jason in the previous example. The remainder of this chapter has as its objective the development of an understanding of the key components of sport, recreation, and leisurely activities, as well as an understanding of people with emotional disabilities and challenging behaviors. This understanding will help facilitate the planning and implementation of developmentally appropriate activities.

Sport, Recreation, and Leisure Goals

Our discussion of goals begins with a review of two approaches to establishing objectives—the process-oriented approach and the product-oriented approach.

Process-Oriented Goals

The term "process" refers to the "journey," the means toward the end, and the technique used in participating. **Process-oriented goals** may be satisfied by all participants. Each person works to improve on some aspect of the skill—physical, cognitive, or social. Positive reinforcement and encouragement is provided frequently as people demonstrate appropriate effort. Process-type goals in the game of horseshoes may include holding the "shoe" with the proper grip, verbally repeating the score before each throw, or alternating turns without argument. If Jason were to play horseshoes at his family reunion picnic, emphasis on any of the above goals would be appropriate.

Product-Oriented Goals

The term "product" refers to the "destination," the end following the means, or the outcome resulting from participation. An emphasis on product means that each person's performance is evaluated with some form of judgment being made as to the quality of that performance. Effort is overshadowed by accomplishment, and technique gives way to results. In our horseshoes example, a **product-oriented goal** may be to earn at least one "ringer" by the end of the game. In baseball a product-goal may be to get at least one hit during the game, while in tennis a product goal would involve serving over the net. Track and field, by nature, is very product oriented. Participants compete against themselves or opponents to run faster, jump higher, or throw farther. One may recognize that sports tend to be product-oriented, while recreation is somewhat less product-focused. Leisure is the least concerned with "product" and the most therapeutic environment for including people who are emotionally at-risk.

Example: Process and Product Goals in Aquatics

Consider aquatics as an illustration of the relationship between "process" and "product" in creating activity goals. A group of emotionally challenged children are spending the day at a swimming pool. Students in group A are asked to participate in a relay race activity in which the winning team earns certificates. Students in group B are asked to participate in a cooperative group activity in which the goal is to work together to move a giant ball across the pool. Students in Group C are working on fitness and are asked to use kick-boards to move about as they wish.

Students in Group A have a product-oriented goal in which there will be a winner and a loser. If the emphasis of the activity was on winning, the students on the losing team will likely react in negative ways. Students in Group B have a process-oriented goal that is social in nature. There are no winners or losers—only progress toward a collective goal. It is the process of teamwork that is reinforced by the comments of the staff. Students in Group C have a process-oriented goal related to fitness. This type of activity lends itself to individual feedback that is helpful to motivate students. Clearly, the activities of groups B and C provide the most success-oriented environments.

Winning

The most pervasive product-oriented goal of all physical activities is to "win," which is seldom productive when working with people who have emotional challenges. If the emphasis of any particular activity is "winning" the potential for behavioral problems significantly increases. This is not to say that competition is to be avoided. On the contrary, competition is an important part of American society, and we are doing our children a disservice to shelter them from the realities of an often cruel and competitive world. The key, however, is to introduce emotionally fragile people to competition in a developmentally appropriate progression—and one that allows individual choice in that progression.

In fact, participating in many activities would become boring and monotonous without eventually working toward some product-oriented goal. Most people enjoy the thrill of victory, but it should not come at the risk of significant emotional trauma, or anxiety resulting from defeat. It is the challenge and responsibility of the person planning the activities to ensure that the participants are developmentally ready for the activity. This is especially true if it involves a winner and a loser.

When planning activities for people with emotional and behavioral disabilities it is helpful to consider goals in the following three domains: physical motor development, cognitive, and social-emotional. Each contributes uniquely to human development.

Physical Development Goals

Physical goals may be classified as either health-related fitness, motor fitness, or physical skill development goals. Health-related fitness goals encompass aerobic endurance, muscular strength, muscular endurance, body composition, and muscular flexibility. Motor fitness includes the development of power, speed, agility, and coordination. Physical skill development goals are activity-specific. While in-line skating, for example, skating backwards is a learned skill. Likewise, paddling a canoe, dribbling a soccer ball, or flipping one's body in gymnastics are all acquired physical skills gained through practice.

Cognitive Development Goals

Cognitive goals relate to understanding and implementation of strategy, as well as knowledge and application of the rules and score. During bowling, students will typically become bored with the act of rolling balls and knocking down pins. It is not until they comprehend score-keeping that the game becomes meaningful and motivating.

Social-Emotional Development Goals

These goals include cooperation, trust-building, risk-taking, self-esteem development, social skill development, stress reduction, and fun. These are the foundation of such time-tested and effective programs as Outward Bound, which helps students to mature socially and emotionally through cooperative outdoor adventure activities. It is no accident that programs serving students with emotional disabilities emphasize these goals, in the process context, in their programming. Physical education programs, summer camps, outreach centers, and numerous other service providers have created alternative curriculums which de-emphasize traditional product-based sports and emphasize process-based recreation and leisure curriculums.

Once goals are developed, the planning process has direction and focus. In order to move from goal-development to program-adaptation one needs to recognize the components, or **"dynamics,"** of each activity. The next section will describe specific dynamics in the social, emotional, physical, and cognitive domains. It will be these dynamics that are the variables to be manipulated in an effort to create developmentally sound activities.

Sport, Recreation, and Leisure Dynamics

The social, emotional, motor-skill, and cognitive dynamics are the variables that are manipulated and adapted to create developmentally appropriate activities. The description and examples that follow are intended to facilitate an understanding of each dynamic, and the manner in which each influences the development of appropriate learning and play environments.

Social Dynamic

The first dynamic, which needs to be considered when planning activities, is social. Specifically, one must consider whether the student will participate individually, with a partner, or as a member of a group or team.

Intrapersonal Participation

The significance of individual participation is that it allows people with complex emotional issues to participate at their own pace, intensity, and duration. We refer to this as **"intrapersonal participation."** The role of the staff supervising intrapersonal activities is to monitor student safety, and provide motivation with verbal reinforcers. Feedback regarding performance is either process or product related. Typically students will group themselves in the environment in which they will be most successful if given the opportunity to choose. Too often, however, the physical space or the equipment limits options. In any given group of 12 or more students there will likely be one or two who will choose independent work.

Interpersonal Participation

There will be others who choose to participate with a partner, and still others who elect to be in a large group. These are examples of **"interpersonal participation."** Interpersonal participation requires more social skills and self-control abilities than intrapersonal participation.

The social dynamic is illustrated in the following example featuring a **progressively competitive level system.**

Example: Progressively Competitive Levels

A physical education program for high school adolescents with emotional disabilities provides five levels of participation status. The five levels are labeled corresponding with the colored-belt system of some martial arts—white, yellow, green, brown, and black belts, respectively. Students on the white belt level are limited to individual participation and receive no reinforcement from staff; only "verbal directions" are given. This intrapersonal participation provides a non-threatening environment in which students only need a minimum of social skills and self-control to be successful.

Following five consecutive days of acceptable participation at the white-belt level, students are promoted to the yellow-belt level. While on the yellow-belt level, students may choose to participate one-on-one with a staff person, or remain solo. Play can be leisurely, recreational, or competitive. The participating staff person provides reinforcement in the form of verbal praise and encouragement. Note that the social progression moves the student from individual play to participation with staff, not a peer. This is because staff is more likely to be mature and therapeutic.

Following five satisfactory days, the student is promoted to the green-belt level in which he or she may choose to participate one-on-one with a peer. Staff supervision is necessary to ensure that the environment remains positive. Staffs need to be actively engaged and attentive. Staffs who are actively involved in the planning, teaching, playing, and officiating are **"engaged staff."** Permissive or negligent supervision is counterproductive. This social situation provides the forum in which staff can model appropriate interaction, responses to officials, and attitudes regarding competition.

Once students demonstrate five days at this level they move to the brown-belt level in which they may elect to participate in small groups with one staff for every one student. The one-to-one ratio is necessary to provide immediate feedback, prevent conflicts, de-escalate students, and control the "competitive climate." At this level, staff is encouraged to increase or decrease their skill level and intensity to keep competitive games close in score. All staff does not accept this strategy of manipulating "competitive climate" easily. Staff typically need to be reminded that their role is to provide for student success, not demonstrate athletic prowess.

Ultimately students may be promoted to the black-belt level in which participation is unrestricted in terms of peer interaction. Typically two staff members support up to 12 peers in cooperative or competitive activities. Staff members need to be active participants, not sideline observers. If the activity is competitive, staff need to be player-officials. That is to say that they play while they officiate. Students with emotional challenges are more likely to accept positive feedback, constructive criticism, and officiating judgments from engaged staff. If the activity is cooperative, recreational, or leisure in nature then staff involvement is in the form of **"facilitation."** Facilitation means providing verbal instructions, suggestions, and praise such that students are kept focused, on task, and positive. Even the most cooperative activity, such as rock climbing, can become hostile and aggressive without the proper staff facilitation.

Social milieu is a critical component in sport, recreation, and/or leisure. Staff should monitor the appropriateness of the social context for students, especially when it is competitive. Some programs, such as the one in the above example, will make the competitive level of play a privilege that must be earned. Students then are afforded a safe and appropriate environment in which to develop from intrapersonal to interpersonal social interaction—from the cooperative to the competitive.

Emotional Dynamics

The emotional dynamics of activities involve the specific risk-characteristics that govern the degree of emotional stress and the potential for anger escalation. A close look at emotional dynamics will lend insight into the trend in special education to shift from competition to cooperation.

Static vs. Dynamic Environments

A **"static environment"** is one in which a student decides when to initiate movement, and is free of any defensive pressures. Examples of static environments include "putting" in golf, shooting a foul shot in basketball, or jumping over a high bar in track. Static environments do not change before or during student involvement. The key element is that the student maintains control; other participants do not influence him or her.

On the other hand, a student who attempts to dribble a basketball past a defender, "set" a volleyball as it flies over the net, or maintain balance while roller-skating in a crowded rink, is experiencing a **"dynamic environment."** Dynamic environments include changes in time, space, object positioning, and body positioning. The most emotionally risky dynamic environments include opponents in a competitive setting. Modifying this variable is critical when planning for students with emotional and behavioral disabilities, and is addressed later in this chapter.

Closed vs. Open Skills

Skills, too, like the environment, may be a contributing risk factor associated with leisure, recreation, and sport activities. **"Closed skills"** are associated with static environments and include movements that are initiated by the performer. The draw and release of a bow in archery is a closed skill. If the target is fixed, then this closed skill is executed in a static environment. Another example includes batting in baseball. Swinging at a ball resting on a tee is a closed skill in a static environment. Other closed skills include the foul shot in basketball, corner kick in soccer, goal kick in football, serve in tennis, and release in bowling.

Open skills on the other hand are associated with dynamic environments and include movements such that initiation depends on outside factors. If the target in archery is swinging on a rope, then the skill becomes "open." Likewise, batting a pitched ball is an open skill. Other examples of open skills include dribbling in basketball and soccer, catching a pass in football, and returning a tennis serve.

Climate

Climate refers to the category of activity and the social requirements necessary for student success. Climates may be combative, competitive, or cooperative. They may include extreme sports, adventure activities, or outdoor pursuits. Climate may even refer to the virtual reality of video game-play, or the local version of favorite games and pastimes.

Combative climates

Combative climates are created in sports in which players defend and attack. Typically they involve aggressive contact between players. Combative team sports include football, rugby, soccer, lacrosse, hockey, and basketball. Combative individual sports include wrestling, boxing, and karate.

Competitive climates

Competitive climates exist in a variety of individual, partner, and team sports. While winning is the goal of the activity, aggressive contact is not typical, and there is no goal to defend or attack. Examples of competitive activities include tennis, badminton, volleyball, baseball, gymnastics, bowling, golf, and track and field.

Cooperative climates

Cooperatives include a variety of individual, partner, and group activities. Cooperatives may be classified into three types of initiatives—trust, social skill, and problem solving.

There are far too many cooperative activities to provide a comprehensive list in this category. The trend in physical education classes across the country is including cooperatives throughout the school year to address the affective needs of students. Summer camps and outdoor education facilities, too, utilize these types of activities as a means to include, motivate, and educate students.

The multi-colored parachute is a familiar piece of cooperative equipment. In one cooperative activity called, "Popcorn," a group of students hold the outer edge of the parachute as they work together to lift and catapult a nerf ball up to the ceiling of the gymnasium. This is but one of many parachute activities to promote teamwork and direction following. It is interesting to note that many students, who find traditional combative-competitive basketball stressful, enjoy parachute basketball. This is where a small group of students lift the parachute to catapult a basketball to the hoop for points.

An example of a trust-initiative involves "trust falling." A group of students links forearms and hands to create a "safe landing" for a student who falls from progressively higher objects—and trusts the group to catch him or her safely.

An example of a problem-solving initiative is the "electric fence." A group of students is given a wooden plank and asked to transport each member across a vaulting box that may not be touched by members.

Extreme activities

Extreme activities have been made popular by Generation X during the 1990s as evidenced by the creation of the X Games and Gravity Games, two Olympic-like events featured on ESPN and MTV Sports. The goal is to effect a physical adrenaline rush and to execute movements in the sport that have yet to be demonstrated. Extreme activities include skate-boarding, in-line skating, snow-boarding, sky-boarding, and free-style biking. The "extreme" is derived from the fact that there is a significant risk of physical injury while executing the performances and stunts.

Adventure activities

Adventure activities include outdoor sports and challenges that include individual demands, as well as partner and group trust and teamwork to accomplish a journey or task. Adventure activities are associated with milder risks than extreme sports and include rock climbing, ice climbing, canoeing, kayaking, whitewater rafting, skydiving, spelunking, bungee jumping, deep-sea diving, hang gliding & parasailing.

Outdoor activities

Outdoor activities differ from adventure activities in that they do not possess the same inherent risks and dangers. Most outdoor activities are either recreational or leisurely in nature. Examples include horse riding (equestrian), hiking, orienteering, mountain biking, road cycling, walking, jogging, running, swimming, snorkeling, archery, hunting, fishing, water skiing, snow skiing, boating, and sailing.

Games and pastime activities

When considering recreational and leisure activities for people with emotional and behavioral challenges, one should not overlook traditional games and pastimes. Many of these activities are culturally specific and may be new and interesting to students with diverse backgrounds. Such activities include, but are not limited to, hopscotch, rope-jumping, marbles, jacks, hide-and-seek, freeze tag, dodge ball, darts, frisbee, billiards, and table tennis. Then there are international games such as bocce ball, cricket, and croquet.

Video games and virtual reality simulation activities

Finally we arrive at the high-tech world of video games and virtual reality simulators. It is interesting to note that the first home-video game "Pong" was introduced to most American homes in the 1970s. Until that time, the closest thing to video games was pinball. Atari followed, only to be superseded by Coleco, Nintendo, and Sony Play Station. The next millennium will feature even more realistic games. Today these home-based video games are as common as televisions themselves. Home computers, too, have created opportunity for expanded video game-play. Add the attraction of the Internet, and as we enter the next millennium one can bet that even more of our children's spare time will be spent playing video games. At local fairs and conventions, virtual reality simulators have gained in popularity. Now it is inexpensive and available to experience driving an Indy racer, flying a jet, or operating a submarine. As far as emotional dynamics, video games are non-threatening and attractive to children with emotional and behavioral disabilities. One needs to ask how much is too much, and at what health-related physical cost are children participating? The common sense answer is for parents and guardians to monitor the appropriateness of game content, and to limit play to allow for other activities such as homework and outside playtime.

Motor-Skill Dynamics

Selecting and adapting activities requires a general recognition of key motor-skill concepts. If a child is easily frustrated by failure and does not possess fine motor skills or eye-hand coordination, then activities requiring these are likely to cause problems. Consider the skill of underhand serving a badminton shuttle. One who understands motor-skill concepts will be able to assist the frustrated child who is growing more impatient with every attempt to serve the shuttle. The teacher shows the student how to extend his or her arm with the racquet face held parallel to the ground. Then the teacher places the shuttle on the center of the strings and the student simply needs to swing the arm forward to "launch" the shuttle over the net. Thus, the skill was adapted to eliminate the coordination and fine-motor components. The following terms will help in understanding more about such modifications.

Fine Motor and Gross Motor

Fine motor activities involve the coordination of limited muscles to perform precise movements. Threading a needle is the classic fine-motor movement. With respect to sports and recreation, fine motor skills are required in serving a badminton shuttle, stabilizing a bow in archery, and throwing a dart at a bull's-eye. Gross motor activities involve large muscles of the body to perform general movements. Kicking a ball, swimming, or pedaling a bicycle are all gross motor movements.

Speed and Strength

Speed is the ability to move from one point to another in as brief a time as possible. Speed is important in racing in track events, swimming, and bicycling. Speed is also important in competitive games where the object is to beat an opponent to the goal. Strength is often associated with speed; however, strength is the ability to perform a maximum muscle contraction without regard to time. Strength would be important in tug-of-war, for example. Strength can be specific to body parts as well. For example, students who choose to use in-line roller skates need the ankle strength to keep their ankles from flexing inward or outward.

Power and Accuracy

Power is the ability to perform a maximum muscle contraction in as short a period as possible. The standing long jump is an example of an explosive muscle contraction that reflects the power of the muscles of the legs. Jumping to receive a rebound in basketball is also a power move. Track events like the discus throw or shot-put are classic power sports. Power requires gross motor movement. Accuracy, on the other hand, requires fine motor movements combined with gross motor. A student can throw for distance, which would rely on power. The same student may throw for accuracy that is a reflection of fine motor control. An example of accuracy in recreation would be throwing darts, using a billiards cue, or shooting a marble.

Coordination and Agility

Coordination is the ability to integrate separate motor groups with separate senses. An example would be combining eyesight with arm movements. Eye-hand coordination is the most common form, and is necessary for successful batting in baseball, serving and returning balls in net sports like tennis, as well as games like jacks. Jumping rope requires the integration of eyes with legs, and adds a component of rhythm for success. Agility is the ability to change the direction of movement quickly and accurately. Activities that incorporate dodging opponents or objects require agility. A relay race is an activity that requires students to run, stop, and change direction quickly. Agility is developed with practice, and is commonly a weak skill for many sedentary students.

Muscular Endurance and Aerobic Endurance

Muscular endurance is the ability of a muscle to work repeatedly without fatigue. Continuous movements like swimming, cycling, and running require muscular endurance. When the muscle fatigues, the activity becomes unpleasant or painful and usually the activity stops. Endurance athletes train their bodies to push past this fatigue point. Running, biking, and swimming are common endurance activities, and when combined make the three events of the triathlon. Aerobic endurance is the ability of the heart and lungs to provide oxygen to muscles to keep them working. The same activities that require muscular endurance require aerobic endurance. When an activity is performed such that the heart rate increases, the activity is aerobic. The increased heart rate is a reflection of the heart working faster to pump blood, and thus oxygen, to the necessary muscles. If the activity requires the student to move faster than his heart can provide oxygen, muscles will quickly fatigue and the student will come to a breathless halt. Limits to student endurance should not be confused with laziness or lack of motivation. These are physiological limitations, and need to be addressed as such—with developmentally appropriate training. It is extremely frustrating for a student to reach the point of muscular or aerobic exhaustion, only to be called lazy by an uninformed coach.

Muscular Flexibility

Muscular flexibility is the ability of a joint to move through a wide range of motion. Students whose muscles are less flexible will have difficulty performing activities at the same degree of ease as their more flexible peers. Some activities, such as racing, throwing, and kicking will be more challenging for the less flexible student. For activities like gymnastics, and contact sports like football, training for flexibility is critical for both student success and safety. It is developmentally appropriate to warm up with low-level walking, or jogging-type activities before muscles are stretched.

Cognitive Dynamics

Students generally need to understand the cognitive dynamics of rules, scoring, and strategy to participate fully in an activity. The first dynamic that needs to be addressed involves rules so that a basic level of interaction can occur.

Example: Cognitive Progression In Bowling

To illustrate the interaction of cognitive dynamics we will use bowling as an example. The first priority is to explain the safety rules and the vocabulary. Keep it simple. Students need to know to handle balls safely, keep them between the gutters, and to roll one at a time. They also need to know what area defines the lane, the gutters, and which buttons return the ball and sweep the lane. Then bowling can begin.

Progressively speaking, the score should be introduced next. Once students are safely rolling balls down the lane, taking turns, and following directions, it is time to give some meaning to knocking down pins. Students will need to understand that they get one point for every pin they knock over. While some students will be able to use pencils and paper, others will need to count manipulatives, such as poker chips, to help them with the math. Computer scoring is wonderful for students who understand the game and need some assistance with math. Many students, however, do not fully understand conceptually how their scores show up on the big overhead screen. This lack of understanding is likely to lead to frustration and acting-out from students with emotional difficulties.

Once rules and score are understood, strategy can be introduced. This means stance, release technique, and spare pick-up. It is extremely upsetting for a student to be coached on technique and strategy before he has a grasp of the rules and score. The same developmental progression is recommended for all sport, recreation, and leisure activities. Since there is less emphasis on score and strategy in recreation, and even less in leisure, it is clear why these activities are less intimidating to youth with emotional disabilities. Adapting these cognitive concepts is even more critical when a learning disability accompanies the emotional disability.

Practical Strategies and Adaptations

This section presents practical strategies that enable students with emotional disabilities and behavioral challenges to participate at a developmentally appropriate level. The following adaptations are offered in the context of the social, emotional, motor-skill, and cognitive dynamics. This is not an all-inclusive list of activities or adaptations. It is intended to stimulate thinking in developmental terms. It does not take a genius or adapted physical education certification to demonstrate appropriate modifications and employ sound instructional strategies. It does, however, take an open mind and an ability to think "outside of the box." Many of these strategies transfer to other activities. Once one understands how to adapt a particular activity, the same principles and practices may be applied to modify other activities. By thinking "outside of the box," one will begin to analyze activities as a series of tasks to be manipulated for student success. One may also recognize that the activities presented in this section are all "traditional sports." These have been included because these are the activities that present the most difficulty for people with emotional disabilities. These are also the activities found in many sport and recreational settings. Whenever possible, people with emotional disabilities should be afforded the opportunity to participate in climates other than combative or competitive.

The following activities are commonly included in schools, recreation programs, summer camps, and family get-togethers. They include basketball, combative sports (soccer, lacrosse, hockey), volleyball, racquet sports (tennis and badminton), and baseball.

Activity: Basketball

Social Dynamics
1. Ask students to elect individual play, partner play, small group social play, or competitive play.
2. More than one individual can participate at the same hoop as long as there is one ball for each player.
3. Individual play can occur with or without staff interaction and feedback.
4. Partners will typically play social shooting games in a leisurely capacity.
5. Small groups playing leisurely should be clear about the rules for sharing the ball.

6.   Any competition at all requires Engaged Staff.

Emotional Dynamics

1.   Use triangulation to make the dynamic environment static.

Players who elect to play competitively may need the environment adapted to be less dynamic. The strategy for doing this is called "Triangulation." Triangulation involves taping or chalking a triangle under each basket such that the base of the triangle is as wide as the "key" area with the point of the triangle extending to the foul line. This provides an area referred to as the "defensive triangle." Players while on defense are required to have at least one foot inside the triangle. The offensive team may advance down-court toward the opponent's goal without the pressure of defensive players "in their face." The offensive players may then execute closed-skill shooting in a static environment.

When offensive players demonstrate readiness, one of the five defenders may be allowed to leave the triangle to put pressure on the advancing offensive dribblers. More defensive players may leave the triangle when the offensive players demonstrate emotional and behavioral readiness for the stress of the progressively more dynamic environment. Triangulation eliminates the fast break and makes a dynamic environment static such that players may participate at their developmental level.

Motor-Skill Dynamics

1.   Recognize the gross motor skills required are dribbling, passing, and shooting.
2.   Ignore dribbling violations to keep game-play moving.
3.   Only permit dribbling behind the half-court line where no defenders may attack.
4.   Require bounce passing to provide more tracking time to less coordinated receivers.
5.   Bounce passes are less likely to hit players while in flight.
6.   Require each player to receive a pass before any player may shoot for equity.
7.   Make dribbling a violation to discourage prolonged hot-dogging that slows the game.
8.   Allow players to score one point for contacting the rim and or backboard.
9.   Create a maximum score such that many games can be played in a brief time period.
10.   Multiple games provide opportunities to change players and cool off from a disappointing loss. These are **"low-stakes games."**
11.   Staff should be actively engaged as player-officials.

Cognitive Dynamics

1.   The rules should be adapted such that violations do not slow the pace of game-play.
2.   Essential rules include contacting the ball but not the opponent.
3.   A primary safety rule is that play stops on any staff whistle.
4.   Rim-players may elect to score one point for rim or backboard contact.
5.   Hoop players may score either two or three points for balls passing through the hoop.
6.   Do not allow defensive players to attack until offensive players cross the half-court line.
7.   Stop play occasionally for teachable moments—choose these opportunities wisely.

Activity: Combative Goal Defending Sports (Soccer, Lacrosse, and Hockey)

Social Dynamics

1. Individuals can work by themselves with teacher guidance.
2. Partners and small groups may work together cooperatively passing and shooting.
3. Any competition at all requires active staff engagement.
4. Teams should be selected using the **"ability partner procedure."** This procedure is a non-threatening and non-embarrassing way to group students. It involves staff pairing students by similar ability and then splitting the pairs to create two groups or teams with comparable ability. Teams should never be selected using the "team-captain" technique, as this alienates the less skilled or disliked students.

Emotional Dynamics

1. There are three primary strategies: hot players, clock-players, and crease players.

Hot players

A hot player participates in the same field of play as his or her peers, only the ball or puck assigned to him or her is a different color and designated as "hot." Hot players may only touch hot balls or pucks. A hot player may be engaged in his or her static environment in the middle of a very competitive dynamic environment. Typically hot players work toward making a shot or goal. They may elect to have one or more defenders in the "actual" game block one of their shots. Hot players take advantage of the fact that the defenders get preoccupied with the "actual" game that affords hot players opportunities to score.

Clock players

A clock player participates as any other player on the field until he or she contacts the game ball or puck. Once the clock player contacts the ball or puck, the official counts down from a predetermined number. A typical clock duration is five seconds. During the countdown no defensive players are permitted to move their feet. This is another method of making the dynamic environment static, and providing a non-threatening environment in which to play. Once the countdown reaches zero, play resumes as normal and defenders may attack.

Crease players

A crease player participates in a designated zone in which only he or she is permitted. Once the ball or puck enters the zone the official sounds a whistle and affords the crease player possession of the ball or puck. Crease players may be positioned on defense or offense. Staff needs to encourage other players to make strategic use of the crease-areas of the field such that crease players develop into valued team players.

2. The crowding rule discourages unfair and threatening double-teaming.

Crowding is called and the whistle is sounded whenever two players from a team make an active defensive play for a ball or puck against one player from the offensive team. This provides a safe, non-threatening environment and communicates staff awareness and engagement.

Motor-Skill Dynamics:

1. Competitive zones are created for ability-matching players.

   "Zoning" involves arranging a team such that half of the players need to remain on the offensive side of the centerline, and the remaining half needs to remain on the defending side. This allows the staff to match the players most likely to go head-to-head. There should be at least one actively engaged staff person playing on each side of the field to monitor play intensity.

2. Adjust the size of the goals to provide for offensive success. Students need to score frequently to keep them motivated.
3. Do not allow a student to goal-tend unless he or she has the appropriate safety equipment. The alternative is to establish a restrictive "goal area" which offensive players may not enter to shoot. This allows defensive players to capture the ball or puck without sacrificing their bodies in front of the goal.
4. Play three-point games. Short games decrease the "high stakes" mentality, provide more opportunities to switch positions, and allow students to forget about "bad calls" or disappointing losses.
5. Brief games provide for needed rest and water breaks.
6. In soccer, lightweight balls are available which are less threatening.
7. In floor hockey, rubber pucks are less dangerous and painful if they hit a player.
8. In floor hockey, practice keeping sticks below knee level, and follow through with penalties or removal for consistent violations (three-strikes policy).
9. In lacrosse, tennis balls, rubber balls, or sponge balls may be used.
10. In lacrosse, allow stick checking only—no body checking with sticks.

Cognitive Dynamics:

1. The most important rules involve safety.
2. Clearly mark a goal area in which offensive players may not enter to shoot.
3. Allow goal-tending only when practiced and padded appropriately.
4. Call offsides penalties whenever players cross the centerline.
5. Clearly mark the goal with the color of the shooting team (i.e., hang a jersey).
6. Reinforce the score by placing each ball or puck scored on top of or inside the goal.
7. Restart a new game after one team scores two points.
8. Stop play occasionally for teachable moments—choose these opportunities wisely.

Activity: Volleyball

Social Dynamics

Volleyball is an activity that is usually considered as a team sport. Keeping with our philosophy of offering the individual, partner, and small group options, therefore requires some non-traditional thinking. The individual options include self-volleying, wall volleying, and wall serving. The equipment may be regulation-type balls or adapted balls, Nerf balls, beach balls, or even balloons. Partner work includes volleying back and forth, serving to a partner across the net, or one partner tossing the ball up for a variety of "hits" over the net. Small groups of students may play some variation of the regulation volleyball game. Note that beach volleyball, which may be played leisurely, recreationally and competitively is played with only two players per team. There is nothing wrong with a group of students simply enjoying a game involving volleying a ball back and forth across the net without keeping score or applying rules. If, however, a group is interested in playing volleyball with score, officiating, and rules, then it is suggested that the game be introduced in a progression of developmental levels. The next section explains the emotional significance of incorporating developmental levels in volleyball. The motor skills section presents a detailed example of the level progression.

Emotional Dynamics

Volleyball is seldom presented to students in a static manner, and even less as a cooperative game. These are the keys to making volleyball a player-friendly activity. Because it is a highly dynamic environment that requires mature motor-skills and social cooperation, it is one of the more challenging activities for students with emotional disabilities. The challenge for educators then becomes how to break down the tasks of the game into developmentally appropriate segments. Students will cooperate and have fun when they can participate successfully. This is the challenge of the educator.

The anxiety associated with being unskilled in front of one's peer group often manifests into participants teasing and provoking students on their team, as well as the other. It is critical that at least two mature staff intervene in this type of activity. At least one staff person needs to be on each team to facilitate positioning (especially during rotation), score-keeping, rule following, and most importantly, positive social interactions. Staff needs to model cheering for teammates, clapping, and pats on the back, and verbal support to teammates who make errors. A positive play environment will decrease student anxiety about participating. It is acceptable for a team to play competitively, but students need to have limits set such that negative comments are discouraged and positive ones are praised and reinforced. Hence, even in a competitive environment, cooperation and positive play can occur. It is more difficult, but still possible to motivate students to congratulate, shake hands, and support the opposing team. The modeling and tone set by the engaged staff is the critical element.

Should students not express interest in playing volleyball competitively, or they need some variety, consider cooperative game-play options. One favorite among students is cage ball volleyball. In this game a 72-inch diameter cage ball (multicolored giant ball) is lifted by the members of the team, which takes tremendous balance. Through teamwork and cooperation, the team then throws the ball over the volleyball net, which is the object of the game. Score can be included, but generally is not necessary for motivation.

Another such cooperative game is parachute volleyball in which students hold the edges of a parachute and launch one or more Nerf-type balls over the net. No score is recorded, as the goal is to successfully propel at least one ball over the net. An opposing team receives the balls and counters with their best effort.

Motor-Skill Dynamics

The motor skills required to play competitive regulation volleyball are advanced, and most people do not possess the skills to be successful playing an official regulation game. Yet, many students are subjected to the embarrassment and frustration of being expected to play at this high level. In response, it is suggested that volleyball be presented to students as a series of seven stages—each progressively more challenging. The seventh level is regulation volleyball play. The following is a description of the rules and adaptations for each of the seven levels.

The following rules are universal for all levels:

1. Teams are positioned as in regulation volleyball.
2. Score is kept as in regulation volleyball.
3. Boundaries are as in regulation volleyball, with the exception of the service line.
4. Players need to roll the ball under the net during side-outs.

Level 1: Bounce-Catch Volleyball

1. The serve may be delivered over the net by tossing or striking the ball.
2. The serving position may be as close to the net as the server chooses.
3. Receiving players may allow the ball to bounce one time before catching or striking it.
4. Receiving players may toss the ball to a teammate who also may catch or strike it.
5. A maximum of three players may touch the ball before returning the ball over the net.
6. The ball may be tossed underhand or struck over the net.

Level 2: Catch Volleyball

1. All rules from level one apply except the ball may not bounce.

Level 3: Serve Volleyball

1. All rules from level 2 apply except the ball must be served with a strike.
2. Either underhand or overhand is permitted; underhand is easiest for success.
3. Serving position may still be chosen by the server.

Level 4: Set Volleyball

1. All rules from level 3 apply except the ball must be returned over the net with a strike.
2. The strike should be a two-hand "set," but any strike is acceptable as long as the ball lands in-bounds.
3. Spiking is not permitted at this level.

Level 5: One-Catch Volleyball

1. All rules from level 4 apply except the first hit for a team must be a strike. The last hit must be a strike as well. Only one catch is permitted between strikes before the ball is returned over the net.
2. The "catch" in between strikes provides a skill-buffer since most initial strikes are not controlled hits, and often difficult to follow with a second set or bump-type strike.
3. Clever students will attempt to toss the ball in position for a "spike." This is acceptable as long as the receiving team has been instructed how to recognize a spike is likely, and as long as the receiving team has the skills to block or dodge the spiked ball safely.

Level 6: Bump-Set Volleyball

1. All rules from level 6 apply except a catch must be preceded by two consecutive strikes by a team.
2. The sequence for receiving served balls is either:

- bump-set-catch (the third person may then set the ball over the net him-or herself)
- set-set-catch (the third person may then set the ball over the net him-or herself)
- bump-bump-catch (the third person may then set the ball over the net him-or herself)

Level 7: Regulation Volleyball (Varsity Or Collegiate)

1. All rules from level 6 apply except no catching is permitted.
2. All 3 hits must be strikes including sets, bumps, or spikes.
3. Servers must remain behind the end-line.

Cognitive Dynamics

Volleyball is a cognitive challenge for students for a variety of reasons. Because most students lack basic skills the game does not progress with consistency. The result is that students do not have the opportunity to observe the volleyball game as a "whole," which is important in learning the rules. It is usually perceived as a fragmented series of complicated procedures. By presenting the game in progressive levels, students are afforded the time necessary to assimilate many of the game's procedures. The following are the cognitive challenges that may confuse students, and strategies for preventing the resulting frustration.

1. There will likely be initial resistance to playing volleyball as a series of levels. Expect it and offer a "promotion agreement." The agreement states that teams need to demonstrate proficiency at each level for at least five minutes or until the staff decides to move to the next level. Students will settle into the game and quickly enjoy their success with the modified rules. It is imperative that engaged staff members play enthusiastically, with the modified rules, to bring credibility to the game. The time needed to demonstrate mastery at each level should increase proportionately. Many high school students, with or without disabilities, are successful and happy to play at levels four and five.

2. Students often become confused about where and when to rotate positions. The first strategy is to include one engaged staff person per team to facilitate and model the rotation procedure. The second strategy is to have a visual and auditory signal to communicate a side-out in the game. The visual would be rolling the ball under the net to the rotating team. The auditory signal is for staff to call, "side-out! rotate!" A third strategy is to mark positions on the court (with tape on gym floors or chalk on asphalt or grass) such that each player has a designated space. This affords the staff to direct a student, "move over to position "C." This also assists players with a concrete boundary outlining their playing space. One of the most frequent causes for emotional outbursts in volleyball is when one player aggressively invades another player's space.

3. Players often get frustrated by the unique manner in which points are awarded in volleyball. It is common for disagreements to occur involving score. Establish a policy that every server must call out the score before serving. Reinforce this with verbal reminders, and award the opposing team the serve if the server does not call out the score. Be prepared for students to be confused if they expect to receive a point when the serving team commits an error. In fact they earn the ball, not a point. Only the serving team is eligible to earn points. Avoid telling students they do not get a point, as they will feel cheated. Re-frame the situation by explaining that teams either get "points" or they get "the serve" following an error by the opposing team.

4. Explain that games end when the score reaches seven points. Several brief games, called **low-stakes games**, are easier to deal with emotionally than one high-stakes game that may not finish before time runs out in the class. Low-stakes games also provide for each team to win at least once, which is often enough to keep emotionally fragile students from acting out in frustration.

5. Always encourage students to shake hands with at least one player on the opposing team. Do not require handshakes with every player, as this takes away a player's choice to avoid an antagonistic opponent.

Activity: Racquet Sports (Tennis and Badminton)

Racquet sports present challenges similar to volleyball in that the skills required to play at the regulation level of game-play exceed those of most students. In addition, equipment and facilities are often less than optimal for promoting student success. Furthermore, it is more difficult to hide one's weaknesses when a game is played one-on-one across a net.

Social Dynamics

Students should be offered the opportunity to work as individuals. Tennis balls may be rallied against walls, and badminton shuttles may be volleyed overhead to oneself. Staff should develop as many creative activities to facilitate individual participation as possible. A variety of solo games can be developed focusing on either consecutive hits, accuracy of hits, or power of hits. When playing indoors, modified high-density foam balls should be used for safety. These balls have the same bounce properties as tennis balls, but do not hurt when they contact the body.

Students may also experience success as part of a large group of individuals playing on the same side of the net. The key to success is that there are more objects to strike with the racquet than students. This affords students the maximum opportunity to find objects on the floor or catch them in flight so they can then strike them back over the net to the opposite group. Typically these mass games include safety rules limiting wild swinging, throwing racquets, or directing shots directly at others. Competition in these mass games is not necessary, and often impedes the value of the activities as opportunities for staff to work one-on-one with many students in a short period of time. In addition, because all students are focused on themselves, they are less likely to antagonize peers. This provides a less threatening environment to practice new skills. Two such mass games are explained in the section that follows.

Mass Activity One: Court Cleaners

Students are arranged in two groups, one on each side of the net. Tennis balls or badminton shuttles are tossed onto the court such that there more objects than players. Players use various striking techniques to propel the objects over the net. Play is stopped occasionally to count the objects on each side. Players with the least number of objects in their court win the round, and another is played. Engaged staff should gauge their intensity such that one group does not dominate the other.

Mass Activity Two: Cooperative Wall Ball

Students participate as members of one large group. Each is positioned in a personal space with a racquet. A staff person tosses one ball against a ball. Students are challenged to remain in their space and strike the ball as it bounces into their space. Multiple balls may be added as student ability allows. Play stops once the ball rolls, which is considered the end of the round.

Emotional Dynamics

Students choosing to play competitively should develop their skills while playing a staff person or a peer of similar ability that is mutually agreed upon. Students should have a variety of objects to strike with a partner. Objects include tennis balls, foam balls, beach balls, balloons, and badminton shuttles. Partners should be allowed to choose to be either cooperative or competitive with their striking. Students who experience success with rallying or volleying objects back and fourth will likely ask to be competitive. Note that it is much easier to lose a game to a "friend." This provides a safer environment for students to develop skills with minimal damage to fragile egos.

Racquet sports are frequently associated with tournament play. Recognize tournament play as extremely volatile for students with emotional challenges. Once skills are developed enough to play competitively students should acquire tournament skills in the following progression: Social-rotation, ladder-rotation, and elimination-rotation.

Social Rotation

It is assumed that multiple courts are set up linearly with several nets strung together end to end. A typical gymnasium may support 6 to 12 courts side by side. Once all games have ended, players on one side of the net remain in place while players on the other side of the net slide one court to the right. The last student on the right will need to walk to the far left court in the empty spot created when players shifted right. This results in a situation where players will compete with opponents with a variety of skill levels. There is no benefit to winning and no consequence to losing. The goal is to complete the game with maximum effort and minimal disagreement. Students should have the right to "waive" a particular round if the opponent who rotates into his or her court is particularly antagonistic. Games should end with a clock-count instead of a score-count. Games should be scheduled such that many low-stakes games can be played in one period.

Ladder Rotation

Given the same linear court layout, the far left is designated as the bottom of the ladder and the far right as the top of the ladder. Students are assigned courts randomly. When a game ends, the winner moves one court to the right (up the ladder) and the loser moves one court to the left (down the ladder). The result is that the less skilled players find themselves competing on the left and the more skilled on the right. If the ladder connotation produces anxiety, consider less stigmatizing terms such as "east" and "west." Be especially careful not to make the higher ladder positions the focus of staff attention. Recognize all players and their efforts equitably.

Elimination Tournaments

Considering the previous tournament options, there is really no need to offer an elimination-type tournament to players with emotional and behavioral disabilities. Losing in an elimination round is traumatic for people without emotional disabilities, and is particularly risky for those who do not handle loss and rejection well. If it is a must, then there should be some activity for players to participate in following the elimination. That is, if a player is eliminated from a tournament, he or she should not sit and observe the remaining games. The student should be re-directed to a success-oriented activity. It would also be helpful to offer every student an award for participating in the tournament.

Motor-Skill Dynamics

The motor skills required to play racquet sports are some of the most demanding of any sport. Net games require eye-hand coordination, timing, agility, speed, aerobic and muscular endurance, power, and accuracy. The progression of development for striking objects begins with the hands striking large soft objects. Games should be practiced involving striking balloons and Nerf balls with the open hand. Gradually smaller balls can be included. When students demonstrate consistency and accuracy in their control, they may earn a racquet. The first racquets should be racquetball-type, as these are shorter and require less coordination to strike objects. The racquets should also be highly durable as new participants are often hard on racquets—striking the ground, dropping, and abusing them during acting-out episodes.

Underhand serving in badminton is particularly challenging for many students. For those who become frustrated by constantly missing the shuttle, encourage them to substitute the "launch." This is when the shuttle is balanced feather-side-down on the face of the racquet with one hand. The opposite arm swings overhead to "launch" the shuttle over the net in a catapult fashion. Students may participate successfully in badminton games and tournaments using the "launch" strategy.

Students may develop their skills individually by rallying against a wall. In addition, students may practice by hitting a tetherball—a string anchored to a pole with a ball attached to one end. Hence, when the ball is struck it swings around the pole in a predictable path. Once a player decides to play with a partner across the net, the following progression should be followed.

Rally/Volley Games

These games involve hitting the ball or shuttle back and forth without the burden of serving or scoring. Students should begin a rally or volley with a toss, and should continue striking as long as the object remains in bounds. Tennis balls should bounce no more than one time and badminton shuttles should not bounce. There is no winner and no loser.

Serving Games

It is assumed once students are ready for serving games they have a basic degree of mastery at rallying or volleying. Repeated rally/volley games become boring after a short period and it is then appropriate to introduce serving and scoring. Just as serving was not a part of the rally/volley type game, returning the object is not allowed in the serving type game. One player continues individual serves to a partner as long as the object travels over the net and lands in bounds. The partner does not return the object, and allows it to hit the ground. The partner then picks up the ball or shuttle from the ground. When the server reaches a designated number of attempts they switch roles. When both partners are proficient, staff should model a regulation type game for the students. Regulation game-play is simply a combination of the serving game and the rallying or volleying game that has already been practiced.

Cognitive Dynamics

As with volleyball, tennis and badminton bring with them rules that are often confusing to students. Both games may be played with an understanding of the following three rules: the net, line, and bounce rules.

Net Rule

The ball or shuttle must travel over the net on the serve. The ball or shuttle may strike the top of the net during a rally or volley as long as it travels over the net in bounds.

Line Rule

The ball or shuttle is considered in play if it lands on or inside the lines. This rule is best understood when the lines forming the boundaries are clearly marked. Bright colored tape, paint, or chalk is helpful. Corners of courts may also be marked with cones. If more than one court shares the same net then tape or ribbon may be placed on the net to mark boundaries.

Bounce Rule

Students need to understand that the ball may not bounce more than once in tennis (rally). They may also hit the ball before it bounces (volley). Explain that badminton is a game in which the shuttle must be returned before it bounces.

Frequent disagreements will occur over which player scored points. It is helpful to explore each of the three rules above as the staff processes with the players. Note that players will sometimes reach an impasse in which neither will compromise on a call. Teach the students to invoke the "replay rule" in these cases. The replay rule simply asks that students agree to disagree, and then play the point over with the score as it was before the serve. This strategy empowers students to solve their own disagreements with minimal staff intervention. Also note that several engaged staff members need to be circulating throughout the courts providing positive feedback and assisting with officiating decisions.

As with volleyball it is imperative that students verbally call out the score before serving. This affords opponents and staff to recognize discrepancies and address them before they turn into major arguments.

Activity: Baseball

Social Dynamics

Baseball is perhaps the easiest of activities to plan, as students can throw, catch, and bat as individuals, with partners, or in groups. One key risk factor associated with baseball is the selection of teams. It is recommended that teams be selected using the ability-grouping procedure. Besides creating equitable teams, it eliminates the embarrassment associated with being among the last selected.

In any baseball related activity, there should be options for individual and partner play. Students who are initially anxious about their skills may become more confident as they practice in the non-threatening partnership with a friend or staff person.

Emotional Dynamics

Striking-out in baseball is one of the top anxiety producing events of any recreation and leisure activity. Consider the stress of having every person involved in the activity focusing on the batter, only to have the batter fail. For some students the anxiety associated with striking-out is so great that they will go to great lengths to not participate. This stress is compounded when the pitcher is a peer. Most students do no have the physical skills or social maturity to pitch the ball consistently and fairly across the plate. This puts unnecessary stress on the pitcher as well.

The duration of an inning is also a factor in planning for success. Typical innings last ten minutes or more, and when one team is hitting well the other team may only bat once in a class period. Imagine the frustration of batting once, or not even at all in an entire activity block. When baseball is played without adaptations, this is often the case. The following strategies are critical in planning baseball activities for students with emotional and behavioral challenges.

Strategies

1. Eliminate the possibility of "striking out." Adopt a no-strike-out policy such that any student receiving two strikes from pitched balls must then choose to "toss" it to him or her self, or strike it from a batting tee. Swings are permitted until fair ball is hit. While this seems unorthodox, it is extremely welcomed by players of all ability. Should a player protest the policy, allow him or her to choose to waive the "toss or tee" option. Then if he or she strikes out it will be due to the student's choice.

2. Adopt a "staff-pitches-only" policy. This means that one staff member can be the pitcher for both teams, or two different staff players may be their team's designated pitcher. If a player expresses the interest and ability to pitch, allow him or her to do so following the "batter's choice" policy. Batter's choice means any batter may choose to have a staff pitcher at any time.

3. Adopt an "everybody bats once" policy. This states that the inning ends when one of the following occurs: the batting team receives three outs or every player has had one batting opportunity. Most of the time the inning will end as a result of all players batting once. This keeps the game moving and affords players many opportunities to both field and bat. It also eliminates the potential for a batting rally that escalates student anxiety.

Motor-Skill Dynamics

The equipment is a fundamental part of planning for student success. It is helpful to use a modified ball to decrease the fear of being hit with a hard ball, and increase student success with catching and throwing. There are many varieties of limited flight indoor and outdoor balls available commercially. Outdoor games should involve the type of ball that may be caught with or without a glove. Indoor games should be played with a bright colored ball that will not hurt if students are hit with a batted or thrown ball. Wiffle-balls and other high-density foam balls are best for indoor play.

A variety of bats should be provided such that students can choose the one that he or she feels will be best for success. Indoor bats should be of the plastic wiffle variety; an outdoor should include both wood and aluminum in a variety of lengths and weights.

The throwing, catching, running, and sliding skills of many students are often less developed than is necessary for including all facets of the game. It is suggested that leading off and stealing be limited, as well as sliding into bases. All runners should remain on the base while the pitcher has the ball, and all runners are restricted from advancing when the pitcher has the ball. In the event of an overthrow, runners should only advance one base.

Cognitive Dynamics

Baseball involves high-level abstract thinking skills. Players often times participate and accept the umpires' decisions without fully understanding the reasons for the decision. Consider the abstract concept of being "forced out." While this seems like a simple concept, concrete thinkers may believe themselves to be safe unless an opponent tagged them. Here lies the genesis of much of the conflict when players with emotional disabilities play baseball. Similar misunderstanding occurs with the "infield-fly rule," "tagging up" after a fly ball is caught, and interpreting fair and foul balls. Staff should anticipate such instances when they are most probable and verbally prompt the students to prepare them. An example is to remind a runner on first base that he or she needs to run on a ground ball, but should wait for a fly ball. Staff that have played our national pastime most of their lives need to reflect on just how complex the game really is, and then task analyze each component for students. There is a direct correlation between student understanding and success.

Planning For Success

The purpose of this section is to provide a framework for planning developmentally appropriate activities for people with emotional disabilities and challenging behaviors. It should be used sequentially as a who, what, when, where, why, and how progression which will facilitate appropriate activity selection. Students may be led through this process with guidance. Parents, guardians, and advocates should be aware of each of the levels in assisting with the selection of sport, recreation, and leisure activities.

The Participants (Who)

Participants may be family members. The implication is that family members are aware of the person's disability and are more likely to accept activity modifications. Family members can also be prepared and oriented to activity adaptations before the person arrives at the event.

Participants may be peers who are friends. The implication is that these participants are likely to have played with the person before—therefore accepting his or her disability and activity modifications.

Participants may be peers who are classmates. The implications are that only some of the people may be accepting. In this situation it is helpful to allow students to choose social groupings. This process will naturally group students who will be compatible.

Participants may be peers who are strangers. The implications are that anxiety is likely to be higher with strangers. Again, choices about social groupings are important in empowering students to choose the right environment for him or her.

Selecting an Activity (What)

This step includes the climate or nature of the activity. The activity may be sport-focused and either combative or competitive. It may be recreation focused and either competitive, cooperative, adventure, or extreme. The activity may be more leisure-focused and either outdoor, pastime, video, or virtual. The degree of emotional risk is highest for the combative sports and lessens progressively as one moves toward the leisurely options.

Developmental Readiness (When)

Students may choose the level at which they believe they can be successful. Keep in mind that activities need to have clearly defined, developmentally appropriate levels of play. Recall the karate-belt system associated with basketball and the seven levels of volleyball. Also note that students may elect to play as an individual, partner, or as part of a group. Once the student and staff agree that he or she is successful, the student should be encouraged to move toward less restrictive play. This process of moving toward more challenging levels of play is referred to as fading. Fading is received most favorably when the student is empowered to make his or her own choices.

Setting (Where)

The setting of an activity may occur in either the private or public environment. In the private setting the student may be involved in an activity in the home with friends or relatives. Friends or neighbors may also participate in some activity that has been started during a social visit. More often than not, students are placed in stressful situations involving activities associated with special occasions like birthday parties. An example would be a birthday party where all of the children were expected to swim in the pool, or a family reunion in which there was peer pressure to play back yard volleyball.

The most anxiety producing environments are public. Students are placed in situations without prior warning and often with acquaintances, strangers, or worse yet, adversaries. These environments include in-school activities such as physical education class, recess, field days, and trips. After-school activities may also be anxiety producing in that intramurals and after-school daycare activities are often led by staff with little experience working with students with special needs. Interscholastic athletics provide an environment that may include coaches with varying degrees of expertise, teaching skill, and empathy. Even in situations where the staff is knowledgeable and therapeutic, interscholastic athletics is often high-stakes and pressure-filled. Community based recreation programs include children with a variety of physical and social skills. This is perhaps the setting in which students with emotional disabilities are most likely to experience difficulties. This may be partly because, for many, this is their first exposure to organized sports. Another factor is the relative inexperience of coaches and officials in these settings.

Purpose of Participation (Why)

When one is planning developmentally appropriate activities for people with emotional disabilities it is important to consider the reasons why the student is participating. What is the child's motivation? Is it intrinsic in that he or she really wants to participate, or extrinsic in that he or she perceives some pressure to participate? It is also significant to ask what the outcomes of participation will be. Will they be process based, such as improving physical or social skills? Might they be product-based, whereby the student is motivated to earn a trophy or title? The implication is that student success is more likely when they choose to participate from an internal desire. They are also more likely to enjoy their experience if the outcome focus is process-oriented instead of product-oriented.

Therapeutic Environments (How)

A learning environment that is success-oriented does not develop by chance. It includes the factors such as the delivery of instruction, as well as teaching/coaching styles. The therapeutic environment is also largely determined by the effectiveness of the behavior management system employed by the supervising staff. The development of the therapeutic environment, as well as behavior management and positive discipline strategies will be discussed in greater detail in Chapter 7.

Key Terms

Ability-Grouping pairing students by similar ability and then splitting the pairs to create two groups or teams with comparable ability

Calling Score verbally repeating score before initiating play to communicate understanding and limit attempts to alter the score

Climate categories of activities and their corresponding requirements for student success

Crowding a penalty in which two or more players double-team a single player from an opposing team, the ball is awarded the solo player

Dynamics the social, emotional, physical, and cognitive components which are manipulated to create developmentally appropriate activities

Dynamic Environment environments in which student movement is in response to changes in time, space, and/or other players

Engaged Staff staff that are actively involved in planning, teaching, playing, and officiating a particular activity

Fading the process of gradually removing restrictive rules and progressing toward more challenging and competitive game-play

Facilitation the process of staff providing verbal feedback, suggestions, and praise such that students are kept on task and positively motivated

Intrapersonal Participation individual participation at one's own pace, intensity, and duration with minimal peer interaction

Interpersonal Participation partner or group interaction requiring social skills and cooperation with peers

Low Stakes Games games that end quickly and decrease anxiety by offering multiple opportunities for success and limit the trauma of "the big loss"

Progressive Levels a series of steps of a game or sport that includes progressively more difficult skills leading from basic to regulation game-play

Process-Oriented Goals goals that involve the means toward an objective with focus on technique and "how" students participate

Product-Oriented Goals goals that involve the end result with focus on outcome and "what" is accomplished

Replay Rule affords players who have an officiating disagreement the choice to replay the point with the score as it was prior to initiating play

Selective Hand-Shakes students are encouraged to shake hands following competition with at least one member of the opposing team, but not all

Static Environment environments that is unchanging such that students may initiate movement when he or she chooses

Tournament Structure establishing one of three levels of tournament: social, ladder, and elimination

Zoning limiting the areas of the field that offensive and defensive players to create ability-grouped zones

Development of Recreation and Leisure Skills Through Art Interventions

Valerie Smitheman-Brown

We human beings enjoy making our mark on the world beginning at a very young age. Before recorded language we find numerous examples of drawings and pictographs enhancing the lives of our ancestors. Cave drawings, ancient tomb drawings and carvings, decorated living spaces, and images detailing the spiritual lives of people relate the natural instincts we have to "tell our story".

Most adults rightly consider art as a naturally forming leisure skill of their children. This is certainly true for the typically developing child who readily picks up a marker or crayon and draws on whatever surface is handy. Drawing a scribble and describing it as a tree or a picture of mother is one of a child's first experiences with control over his/her environment. Observant parents and educators are aware that children scribble first, draw stick figures, and then move on to more representational artwork.

Lowenfeld & Brittain (1987) observed that in order to develop a deeper understanding of the lives of children it is of great importance that even their scribbling be recognized as a part of the total growth pattern. A child's intellectual and emotional development is often reflected in their creative work. Mirroring the theoretical developmental work of Piaget & Inhelder (1971), Lowenfeld & Brittain recognized that creative growth in children can be followed by observing an orderly sequence of developmental stages that coincide with their physical, gross/fine motor, cognitive, and emotional progress.

In their book *Creative and Mental Growth (8th edition)*, Lowenfeld & Brittain's (1987) theories of creative growth can be joined with that of a number of other psychological theorists who base their work with children with emotional and behavioral challenges by comparison to what is considered "typical progressing development of artistic abilities." In other words, comparisons of the art work of typically developing youngsters with that of youngsters with emotional or behavioral challenges can lead to a more complete understanding of the issues a child faces and the developmental area in which the child has arrested. Once we understand where a child is in his creative development then we can more safely guide him in moving forward to utilize art as a tool for further development of emotional, recreational, and leisure skill progress.

In regular education schools throughout the world, children's artwork is displayed and admired. Art time is considered downtime and students are encouraged to draw as a leisure skill. Large art projects are often created by groups of students, papier-mâché sculptures adorn classrooms and hallways, and markers and crayons can be produced at a moment's notice. Sweet little art projects are the mainstay of classrooms for holidays and special occasions. In a school setting we take the addition of art materials to the classroom or to the lesson as a naturally occurring tool that is deemed pleasurable to all students.

Inclusion has changed the face of a regular education classroom or school and has brought students with emotional and behavioral challenges into the setting, sometimes upsetting the traditional balance of what has been previously considered a "fun" activity. Teaching staff often cannot quite understand why a student might not want to engage in a "fun" drawing project or a group mural. The fear or anxiety a child exhibits when faced with a blank piece of paper or working alongside others is often considered disruptive or non-compliant behavior. What might be fun for other students in the classroom can be extremely frightening to a student with emotional or behavioral challenges.

In the artwork of children in a special education setting it is even more essential for the teacher, therapist, and art/music facilitator to recognize the powerful impact that creativity has on a child with emotional or behavioral challenges. Recognizing that an orderly development of skills is equally as evident in art as it is in mathematics or reading will assist the special education provider to plan for the introduction of interventions to further a student's growth in a non-threatening manner. Understanding that the artwork a child produces can be the first sign of the area of arrested development can be a big advantage to the special educator and therapist in planning the educational program and mental health programming for a child with special needs.

The educator, special educator, related service provider, and art/music facilitator are faced with the challenge of providing creative outlets for the expansion of recreation and leisure skills for children with emotional and behavioral challenges. While all teaching and related service staff cannot be licensed to carry crayons, there are some techniques and interventions that can be utilized that will help us to understand and work more effectively with students who are challenged cognitively, emotionally or behaviorally. The techniques shared here are not guaranteed to be effective all of the time or with all children; however, these techniques have been observed, studied, and researched over time by a multitude of psychologists, clinical art therapists, and theorists. These techniques should be considered jumping-off points for the further development of recreation and leisure skills through creative activities.

Mandala Drawing

By way of explanation, a mandala is a circle in which any manner of design or drawing can be imaged. Circular designs have been used throughout time in all cultures in religious, spiritual, and meditative situations. In a meditative sense the circular design represents infinity or eternity, having no beginning and no end. Jung, (1972) speaks of the ability to formulate inner symbolism within the structure of the mandala. According to Kellogg (1978, 1984), the mandala form presents a structural device on which to concentrate and can be approached as a drawing of the ongoing process of creation. From the point of creative development, the ability to draw a circle appears to be crucial to further pictorial advancement. The extensive work of Lowenfeld & Brittain (1987) describes the circle as the first recognizable form drawn by children in the post-scribble stage.

A recent study by Smitheman-Brown & Church (1996), using a single subject, multiple-baseline design investigated the creative growth and behavioral changes precipitated by the work done in art therapy through the employment of the mandala as an active centering device with children who have been diagnosed with Attention-Deficit Disorder (ADD) or Attention-Deficit Hyperactivity Disorder (ADHD) and a history of impulsive behaviors. By introducing the drawing of a mandala at the beginning of each art therapy session as an active centering device, it was expected that there would be evidence of an increase in attention span, a decrease in impulsive behaviors, and the furthering of development of artistic ability according to the stages noted in Lowenfeld & Brittain (1987). It was theorized that an active focusing device, such as drawing, is oftentimes easier for an impulsive or low attention span student to tackle than a passive focusing device such as music or quiet time. It is as though by providing active drawing, the facilitator is meeting the student at her high energy level rather then expecting her to relax through being sedentary.

For this research project, a circle about the size of a medium-width dinner plate was pre-drawn in pencil on white paper and many colored markers were supplied for the student's use. The circular form limited the surface to be covered and challenged even the most impulsive to stay within the line. Throughout the study it was noted that children with emotional and behavioral issues were drawn to the structure represented by the pre-drawn circle. At first they approached the project tentatively, but the consistency of approach and the familiarity developed with the mandala form allowed them to experiment and eased the natural fear of a big, blank, white piece of paper. As expected, it was noted that the content of what was drawn within the circle was of less significance than the actual motion and rhythm of drawing. In fact it is highly suggested that the content not be discussed with the student immediately, but rather in review at another time. Unconditional acceptance of the subject matter of the drawing will certainly build confidence in the relationship being developed.

The results of the study, held over a one-year period, were measured by observation and by the use of the Formal Elements Art Therapy Scale (Gantt, 1990) and Brown Assessment of Visual Representation (Smitheman-Brown, 1997). Both of these scales are criterion-referenced instruments using age/grade normative studies of artwork from typically developing children as the baseline. The subjects of the study were children with a history of impulsivity and short attention span. A comparison of baseline and performance data over time for the subjects showed an improvement in attention span of an average of 23% and a decrease of impulsivity of 24% average. The control group of students without impulsive behaviors and average attention span exhibited an increase of attention a bit less than 10% and decrease of any normal childhood impulsive behaviors by 12%.

The outcome of the study indicated that the intervention had some promising results. To that end, the research was expanded from individual sessions to classroom groups. In this segment of the study the students in a classroom were expected to draw within a mandala when they returned from a less structured setting such as gym or play-ground as a means of settling them down and preparing them for further instructional time. This study was conducted over a two-year period and proved to be extremely successful in classrooms with special needs students. Over time the class was able to exhibit growth in attention span as displayed by their ability to transition into a teaching situation in a shorter amount of time. Settling down time defined as inappropriate movement, rapid talking, and out of seat behavior when arriving in class from a less structured session was reduced from an average of six minutes to two minutes after the intervention was introduced. In addition, progress was shown in the language arts lesson that followed the mandala.

The intervention is very simple. In a classroom situation, staff provides the student or students with a piece of drawing paper "8" by "11" pre-drawn with a pencil circle. On this size paper the circle should cover most of the page. Provide the student or students with magic markers or crayons. Instruct them that they will draw anything they like in silence for two minutes within the circle. Ideally the paper and drawing materials should be on the desk before the students arrive back into the classroom. It works well to set a bell timer. At the end of the session quietly pick up the drawings and/or materials and immediately start into the lesson. No discussion of the drawing is appropriate and you should accept anything the student draws. If you are working in a 1:1 with a student the drawing can last more than two minutes if it is appropriate and it would be ideal if the paper were already on the desk when the student arrived.

This intervention can be used at home as well to reduce anxiety prior to bedtime or mealtime, in the form of a journal of drawings that can be developed in a blank sketch book, and as a method of relaxation during periods of stress or after behavioral outbursts. At all times it is important to unconditionally accept all that is drawn as the feelings of the moment. The use of the mandala normally becomes a natural process and develops into a method of self-initiated relaxation and leisure as children become more self-contained and self-actuated.

The circular form, the mandala, has proven to be a powerful tool throughout recorded time and can be utilized effectively with children with emotional or behavioral issues. The key to utilizing this intervention for optimum effect is preparation and acceptance. The materials required are very inexpensive and portable.

Developmental Levels of Intervention

As mentioned earlier, Lowenfeld & Brittain (1987) were the first to recognize that creative development mirrored the orderly stages of development of a child's other skills. In recognizing this correlation they set up a more orderly scenario for teaching and experimenting with art materials that is age appropriate. There are several "how-to" books available in the art therapy and art education worlds. One in particular is *Developmental Art Therapy* by Williams & Wood (1977). In this volume the authors use Lowenfeld & Brittain's theories and join them with psychological theorists to develop a recipe for use of art materials according to the developmental stage of a child or group of children. If you combine this with knowledge of the innate properties of all art media as defined in *Imagery and Visual Expression in Therapy* by Lusebrink (1990) you should be able to develop an appropriate plan of action for each individual child that will assist in the expansion of recreation and leisure skills using art materials.

Using all the above mentioned resources, personal research and nine years experience as a clinical art therapist, the following suggestions have been developed for opening up the doors of creativity for youngsters with emotional and behavioral disorders. The interventions suggested below are based on the developmental level of the child. However, since children with emotional and behavioral disorders often exhibit significantly arrested development, a test of their creative level is suggested prior to using the intervention. A description of the Brown Assessment of Visual Representation is included in this chapter.

Scribble Stage   Responding to the environment with pleasure

In this stage of development a child is in the pre-symbol formation stage, typically described as between ages 2-4. Lowenfeld & Brittain describe this stage as being characterized by kinesthetic pleasure, starting out disordered and developing a more controlled movement pattern. Color does not play a big role in the drawing process, content is not significant. By age 3 a child can copy a circle but not manage a square until the next stage of development.

Art materials used during the scribble stage should be on the kinesthetic level, simple and semi-fluid. Oftentimes natural materials make the best "art play." In the case of a typically developing child, the act of splashing in colored water or drawing with pudding, etc. can be a very pleasant sensory experience. In working with a young child with emotional or behavior issues, a safer approach would be utilizing a more controlled media as noted below. While fluid materials will evoke a random response and give the appearance of fun, these materials can also cause a child to lose what little control he has and actually increase the likelihood of a behavioral incident.

Drawing: Broken, unwrapped pieces of crayon (eight colors)
                Scented magic markers, wide point
                Soft, lead-colored pencils
                Hard, colored chalks
Sculpture: Soft, small bundles of clay
                Cookie cutters
                Beads
                Various plastic bottles and pieces for mobiles
                Glue

Pastels, acrylics, watercolors, and other painting materials are not recommended for children with emotional or behavioral disorders in the scribble stage because the material is too uncontrollable and messy. Naturally available sensory materials are an excellent tool for developing leisure and recreational skills. By using the senses the limitations are only in the imagination. Examples of sensory materials are: *Taste:* spices, fruit, candy, marshmallows; *Hearing:* clicking of lights, recordings, crumpling paper, paperclips, water dripping; *Smell:* food products, soaps, toothpaste; *Touch:* fabric, cotton balls, sponges.

Pre-Schematic Stage   Responding to the environment with success

This stage is described by Lowenfeld & Brittain as when a child is engaged in exploration and uses art as a communication tool usually occurring between the ages of 5-7. Spatial relationships are according to the emotional response of the child. There is flexibility of symbol, i.e., the same drawing can be described as mother one minute and the pet dog another. The importance of this stage is the development of the concept that our marks have meaning. During this stage of development the actions of the child are more meaningful and representative to them. The child is more aware of his/her environment and wants to depict his/her involvement in that environment. This is an excellent time in which to develop the recreational and leisure skills of a child. Because these children have only their personal standards of artwork to rely on they can be more creative and are not restrained by what is considered "good." Color is also more relevant to the pre-schematic artist but not necessarily representative. Objects may float in space and the drawing may appear disorganized but there is order according to the individual child's perception.

The methods and materials recommended for the typically developing pre-schematic child are similar to the emotionally and behaviorally disordered child with the exception of lose and fluid materials. These materials are still considered unsafe for children that do not have internal control. Suggested materials and projects that can be added to the pre-schematic performer are:

Drawing: Crayons that are whole and a larger variety
Colored pencils
Markers with wide and fine points
Sidewalk chalks
Magazine pictures for collage work

Sculpture: Mixed media: a variety of naturally occurring objects
Clay in larger amounts
Mosaics
Tissue paper
Yarn

As with the scribble stage, materials that are too fluid are not recommended for children with emotional or behavioral disorders. Sensory intake is still very applicable in this stage.

Schematic Stage   Learning skills for successful group participation

When a child reaches the point of the development of a form concept that she can repeat continuously, she is considered to have reached the schematic stage of creative growth. A schema is a representation of an object or objects in the environment that is constant, likened to Piaget's pre-operational stage. Children may have a schema specific to themselves, but in general the representation is egocentric and self-centered. An example of this is a drawing where the self-representation is larger than a tree or house. There is the establishment of a baseline and some personalized order to the drawing. At the beginning of this stage, the depiction of human and animal forms tend toward the traditional stick figure, trees may look like lollipops and objects are often lined up on the baseline. The sky is depicted as color at the top of the paper and does not come down to meet the baseline. Towards the close of the schematic stage the images of people and objects become fuller and more three-dimensional. Color now becomes more of an element in the drawing, telling us that the child is increasingly involved with his/her environment, ready to interact more appropriately, and attempts to image the environment correctly.

Art materials and projects for the typically developing schematic stage artist represent development of greater self-esteem, awareness of membership in a group, and basic sharing processes. For the emotionally and behaviorally challenged child there are still cautions to be observed with lose materials. In addition, while group mentality is typical at this stage, the challenged child is more likely to be threatened by too many or too large a group experience. Some additional materials can be offered at this stage:

Drawing: Crapes and crapes resist projects
64 or more crayons
A variety of sizes of pencil
Print making materials
Rubbings

Sculpture: Mobiles using natural materials
A wide variety of collage materials
Free-form clay
Diorama materials
Model building

	Papier-mâché
	Wire or pipe cleaner sculpture
Miscellaneous	Sand
	Stitchery
	Tie-dying
	Wood structures

Dawning Realism   Investing in group process

In this stage of creative development peer influences are evident: more attention to detail in the artwork, a more realistic approach to imagery, use of shades, hues of color, use of art for decoration (drawing on your notebook), and the sky meets the earth in a picture. People are depicted as full bodied, clothing is important, and the environment is drawn in perspective to size and distance. Color is not idiosyncratic but rather very realistic.

An important part of the dawning realism stage is that the typically developing artist is definitely influenced by the reaction to peers. The artist starts to become more self-conscious and actually less spontaneously creative. In the case of youngsters with emotional and behavioral challenges, the drawing realism artist is often less invested in-group process because his/her self-esteem is significantly lower than a typically developing peer. This is the time when content of drawings and paintings may become more significant for review with the youngster and with the therapist. A more sophisticated approach to art materials can be used with the addition of batik work, candle making, charcoal, soft pastels, carving, jewelry, wood sculptures, fiber arts, and woodworking.

One of the most satisfying materials that is used by burgeoning artists, especially those in the dawning realism stage, is clay, tons and tons of clay. Clay is malleable, sensory, concrete, explorative, three-dimensional, and flexible. In my experience as a clinical art therapist I have used as many as 300 lbs. of clay each school year in working with adolescents with emotional and behavioral challenges. I fired the kiln five days a week during certain periods.

Clay allows for change in content. A teenager can fix his/her errors in clay. A teenager can develop something inappropriate and then smash it, thus sublimating his/her unsuitable thoughts in a less threatening acting-out behavior. Clay allows.

Conclusion

All of the suggested materials and projects are available to both typically and atypically developing children. There are suggestions for therapeutic interventions and recreational and leisure skill activities. Artwork can become a solitary and insightful experience or it can be a group experience. It is strongly recommended that when one is working with emotionally or behaviorally challenged children that a deeper understanding of the creative developmental stage be determined before attempting to guide the child toward a particular method or material for their artwork. By taking the precaution of determining the correct developmental stage of visual representation, an adult can lessen the chance that an art project or an art material will become stressful or disturbing to the child.

One way of determining the developmental stage of visual representation is through the use of the Brown Assessment of Visual Representation. As growth in cognitive strength is exhibited, change can be observed in the child's development of visual representation. As emotional components are brought under control through treatment, clinicians can observe the inherent potential of the client that is now exhibited in their advance in visual representation. Both Piaget and Lowenfeld & Brittain espoused the sense that the child is positioned as a builder in his/her attempt to develop an understanding of how the world functions for them. In this perspective, the drawings of a child are correctly seen as his/her active knowledge, not wrong or false, but rather a direct reflection of their present understanding of the world at the time of the drawing task.

The Brown Assessment of Visual Representation (BAVR) was developed according to the stage theory of Lowenfeld & Brittain. This assessment is based on an extensive normative study of 1,250 typically developing students ages 5-18. A portion of the BAVR was originally adapted with permission from a section of the Formal Elements Art Therapy Scale (Gantt, 1990) whose published work is directed toward applying the FEATS to measuring signposts of pathology through analysis of client artwork. After experience with the FEATS it was decided that rather than attempt to track the fuzzy trail of pathology for children, the BAVR would be better served to closely parallel Lowenfeld & Brittain's more concrete approach to probing the principles of artwork as an infrastructure. By utilizing the structural principles of artwork, the BAVR can provide an objective measurement of growth in visual representation skills on a developmental and mastery level.

The BAVR is very simple to use and follows a child through growth in developmental stages. The BAVR requires a piece of white paper 12" × 18," a set of 12 magic markers, and the direction to the student to draw a picture of a person picking an apple from a tree. Encouragement to continue is required, but no help is suggested for a better understanding of the child. After 1,250 drawings in the research project I found that this is an enjoyable picture for youngsters to draw and I have never had any complaints about the subject matter.

When the drawing is completed to the student's satisfaction, the drawing is scored according to the attached scale and a developmental level is determined. Once there is a determination of developmental level, then the adult should be more comfortable in using materials, methods, and suggestions noted in this chapter.

Art can be a pleasant experience and a true recreation and leisure skill. Art can be done in a group or alone, can be extroverted in its expression or can be inward seeking, never meant to be shared with others. Either way it is a non-threatening, non-verbal mode of expression that should be explored by all in a non-judgmental atmosphere of unconditional regard.

References

Gantt, L. (1990). The validity study of the Formal Elements Art Therapy Scale (FEATS) for measuring diagnostic information through assessing formal variables in patients' drawings. Unpublished dissertation, University of Pittsburgh, Pittsburgh, PA, USA.

Jung, C. (1964). *Man and his symbols*. London: Aldus Books Limited.

Kellogg, J. (1978, 1984). *Mandala, path of beauty*. Lightfoot, VA: MARI

Lowenfeld, V., & Brittain, W.L. (1987). *Creative and mental growth* (8th ed). New York: MacMillan.

Lusebrink, V.B. (1990). *Imagery and visual expression in therapy*. New York & London: Plenum Press.

Piaget, J. (1955). *The language and thought of the child*. New York: Meridian.

Smitheman-Brown, V. (2000). Brown Assessment of Visual Representation: Rating Scale and Guidebook. (Unpublished).

Smitheman-Brown, V., & Church, R. (1996). Mandala drawing: Facilitation creative growth in children with ADD & ADHD. *Art Therapy: Journal of the American Art Therapy Association, 13*(4), 252-262.

Williams G., & Wood, M. (1977). *Developmental art therapy.* Austin, TX: Pro-Ed, Inc.

Collaborative Intervention: Creating Interagency Partnerships

Carol Ann Baglin

M. E. B. Lewis

No one wants to feel isolated or shoulder the full burden of addressing behavior problems in children. Teamwork and emotional support concentrate efforts on collaboration, increasing the skills of providers and impact of services. Shared responsibility and accountability for children's behavior and learning requires an innovative approach to education and community relationships. Students can also be engaged in taking responsibility for their own behaviors. This framework (Conzemius & O'Neill, 2001) focuses not only on shared responsibility but also on reflection on strategies for goal attainment, and collaboration as a means to bring people together to share ideas. This strategy of collaboration is essential to accomplish necessary and significant changes for children with emotional and behavior problems and to assist their families. These families require a broad array of services unlikely to be fully available through any single public or private agency. In many cases these services are initiated as crisis-oriented interventions after prior efforts have been largely ineffective.

Community-based planning is the context within which services can be designed to provide a workable collaborative environment for practitioners and service providers. This may require a readjustment on the part of agency personnel in terms of service roles, job definitions, and the service delivery process. In this type of system, parents have a greater role in negotiating the necessary services for their child and family. Parents must first be provided with opportunities to improve their skills and develop successful parenting strategies. Programs to improve skills may focus on improving parenting, changing parent attitudes, and increasing knowledge related to their children's mental health problems.

Collaboration is a progressive process of developing many interdependent relationships with a common purpose. Interagency coordination is an unnatural process for many discipline specific service provider agencies, and the process requires a significant adjustment in attitude. It is an ongoing, active concept that can lead to solutions for some very difficult problems. To achieve this model, professionals involved in interagency activities can no longer operate independently but must seek to work together as a team. Coordination of multiple services can have a pervasive impact on the child and family. Coordinated services can provide parents and professionals with the support and the skills needed to access their own strengths, resulting in a higher quality of intervention as well as a financial savings.

In today's era of managed care, the development of many community-based service systems is to coordinate existing services and identify additional federal, state, and local initiatives. Professionals and families have long recognized the separations that exist among the traditionally self-directed medical, human service, and education communities. These diverse disciplines have maintained that their basic responsibilities to children with mental health problems were separate and distinct.

In reality the services available over the last three decades through a wide variety of governmental programs for children and their families have necessarily blurred distinctions among these health, human service, and educational programs. Mandated services to provide for the needs of children of all ages now transcend many of the traditional boundaries of established service systems. Along with this attitudinal change, a broadening of perceptions of children and family needs has emerged for children with emotional problems and long-term mental health needs.

Historical Perspective of Services

Interest in children with disabilities can be characterized as a series of broad trends at the federal level beginning with a growing awareness and gradual maturing in American society coupled with a sense of external responsibility for its citizens (Gallagher, 2000). Currently, there is broad support for education and services for all children with disabilities and this has resulted in a combination of mandates, regulations, incentives, and complex program and funding initiatives.

These interventions were initiated throughout the 1900s by the establishment of The Children's Bureau in 1912, and through governmental support of maternal and child health and practices designed to promote the well being of all children. In 1930, the White House Conference on Child Health and Protection recommended that programs for "crippled children" be made available. In 1935, the Social Security Act established Maternal and Child Health Services that specifically included children with disabilities (Weintraub, Abeson, Ballard, & LaVor, 1976).

Current efforts on behalf of children with disabilities began in the 1960s as part of an overall effort by society to become more socially responsible. Disadvantaged children were initially helped through Head Start, a program designed during President Johnson's term to be part of the Great Society's War on Poverty. This program was significant in that it targeted at-risk children, included an emphasis on the central role of parents, and eventually required that the enrollment of Head Start be composed of at least 10% of children with disabilities (Gallagher, 2000; Hebbeler et al., 1991).

In 1965, P. L. 89-10, the Elementary and Secondary Education Act (ESEA), was passed, increasing the appropriations for the Office of Education. In 1966, the Bureau of Education the Handicapped (BEH) was established through P. L. 89-750 and included a State Grant program to provide financial support for the education of students with disabilities. Enacted in 1968, P. L. 90-538, the Handicapped Children's Early Education Program (HCEEP), provided funding for exemplary programs to demonstrate that early intervention could work. HCEEP was the first federal special education program targeted exclusively for young children with disabilities (Hebbeler et al., 1991).

Beginning with HCEEP in 1968, initial efforts were focused at the local level to stimulate models that were community oriented and amenable to replication. As these programs were funded throughout the nation, interest in expansion and support for providing services to children with disabilities increased and, by the 1970s, the focus shifted to the state level and increased regulation and program requirements. In 1974, amendments to the ESEA legislation, which were given the short title of "Education of the Handicapped Act," established a program of grants to assist in the provision of educational services and required a state plan to support local educational agencies.

The landmark P. L. 94-142, the federal Education for All Handicapped Children Act of 1975, was a comprehensive rewrite of Part B of the Education of the Handicapped Act. P. L. 94-142 regulated the provision of special education and provided funding that built the state infrastructure for special education (Hebbeler et al., 1991). While this piece of legislation was the most noteworthy and it established the right to a free and appropriate public education (FAPE) for all school-age children with disabilities, the very youngest of children were not included, and there were limitations related to the provision of services for young children with disabilities from ages three through five (Gallagher, 2000).

The 1980s yielded a continued progression of federal legislation and funding that would first encourage—and then require—that the states provide services to all children, including children with behavior problems. The 1983 Amendments to the Education of the Handicapped Act (P. L. 98-199) provided states with grants to develop a state system of interventions and services for children birth to five years. In 1986, Congress passed P. L. 99-457, the Education of the Handicapped Act Amendments, which mandated services for children and their families from birth to three and extended the protections of Part B to preschoolers between the ages of three and first entry to school. This created incentives for a comprehensive, collaborative system of service delivery for children with disabilities from birth to age three, and a "seamless" set of educational services for children and youth between the ages of three and 21.

While the federal government has played a pivotal role in special education through legislative initiatives, the courts have also played a significant role in a number of cases during this same period, including:

- *Brown v. Board of Education* in 1954, which addressed the issue of segregation and right to education, requiring that all children, regardless of race, were entitled to equal educational opportunities;
- *PARC v. Commonwealth of Pennsylvania* in 1972, which required access to school for all children with mental retardation regardless of the severity of their disability under the 14th amendment; and
- *Mills v. Board of Education* in 1973, which required services for all students regardless of budget constraints and established equal protection under the 14th amendment.

Early intervention for children with disabilities evolved as a natural product of the interface between early childhood education and the right to special education. As both of these fields matured, access for children with disabilities to education became guaranteed through legal mechanisms and supported through research findings demonstrating the importance and long-term benefits of early intervention for children.

Federal Legislation in Support of Special Education

Year	Legislation
1965	P. L. 89-313 Payments to states for children, birth through 20, with disabilities in state-owned and state-operated programs.
1968	P. L. 90-538 Established Handicapped Children's Early Education Act that established the HCEEP.
1970	P. L. 91-230 HCEEP consolidated with other federal special education programs; states were provided direct financial support for programs for children ages three through five.
1974	P. L. 93-380 Education Amendments of 1974 enacted new requirements for special education for preschool, elementary, and secondary students; increased authorization levels for the basis state grant program.
1975	P. L. 94-142, Education of All Handicapped Children Act; free appropriate public education required for children, six through 18; Preschool Incentive Grants established; state awards based on child count which included three through five year olds.
1983	P. L. 98-199 State Planning Grants established for handicapped children birth through five years of age; broadened use of funds to include children birth through five.
1986	P. L. 99-457 Handicapped Infants and Toddlers Program, Part H, was established to provide services for infants and toddlers with developmental disabilities and their families; extended the mandate for full services under Part B to three year olds and increased funding.
1990	P. L. 101-476 renamed the Education of the Handicapped (EHA) as the Individuals with Disabilities Education Act (IDEA).
1997	P. L. 105-17 Individuals with Disabilities Education Act Amendments redefined special education to be a service for support of student achievement rather than a place; ensured access to the general curriculum.

Note. Sources: Hebbeler, et al., (1991) and Gallagher (2000)

While education services were evolving through the courts and legislative system, the human service agencies were adapting their systems to incorporate the physical health and mental health status of children into planning for the psychosocial and economic well being of the whole family. The emphasis in recent years has been on wrap-around family support systems and interventions based on each family's identified needs.

The need for changes resulted in enormous pressures for service in the 1980s and 1990s. Historically, the development of equal access to services for handicapped individuals and their families characterized the theme of the 1970s. During the 1980s, greater sensitivity to the needs of these individuals led to describing as individuals with *disabilities*, rather than individuals with handicaps. Under this law, all children with disabilities are guaranteed a free, appropriate public education. Educational agencies were required to identify and evaluate children with special needs and to assure the provision of education and related services. This resulted in the expansion of health—related support services such as physical therapy and occupational therapy, not previously included within educational programs. Section 504 of the Rehabilitation Act (the "Civil Rights" law for the handicapped population) mandated comprehensive, non-discriminatory services for individuals with disabilities.

With the continued consolidation of programs into block grants and dwindling resources due to regulatory changes and budgetary and personnel cuts, the challenge of the 1980s and 1990s was to provide coordinated, collaborative, and cost-effective services in the health, human service, and education areas. The 1990s manifest an approach that focused services for children and their families on the "whole" child. This focus reinforced the need for coordination, communication, and collaboration among a variety of disciplines in order to meet the needs of these disabled children. Systems of comprehensive care began to rely heavily on the family as the primary provider of services. In 1982 the "Katie Beckett" Waiver, named after the first child to receive the waiver, recognized the importance of the family role in providing care to medically fragile children. This waiver permitted states an option to provide for services at a lower medical cost in the home. These children would otherwise remain institutionalized because their return to their home would have resulted in the loss of SSI and Medicaid eligibility.

In 1986 Congress enacted the Children's Justice Act that initiated temporary non-medical childcare in the form of respite services for families of children with disabling conditions or chronic illness. This Act provided a means to alleviate the stress on the family and prevent the unnecessary institutionalization and the permanent break up of the family system. On September 2, 1987 President Reagan signed Executive Order 12606 which ordered that the autonomy and rights of the family be considered by all departments and agencies in both the formulation and implementation of governmental policies. This order required that federal agencies recognize the role of the family as the primary force in the child's life. Historically, parenting has been viewed as a quality that can be learned. The link between the mental health of children and the well-being of the family is inescapable. Effective parenting requires knowledge and skills that create a multidisciplinary approach emphasizing social-emotional environments interwoven with child rearing and stress management strategies.

Effectiveness of Collaborative Strategies

Agencies providing services for children share similar goals for providing both cost-effective and efficient educational and mental health services. At the same time, it is necessary to recognize and integrate into practice the different nuances in the approach of these agencies. The discreet service communities of each agency have developed their own language, intervention techniques, and training plans. The current practice toward specialization has contributed significantly to the polarity among these service communities that has resulted in duplication and gaps in services.

Some of the different agency approaches are due to legislative mandates. For example, state and local education agencies have mandated free services for handicapped children, requiring the delivery of all necessary education and related services, without regard to funding levels. Health agencies also may have legislative mandates (e.g., health departments are required to assist in school health programs), but generally have a more specific service orientation with finite budgets. Services may be paid for through private providers or clinic fees, income maintenance, or a targeted grant program. A variety of human services are made available according to specific age and disability, in combination with income eligibility. Eligibility criteria for health and human services can include age, diagnosis of disease or disorder, financial need, geographic catchments area, and targeted areas of need. Eligibility criteria vary from program to program, and can be based on agency mandates, policies, state and local priorities, and limitations on resources.

There are also differences in the structure of services provided by health, human service and education agencies. State Departments of Education primarily provide management services, such as administration, monitoring, technical assistance, and fund distribution to local educational agencies (LEAs). State health and human service agencies frequently provide direct services through state-operated local agencies. These services may include medical evaluation and treatment services, therapy, counseling, recreation, income maintenance and a variety of support services to children and their families.

Children who need mental health services are not a homogeneous group, including varieties of family background and demographics (Walrath, Nickerson, Crowel, & Leaf, 1998). Education, health and human service agencies all may operate through a categorical approach to service delivery. Following some type of screening and diagnosis, specific probable services are indicated. Services by health and human service agencies are often provided based upon income eligibility, court related issues or disabilities with definitions that may differ from those utilized by educational agencies in implementing programs for the disabled.

While legislative mandates and agency structures may differ, common services goals among the programs can be identified and woven into a responsive system. Health, social service, and educational programs for children may be provided through the public or private sector, may be state or locally funded, large or small, generic or individualized.

Health Delivery System

Innovative connections of health departments with schools and community resources have been a phenomenon of the last decade of the twentieth century, and hopefully, a trend in the new millennium. The health delivery system is also a source of referral to the mental health delivery system. An individual who enters a hospital emergency room after overdosing on drugs or over-indulging in alcohol may be referred for a psychiatric evaluation. This is certainly the case when an individual attempts self-harm (suicide, anorexia, bulimia). Additionally, a patient who shows evidence of abusing any substance would be referred for ongoing treatment of addictions by a mental health professional, in conjunction with a physician or psychiatrist. In some communities, where the coordination of services means traveling throughout the community or city to get to the agencies or clinical settings, there is a real risk that appointments will be missed or not made at all, and wellness care, an excellent and easily provided service, will be lost. To that end, many hospitals have placed outreach clinics directly in communities, near or in schools. These resources allow for preventive care (check-ups, vaccinations, basic treatment) and also the opportunity for referrals to specialists makes them a good investment for any community.

Some health care systems (through managed care or other corporate structures) offer partnership with other agencies through on-site clinics. This can include such services as Well-Child clinics in schools or workplaces, traveling screening centers that go to malls, schools, libraries or other community sites to offer screenings, allergy shots, vaccinations, or pre-natal care. Hospitals may join with the school system in a community to consolidate services in order to get parents and children together in a single setting in order to evaluate needs, prescribe treatment or medication, and do ongoing follow up of treatment outcomes.

Such participation by health professionals can also be arranged when the clinic cannot come to the community. Setting up of on-site "clinic days" with space provided for visiting nurses, pediatricians, pediatric nurse-practitioners, general nurse-practitioners, or other health personnel, can be used to suffice. There can be a schedule of appointments (monthly or bi-monthly) in a general space in a school (health suite, office, even the lunch room or library), providing the time and space for parents or other caregivers to give children and adolescents scheduled care, including the monitoring of medications.

In the case of students with emotional and behavior problems, this model can include needed assessment and therapy, allowing for appropriate record keeping and reporting to families and schools (to the extent appropriate). When therapeutic offerings by the school district are limited in availability, this option can be quite helpful. This model allows for a variety of therapeutic strategies to be used (play therapy, psycho-therapy, art therapy, music therapy, or recreational therapy) because the specific therapist might be more readily available on an "itinerant" basis, traveling to a region of schools, rather than staffing a district with this rare commodity of specialized therapeutic staff.

An additional value in the collaborative model is the communication it affords teachers and medical/therapeutic professionals. Not only can these adults provide services to children with emotional disorders and students with emotional problems, they see each other and talk about cases, share professional development training opportunities, and function within an interrelated environment. All educators continue their professional development while teaching or otherwise serving students, and the same is true of medical and therapeutic professionals. These training sessions can be shared opportunities for all professionals to learn how their work coincides and collaborates with the efforts of others in serving the needs of children and adolescents with emotional, behavioral and learning disorders.

Treatment professionals who previously were found in clinics (pediatricians, psychiatrists, nurses, nurse-practitioners, occupational therapists, physical therapists and speech/language pathologists) are now brought into schools to become part of a team that creates and implements individual educational plans from diagnostic data. Many of these services are provided as *itinerant* services, with the professionals working directly in the school buildings on a daily or weekly schedule. When children or adolescents have problems of an emotional or behavioral nature, mental health or behavioral psychology staff also provide services in the school setting.

The benefit of this collaborative arrangement is obvious. The children and adolescents get direct service on a meaningful and convenient schedule, in a setting they are already familiar with and visiting daily. Paperwork related to service can be managed from the school site as well as any health care site. School staff can be trained to assist families in the completion of insurance and educational forms that will provide comprehensive services with accountability from both the education and health perspectives.

School Linked Services

Schools are learning communities, and as such, represent the same issues and problems of all communities. The concern of the "over-scheduled" child, with so much to do and such a limited amount of time for non-school related tasks, is a condition of national concern. Conversely, the "under-scheduled" child, with so much time on her hands because she either has no access to extracurricular activities that might challenge her social and intellectual skills or no interest in such activities, is another side to that coin.

As has been mentioned elsewhere in this book, students with emotional, attentional, and behavioral issues must be motivated appropriately for their participation in activities. In some schools, outside agencies and organizations ally with the school to provide time and service to children. Police Athletic Leagues, Boys and Girls Clubs, Boy Scouts and Girl Scouts, and large corporations are examples of this connection. The alliance of these organizations with schools provides community service projects for the agencies, organizations and companies. The further alliance with the medical and mental health agencies mentioned above allows for proper training of the adult participants so that the goals of the recreational/therapeutic experience can be met. An additional benefit or this close collaborative effort is the data collection and analysis that may be done. Teachers and other school staff can observe and assess student learning and social behaviors by reporting with logs, checklists, etc. for those providing therapeutic or other intervention services. This can provide necessary information for changes to protocols for behavior management as well as information related to medication regimens.

Another resource to schools is the teacher preparation and therapeutic training institutions near the school districts. Teachers in training need field experiences to prepare them for eventual teaching, and those in training as social workers, psychologists, art, music and recreational therapists, also need to connect to their prospective clients by observing and practicing skills under supervision.

As mentioned earlier, finite budgets make the realistic provision of services in compliance with somewhat altruistic legislative and social initiatives problematic. Therefore, it is vital that the interagency collaborations mentioned here are implemented, and even more creative and meaningful services are designed. When services are coordinated effectively, students benefit, cost effective solutions flourish, and greater inclusion opportunities may result.

Who Delivers the Service?

Services to students with emotional, behavioral, attentional, and learning disorders are most often delivered directly in the classroom and school throughout the school day or in supplemental before or after school programs. Depending on the service, the person delivering the service may vary.

It is often the function of a Child Study Team, or other team based in the school to determine the services that will be delivered to an individual child and his or her family. This depends on effective and appropriate assessment of need. Once the needed service has been determined and agreed upon, any number of persons may join the intervention team to develop the social and learning skills of the child or adolescent. Let's start in the classroom.

Traditionally, the classroom was the domain of the teacher, but what constitutes the background and training of teachers has changed. The current mode in education is for greater variety in the staffing of classrooms. Teachers, whose undergraduate studies were in education, preparing them to teach from their earliest college experiences, provide educational services. More and more, teachers are coming from colleges and universities where they majored in a content area, such as English, mathematics, one of the sciences, or history. These individuals may enter the profession through initiatives such as Teach for America, or AmeriCorps. They train for the classroom through graduate education such as Master of Arts In Teaching (MAT) or other graduate education programs. Additionally, some people enter the teaching profession having already worked in another field, and having returned to graduate school for their education training. This means that individuals with varying amounts of experience and training are teaching, and their participation on teams is very important, for it is there that they can be mentored and assisted by more experienced professionals in understanding and serving students with emotional and other needs.

Teachers coordinate, pace and assess instruction, they observe and assess students and provide feedback data so that the impact of services can be determined and changed as needed. They connect to the other therapeutic professionals on the team for this. Here are some of the other service providers that a student and his or her family may encounter:

Psychologist	This is a mental health professional with a degree in psychology, the study of human development and behavior. They may do testing of intellectual capacity, observe and assess behaviors related to emotional growth and stability, and may interview family members in order to determine the larger picture of how the child functions socially.
Psychiatrist	This is a physician, trained in mental health issues, brain-related conditions that relate to mental health, and the role of medication and therapeutic interventions for the improvement of mental health. This person can prescribe medication, and can refer individuals for hospitalization or other clinical treatment when needed.
Social Worker	This person has advanced training and licensure for working with individuals and their families in a therapeutic format, and they can also connect individuals and families to community and health services. Social workers work in social service agencies, and are also connected to schools in some cases.
Guidance Counselor	This is a specially trained person, sometimes an educator by background, familiar with the issues of child and adolescent growth and development, and how to discuss and guide the individual through situations directly related to school performance. They can connect students and families to agencies and clinical professionals for more in-depth service.
Art Therapist	This is a specially trained mental health professional, not an art teacher. Art therapists assist individuals in handling issues of social, emotional or behavioral crisis through the use of art (drawing, painting, sculpture, etc.). This is often helpful for those whose abilities to express their problems verbally are limited or non-existent. The art therapist is trained in the interpretation of the art products of the individual as expressions of psychological perspectives.
Music Therapist	This is a specially trained mental health professional, not a music teacher. Through the use of music, a highly evocative medium, the therapist can evoke an emotional response from an individual whose ability to express feelings verbally is limited or non-existent.

Movement or Recreational Therapist	This is a specially trained mental health professional, not a physical education teacher or physical therapist. This person uses dance, general physical activity and movement to bring out emotional or behavioral expression from the individual with a need for such expression. The individual may not be able to express feelings through verbal, artistic or musical media.
Nurse	This is a licensed medically trained person who offers direct health care to children or adolescents. In a school setting, the nurse may handle general health matters, but may also distribute medications.
Nurse/Practitioner	This is a nurse with advanced medical training that may include the ability to prescribe certain medications. When a physician is not available or is not practical to have on site in a school, a nurse practitioner can perform some of the duties of a doctor, such as conducting physical examinations.
Behavioral Specialist	This may be an educator with advanced training or a mental health professional with special training in understanding human behavior and how to shape it positively. This person may have training in how to observe and assess behaviors in order to develop a behavior plan that increases positive and cooperative behaviors while decreasing or eliminating inappropriate behaviors. These professionals may also be trained in the management of physically out of control children and adolescents, and the effective use of strategies such as time out, token economies and behavioral contracts. They frequently consult with classroom teachers.
Psychotherapist	This is a mental health professional who is trained to talk to individuals or groups in order to assist them in addressing their emotional, social and behavioral problems. This person may use play as a form of therapy with a child, in order to see how the child views toys as extensions of their world. The therapist may use puppets or other "props" to interact with an individual as a means of getting a response emotionally. Psychotherapy takes time, and a trusting relationship must be built between the child, adolescent and family in order for this therapy to work effectively.

Any of these mental health or educational professionals may work with the child with emotional, social or behavioral issues that interfere with daily living. They can also contribute to the assessments and determination of services that appear on Individualized Education Programs (IEPs). They often contribute to team meetings that determine and monitor services to children and their families. Their services are often coordinated through schools, but they may also work in the community and consult to schools or other agencies.

Collaborative Services: Coordination of Health, Human Service, and Educational Agencies

Conceptualizing both coordination and collaboration has resulted in repeated attempts to clarify terminology and facilitate a sense of specific levels of success in approaching complex systems of service delivery (Elder, 1979; Intrilligator & Goldman, 1989). This new model of intervention necessitates a focused and effective structure for structuring the process and focusing the goals.

The major goals (Bender & Baglin, 1992) of interagency collaboration are:

- To identify services and programs for students with emotional and behavior problems with disabilities;
- To promote awareness of specific agency and program mandates and responsibilities;
- To assure exchange of information and ideas among professionals;
- To facilitate coordinated service delivery on state and local levels through integration of services and policies;
- To maximize the use of existing resources;
- To reduce gaps and eliminate unnecessary duplication of services;
- To increase the cost-effectiveness of service delivery plans;
- To facilitate data-collection efforts through interagency systems;
- To improve the effectiveness of family-centered programs and early intervention services; and
- To promote a core of quality services throughout the state.

To meet these goals, health, human service, and education service providers will have to make a specific commitment to the team approach of working in family-centered care. Service planners must work on the development and management of comprehensive service systems to ensure long-term coordinated approaches.

Efforts to meet the comprehensive needs of students with emotional and behavior problems and their families involve the sharing of knowledge and meaningful coordination of services among disciplines. Many programs may retain a primarily educational, medical, or family emphasis; however, there will need to be recognition of the value of the interdisciplinary approach in addressing the child in the context of their family.

Although many different services are provided by health, human service, and educational agencies, nearly all of these programs have some activities in common. These include prevention, referral, screening and diagnosis, as well as service delivery.

Health, human service providers, and educational agencies all focus on the early identification of conditions in order to prevent childhood disability and to reduce the long-term costs to families and society. The effectiveness of these efforts is measured in terms of maintaining a child's development within normal limits, improving mental health rate, reducing the secondary impact of the disability, and assisting the family to function more effectively in response to the child's needs. The major disciplines with the capabilities and mandated responsibilities for the delivery of educational and mental health services are education and health.

Positive behavior interventions is a proactive systems approach that recognizes the realities we all deal with each day. Increasing numbers of students are more different from than similar to each other. Students with severe problem behaviors increasingly are in need of a broad range of services and supports to continue within their community environment. Suspension is one of the most frequent reasons students drop out of school and punishment is among the least effective responses to violent behavior in schools.

Positive behavior interventions focuses on prevention. One of the key components is instruction. As simple as it seems, behavioral expectations need to be taught directly just like academic skills. Supporting and educating students with severe problem behavior is possible only if an effective and efficient school-wide system of positive behavior supports is in place. Supporting and educating students who exhibit problem behavior in schools is a formidable task.

All agencies involved in the location and identification of students with emotional and behavior problems with mental health or with conditions that result in do not implement the same outreach or procedures. State agencies may share a joint responsibility for identification or may decide that one agency will be responsible for identification of children, depending on age ranges, disability, or eligibility categories.

A thorough understanding of all available educational and mental health services will assist primary referral sources and facilitate the process of referring students with emotional and behavior problems and their families for appropriate assistance. Referral resources must recognize the types of services providers and agencies, what the services are, where the services can be provided, who the contacts are, what the referral process is, including coordination and follow-up. Knowledge of the referral process is essential to provide appropriate and responsive assistance to families. The referral process is a critical point of coordination in the service delivery system. This is the point at which the child and family is provided adequate information and supports, or are lost in the confusion of local and state bureaucracies.

Screening is the ongoing process of identifying children who present a likelihood of having mental health needs. The purpose of screening is to obtain sufficient information about students with emotional and behavior problems to determine the need for a thorough assessment. An increasing number of medical, emotional, and social characteristics have been identified which indicate that a child may be "at risk" for mental health problems. Health, human service, and education personnel have placed increasing emphasis on providing these children with adequate educational and mental health services. Effective universal screening helps produce success in service intervention efforts. Coordination of screening activities is significant in the development of any collaborative system of service delivery.

Comprehensive screening processes can detect abnormalities in physical development, general health and vision, hearing, language, cognitive, motor, social, and emotional functions. Development of screening responsibilities, procedures for access to screening data results, and strategies for coordinating screening activities among local educational agencies, local health departments, primary care providers, and other providers are essential to ensure successful screening efforts. Identification of screening instruments, record keeping, data collection, tracking of screening results, parental/family involvement, utilization of community resources, follow-up, and continuity of services can be addressed through interagency procedures.

Assessment is a systematic process that measures a student's physical, social or emotional status against established mental health standards. The result is a description of strengths and weaknesses, behavioral patterns, and level of functioning in a variety of areas. Assessment provides information to document the nature of mental health and other conditions and supports recommendations for appropriate intervention. Assessment is both an educational and a medical term. The medical community goes through a similar process that results in a medical diagnosis. The diagnosis and description of conditions and medical functioning provide important information for planning appropriate services. It necessitates a comprehensive approach to the family system and incorporates the development of the child as a significant factor in the functioning of the family.

Multidisciplinary evaluation of children who are suspected of having a mental health is crucial. Local systems should pursue collaborative arrangements to identify potential mental health problems, to obtain assessment data results, to avoid duplication of testing among agencies, to develop procedures for tracking high-risk students, and to coordinate a process for multiagency involvement in the determination of mental health. Cooperation of all agencies involved during the evaluation process ensures the accuracy of the diagnosis/assessment and promotes smooth transition to family-centered program planning.

Individualized planning is a characteristic of health and human services, as well as educational services for children with needs. An important issue among service providers and state agencies is the possibility of integrating various mandated requirements into a single coordinated plan. Federal agencies through targeted grants have encouraged health-related professionals and education professionals to use interdisciplinary team approaches to develop individualized plans. When more than one type of plan has been required, agencies were encouraged to develop a consolidated plan as long as it contained all required information and all necessary parties participate in its development. The comprehensive plan of services required under educational and mental health services focuses on a comprehensive approach to goals and outcomes and on the method and criteria for provision of interagency service delivery.

The successful implementation of individualized plans depends partially upon effective interagency and local/state agreements. These agreements set the framework for implementation by describing the decision-making process for service provision and by defining which services will be provided by health, social service professionals and which services educators will provide.

Service Delivery Models

Health, human service, and education providers provide a wide variety of services to children and their families. Agency officials often wonder which agency has primary responsibility for which services. Certain services are unique to agency mandates or regulations and are not usually duplicated, such as certain educational services or medical care. However, there is confusion in applicable federal and state statutes for those services that might be provided by several agencies. Ideally services should not be withheld by one agency based upon another agency having primary responsibility. Still, agencies must determine which agency will bear the cost of specific services needed by the student and their family. These services need to be justified within a specific agency budget and represent the statutory intent or limitations of that agency.

One of the ways agencies can determine the appropriate funding source is through an interagency agreement, which should involve participants from the service delivery programs. In addition, other public and private agencies that provide funds or services for children and families should be involved. In developing the agreement, a number of criteria may be used to establish responsibility for financing services and delivering the services in a coordinated, effective manner. The criteria may include the geographical location of the service being delivered, the qualifications of personnel furnishing the service, the financial eligibility of the family, the overall purpose of the agency providing the service, the time period in which the service is provided, and the availability of personnel and resources in the community. Deciding which agency provides personnel or funding for a given service depends on a careful assessment of state and local factors and can be clarified through the process of coordination and collaboration.

Service delivery settings include a wide range of options including the community school, targeting classrooms with multiple behavioral supports and crisis intervention, nonpublic special education schools, and residential treatment centers. Mental health needs of children suggest that mechanisms for supporting the needs of all children are most effective when implemented with the support of the entire community (Koller & Svoboda, 2002).

Strategies for Coordination

Service coordination among multiple agencies is an ongoing process. All levels of government need to be involved in coordination efforts. In order to ensure long-term collaborative approaches, formal arrangements should be made for interagency commitments, assignment of financial responsibilities, and service agreements. While informal coordination activities have been conducted among professionals in many communities, the lack of formal, written policies and procedures can create problems in continuity of activities when the primary personnel important in the coordination process are no longer employed by their respective agencies. Turnover in personnel at the state and local level can also disrupt even the most successful coordination efforts if those efforts have been based solely on informal interactions among existing personnel.

The Office of Special Education Programs (OSEP) identifies service coordination (34 C.F.R. Part 300) as a strategy to effect the coordination of services among multiple agencies and multiple service providers (Assistance to States for the Education of Children with Disabilities, 1999). The impact of preventing children from receiving effective service coordination may result in a greater impact on children with mental health problems because their disability is invisible (Callegary, 2002).

Interagency coordination and collaboration require time, patience, and communication at all levels. Agency personnel need to be prepared to make appropriate modifications as their needs change. All professionals must carefully examine and re-examine their roles in this process and every effort should be made to facilitate, rather than hinder, the flow of services and information. The first step is to document the needs, rationale, and target the interagency needs. The parameters of the target populations must be defined, including the definition of the family to be used. Also, agencies and programs serving the target population should be identified. The needs of the target populations, in this case students with emotional and behavior problems and their families, should be clearly delineated.

Next, the policies and service responsibilities of providers, especially those of identical or similar agencies or programs, need to be clarified. These programs then can be compared to identify duplications or gaps in services. Recommended program changes for improved collaboration and coordination can then be made. Because various funding options and constraints must also be determined, professionals need to be creative in the use of these funds and other available resources. Different combinations and possibilities should be considered.

The organization and authority for decision making must be clearly established. It may take the form of a council composed of consumers, local providers, and state agency representatives. It may be a separate state authority or agency. Or, it could be principally an advisory group or board with decision-making powers.

Negotiating specific interagency agreements between service providers to improve coordination is a key step in the coordination process. Some programs that serve children with handicaps are required to develop cooperative agreements according to federal laws. The purpose of these agreements is to ensure that the services provided under state plans are coordinated with other public and private agencies providing services to disabled children. Also, efforts are made to use existing resources and to obtain appropriate financial support from other agencies (Bender & Baglin, 1992).

Strategies for implementing program changes should then be determined. State and local planners need to decide the best techniques for bringing about change in the way that agencies and professionals relate to each other in the provision of services to the target population. A last step in the process, which should continue indefinitely, is to ensure the implementation of program changes at the service delivery level. This includes state and local involvement in the management, education, technical assistance, professional development, and follow-up and program evaluation.

Interagency Agreements

Written cooperative agreements are the foundation for most enduring coordination efforts among agencies. Such agreements provide a basis for professionals to begin working together, maximizing funds and resources. These agreements generally include:

- Overall and agency-specific goals and objectives of the agreement;
- Definitions of terms and jargon;
- Responsibilities of each agency/provider listed, including clarification of services provided at the state and local levels;
- Geographic catchment area of each agency and program;
- A system for referrals between agencies and transfer of records;
- Allocation of agency funds and resources;
- Uniform processes, forms, and standards for implementing similar programs by different agencies;
- A case management system to ensure follow-up on services provided;
- A mechanism to ensure continuing cooperation;
- The designation of staff who will be responsible for coordination activities at local and state levels;
- A system for sharing information and data collection;
- Confidentiality assurances regarding sharing of information under differing regulatory systems;
- Specification of time period for the agreement;
- Periodic reviews of the agreement;
- Signatures of all parties responsible for implementation of the agreement; and
- Evaluations of measurable outcomes at set intervals (Baglin & Bender, 1992).

Interagency agreements can be simple memorandums of understanding describing financial arrangements or the allocation of agency resources for accomplishing mutual objectives. Others may direct the establishment of common standards for similar programs and include provisions for maintaining uniform procedures, forms, and activities by agencies offering educational and mental health services (Bender & Baglin, 1992).

Commitment by key agency professionals is necessary to ensure the effectiveness of interagency agreements. It is helpful to identify a person from each agency to coordinate the development and implementation of the agreement. The roles and responsibilities of this person should be defined clearly so that coordination can continue if the designated person should leave the agency. In addition to identifying resources and services needed, agencies should identify the benefits to each participant in the interagency process. Professionals should monitor the effect of the agreement on services to ensure that the outcomes are beneficial to the agencies and to the children and their families.

Coordination is carried out through the management and monitoring of services provided to the family. The ongoing supervision of service delivery enables health, human service, and education professionals to work cooperatively to ensure that the most responsive services are provided. Professionals need to work closely with the families in this process. Professionals can assist each other by sharing information and resources. Joint efforts in service delivery will improve the quality of services provided and facilitate the management and monitoring of services.

Barriers in Interagency Coordination

Agency coordination is often a difficult process that must overcome many barriers, many of which may have long existed. The absence of effective professional and interagency coordination and collaboration usually results in increased problems for students with emotional and behavior problems and their families in obtaining services in the community, fewer referrals between programs, and inadequate services. This comes at a time when families are least able to cope with additional stresses or unresponsive systems. Therefore, professionals must examine their agencies, their individual working styles, their interventions, and the modifications necessary to promote better coordination.

The impact of service barriers can impact greater upon children with mental illnesses because their disability is often unknown or invisible. The stigma associated with mental illness can lead to confusion and concern over the "volitional" component of the disability (Callegary, 2002). Children with emotional problems have serious problems over long periods of time, demonstrating coping problems at school, home, and in the community. Parents may be blamed or even held financially responsible for the behaviors of their children, yet may feel powerless to change the course of their lives. Families need help in understanding their children's problems and assisted in coping.

Working cooperatively requires sharing, effort, and mutual trust and respect and an awareness of the impediments to cooperative planning and service delivery. Barriers to impacting behavior can be overcome through an interconnected continuum of systems linking systems of prevention with community systems of care (Adelman & Taylor, 2002). Systemic change requires readiness within the institutional structures and the coinciding of personnel with vision and a sense of renewal.

A wide range of variables can impact the development of formal relationships. Negotiating agreements among multiple service providers frequently involves effectively resolving significant concerns around the wide range of structures and barriers (Bender & Baglin, 1992):

- Territoriality among agencies
- Competition for funding between similar services/programs
- Categorical programming for target populations within the family
- Different approaches inherent in utilization

- Absence of the "holistic approach" to the family
- Lack of communication among professionals
- Lack of understanding of roles of other professionals or agency policies and procedures
- Professional terminology and languages that accompany knowledge
- Agency policies and practices and program priorities
- Differences in program eligibility requirements creating confusion and contributing to incomplete service plans
- Agencies discouraging the need for additional intervention through another agency
- Perceived threats to agency's autonomy
- Increase in workloads for professionals
- Varying agency priorities, mandates, and responsibilities
- Conflicting organizational frameworks
- Perceived confidentiality issues which limit information sharing
- Narrow focus of agencies on the problem rather than the child or family (Bender & Baglin, 1992).

Who Delivers the Service in a Collaborative System?

Many eligible students with emotional and behavior problems and their families are already receiving educational and mental health services in some form from public or private agencies. In many instances, prior to the implementation of educational and mental health services, these services were being provided in a vacuum, independent and unrelated to services being provided elsewhere in the system.

Agency-specific service delivery systems frequently operate under specified regulations and specific functions. Children with disabilities present a variety of health, social service, and educational issues. While interventions can take place in a variety of settings, the parent is the primary agent and may be taught mental health, therapeutic and teaching strategies. The characteristics of the children and family will affect the outcome of any strategies.

Services to these complex children must cross traditional boundaries of health, human service, and educational planning for comprehensive services. Communities have unique characteristics, needs, and resources. State agencies also have varying legislative mandates and responsibilities. Health, human service, and education providers must be familiar with the roles and duties of each other's agencies and with private providers in the community (Bender & Baglin, 1992).

A main purpose of collaboration is to ensure planning and coordination of educational and mental health services for students with emotional and behavior problems, birth to age three, and their families. Accomplishing the promise of this legislative is dependent upon the extent to which local jurisdictions can and are willing to develop their own capacity for coordinated and community-based service delivery systems. Agencies within any setting are competing for the same fixed resources, both dollar and human. There is a reluctance to support a new initiative that is perceived to be competing for the same resources. When this mandate emerges from an external agency, such as federal or state government, there can also be a reduced commitment to implement these collaborative efforts.

State interagency policy efforts need to provide direction for the coordination of educational and mental health services. We are working to develop policies and procedures to facilitate community-based planning. Successful initiatives at the local level, however, will be the product of community activities that bring about the desired changes.

Interagency coordination is both a process and an attitude. It is an ongoing, active concept that leads to solutions for some difficult problems. Professionals involved in these activities no longer can operate independently but must work together as a team. The overall result can be improved and less costly services for children and their families.

Effective Services for the Family

Service delivery programs are being asked to look at families in a new way. The family is much different today than ten years ago with more mothers working. Responsive services for these families can provide parents with the support and the coping skills that will enable the family to effectively access a coordinated system, resulting in a financial and human savings. Coordination of services through interagency collaboration of resources represents a significant opportunity to demonstrate the effectiveness of services designed for individuals with unique needs—which are supportive to their families, and reflective of the community.

Families and providers face the same challenges in addressing the needs of these difficult children. Each member of this partnership presumes mutual values, bringing a wide range of assets to the relationship. Within this context, the funding, advocacy, and service delivery is implemented.

References

Adelman, H.S., & Taylor, L. (2002). Building comprehensive, multifaceted, and integrated approaches to address barriers to student learning. *Childhood Education Infancy Through Early Adolescence Annual Theme, Association for Childhood Educational International, 78*(5), 261-268.

Assistance to States for the Education of Children with Disabilities, 34 CFR § 300.7(4), (1999).

Bender, M., & Baglin, C.A. (Eds.). (1992). *Infants and toddlers: A resource guide for practitioners.* San Diego, CA: Singular Publishing Group Inc.

Burke, R.W., & Myers, B.K. (2002). Our crisis in children's mental health: Frameworks for understanding and action. *Childhood Education Infancy Through Early Adolescence Annual Theme, Association for Childhood Educational International, 78*(5), 258-260.

Callegary, E.A. (2002). The IDEA's promise unfulfilled: A second look at special education & related services for children with mental health needs after Garret F. *Journal of Health Care Law & Policy, 5*(1), 164-207.

Conzemius, A., & O'Neill, J. (2001). *Building shared responsibility for student learning.* Alexandria, VA: Association for Supervision and Curriculum Development.

Elder, J.O. (1980). Writing interagency agreements. In J.O. Elder, & P.R. Magrab (Eds.), *Coordinating services to handicapped children* (pp. 203-207). Baltimore: Paul H. Brookes.

Gallagher, J.J. (2000). The beginnings of federal help for young children with disabilities. *Topics in Early Childhood Special Education, 20*(1), 3-6.

Hall, H.B. (1980). The intangible human factor. In J.O. Elder & P.R. Magrab (Eds.), *Coordinating services to handicapped children* (pp. 45-62). Baltimore: Paul H. Brookes.

Harbin, G.L., & Terry, D.V. (1991). *Interagency Service Coordination: Initial Findings From Six States.* Carolina Policy Studies Program.

Hebbeler, K.M. (1991). Creating a national database on early intervention services. *Journal of Early Intervention, 15(1),* 106-112.

Hebbeler, K.M., Smith, B.J., & Black, T.L. (1991). Federal early childhood special education policy: A model for the improvement of services for children with disabilities. *Exceptional Children, 58*(2), 104-112.

Intrilligator, B.A., & Goldman, H. (1989). *The part H initiative: Toward a community- based service delivery system for infants and toddlers with handicaps and their families.* ICA. Arlington, VA: 4212 S. 32nd Street.

Koller, J.R., & Svoboda, S.K. (2002). The application of a strengths-based mental health approach in schools. *Childhood Education Infancy Through Early Adolescence Annual Theme, Association for Childhood Educational International, 78*(5), 291-294.

Magrab, P., Flynn, C., & Pelosi, J. (1985). *Assessing interagency coordination through evaluation.* Chapel Hill, N.C.: University of North Carolina, Grant #GOO-84C-3515, START.

Magrab, P.R., & Schmidt, L.M. (1980). Interdisciplinary Collaboration. In J.O. Elder, & P. R. Magrab (Eds.), *Coordinating services to handicapped children* (pp. 13-23). Baltimore: Paul H. Brookes.

McLaughlin, J.A., & Covert, R.C. (1984). *Evaluating interagency collaborations.* TADS, University of Chapel Hill, Chapel Hill, NC: 500 NCNB Plaza.

Peterson, N.L. (1991). Interagency collaboration under part h: The key to comprehensive, multidisciplinary, coordinated infant/toddler intervention services. *Journal of Early Intervention, 15(1),* 89-105.

Public Law 99-457 (1986). Amendments to the Education of the Handicapped Act.

Smith, B.J. (1986). *A comparative analysis of selected federal programs serving young children.* Chapel Hill, N.C.: University of North Carolina, Grant # GOO-84C-3515, START.

Smith, B. (Ed). (1988). *Mapping the future for children with special needs* P.L. 99-457. University Affiliated Programs, University of Iowa.

Walrath, C.M., Nickerson, K.J., Crowel, R.L., & Leaf, P.J. (1998). Serving children with serious emotional disturbance in a system of care: Do mental health and non-mental health agency referrals look the same? *Journal of Emotional and Behavioral Disorders, 6*(4), 205-213.

Weintraub, J., Abeson, A., Ballard, J., & LaVor, M.L. (Eds.). (1976). *Public policy and the education of exceptional children.* Reston, VA: Council for Exceptional Children.

Zeller, R.W. (1980). Direction service. In J.O. Elder, & P. R. Magrab (Eds.), *Coordinating services to handicapped children* (pp. 65-97). Baltimore: Paul H. Brookes.

Treatment Models With Recreation and Leisure Components

Buzz Williams

The Unique Needs of Children and Adolescents With Emotional Disabilities Treatment Defined

The term treatment may mean different things to different people. Treatments may be medical, psychological, physical, emotional, social, or even spiritual. The treatment process is influenced by the particular philosophy, beliefs, and chosen discipline of the treating professional. A person with a serious behavioral disorder may be treated with medication by a psychiatrist or an exorcism from a priest. Our reference to treatment includes an educational and behavioral approach. Treatment as we define it is psych-educational, meaning it is rooted in both behavioral psychology and instructional methodology. Treatment includes recognizing the characteristics of the individual and making therapeutic adaptations to the tasks and the environment. Our discussion of treatment must begin with an understanding of the interaction between the individual, task, and environment.

Individual Factors

Providers of leisure, recreation, and sport opportunities need to recognize three domains in the children and adolescents served–cognitive (thinking), motor (moving), and affective (emotions and behavior). During the past three decades there has been great progress in including children with learning and physical disabilities. It is commonly accepted practice to modify instruction for a player with a learning disability or to adapt equipment for a player with a physical disability. But what about the child who curses, tantrums, threatens, or fights? Just as teachers, coaches, and youth leaders have learned to include children and adolescents with cognitive and physical disabilities, they must also learn to include those who act out emotionally and behaviorally.

Task Factors

Task factors are specific requirements that allow people to do the things that are asked of them. In baseball, batting is a task that includes many task factors. For example, the size and weight of the bat is a task factor. So, too, are the size, distance, speed, and trajectory of the ball. For a student who is highly anxious about striking out it would be appropriate to adapt the bat, ball, and pitch for success.

Environmental Factors

Environmental factors, unlike biological ones, influence the individual from the outside. We recognize that environmental factors can affect people's emotional development either positively or negatively.

The following chart illustrates several environmental and individual factors that put children at risk for social and emotional disorders (Nelson, 1991). For the teacher or coach, adapting both the task and environmental factors is critical in understanding and implementing psycho-educational treatment models.

Identifying The Need For Treatment

As discussed in chapter two, children and adolescents with special needs in emotional development and behavioral structure require systematic and consistent design in all of their activities. This can be difficult when one thinks of recreational or leisure time as "unstructured" or "less structured" time in our lives. Without attention to these elements of daily activities for these individuals, risks are present that can influence or threaten the success of continued socialization, as well as effective use of personal time. Those working with children and adolescents must be aware of the effect of inappropriate social skills on the adult arenas of family life, peer interaction, and the formation of lifelong habits of effective time management and employment. These habits are formed early in life, even before the first formal social experience of school.

Before treatment approaches can be developed and implemented it is necessary to accurately identify those in need of treatment. To this end, researchers have long studied the distinct differences among those whose behaviors deviate from what is called "normal," essentially, that which is expected of the majority of individuals. Since the middle of the twentieth century, studies have been performed to differentiate types of behavior so that they can be addressed with effective treatment methodologies (Achenbach, 1966; Achenbach & Edelbrock, 1980, 1981; Ackerson, 1942; Hewitt & Jenkins, 1946; Peterson, 1961; Von Isser, Quay & Love, 1980; Lambros, Ward, Bocian, MacMillan, and Gresham, 1998).

From this research and the interpretation of the data that was generated from those studies, clusters or distinct categories of disabilities have resulted. Some of the categories include:

Conduct Disorders—behaviors that conflict with the expectations of society, including overtly disruptive behaviors such as aggression, threatening verbal or physical gestures, defiance, and general negativism.

Anxiety Withdrawal Disorders—behaviors that isolate an individual from more social or outgoing individuals, including shyness, trepidation, over-sensitivity, seclusiveness, and over-anxiety.

Immaturity—behaviors resulting from developmental delays, including infantile actions, tantrums, inattentiveness or preoccupation, daydreaming, sluggish responses, or passivity.

Socialized Aggressive Disorders—behaviors considered antisocial, non-conformist, or criminal, including gang activities, truancy, stealing, or other participation in the activities of a delinquent subculture.

The Teachers' And Coaches' Role
In Identifying Behavioral Needs

Clinicians use classifications to create treatment plans. Many individuals act as clinicians in the lives of individuals with emotional or behavioral problems. These "clinicians" include psychologists, psychiatrists, social workers, family therapists, play therapists, art therapists, music and movement therapists, and counselors. As mentioned earlier in this book, teachers, coaches, and other youth leaders are the daily "clinicians," implementing plans and programs *within* daily instruction. Their therapeutic training is not as extensive or detailed as that of the persons named above, and therefore, it is important to look at how these trained professionals construct plans for treating the needs of individuals whose behavioral responses are troubling, disruptive, or ineffective.

Although teachers and coaches are not clinical diagnosticians, their observations of behaviors in the learning environment, coupled with their partnership with family members as observers, can assist mental health professionals in characterizing behaviors. The reports are especially helpful in identifying the nature of the behavior in terms of appropriateness, adaptability, severity of deviation from expected behaviors, and activity levels (Lambros, Ward, Bocian, MacMillan, & Gresham, 1998).

Working Together With Parents To Identify Needs

Teachers and coaches are not expected to use clinical diagnostic labels, but Wood (1982), and Wood and Smith (1985) offer a simple way to look at behaviors to determine how to characterize them. Each category is important to help determine the elements of the behavior. In addition, a clinician may find it helpful to compare the results from many different observers (i.e. parent, teacher, coach, babysitter, etc.) in order to identify patterns related to the cause and effect of behavior.

An extension of Wood's criteria is in the following chart, allowing a teacher, coach, family member, or other observer to clearly describe a problem behavior and to assess the seriousness of the behavior.

BEHAVIOR CHECKLIST

Date: __/__/__ Day: M T W R F
Observer:_____   Time: __:__   AM PM

OBSERVATION OF BEHAVIOR

Who is causing the problem?

What is the problem?

❏ is too loud
❏ uses disrespectful gestures
❏ makes threats of harm to self
❏ yells at me when I speak to him/her
❏ defies me by not following my directions
❏ disrupts the activities or work of others
❏ tantrums when denied something
❏ harms himself/herself
❏ hides in a trusted or special place
❏ runs away by bolting into the community
❏ refuses to complete activities
❏ takes a long time to complete tasks
❏ seems unable to remain relatively still
❏ uses belongings of others without asking
❏ hordes personal belongings
❏ challenges my authority in front of others
❏ overreacts to situations by showing anger
❏ overreacts to situations by being fearful
❏ eats too much
❏ sleeps too much
❏ talks too much
❏ refuses to try new things
❏ insists on being helped
❏ daydreams or gazes into space
❏ seems fearful of individuals
❏ stops personal hygiene habits
❏ is irritable
❏ refuses to go to school or other places
❏ talks a lot about a single thing
❏ spends excessive time with video games
❏ has no friends
❏ communicates with "imaginary" friends
❏ chooses to communicate with select people
Other notes on the behavior:

❏ uses disrespectful language
❏ makes threats of harm to others
❏ ignores me when I speak to him/her
❏ screams to drown out voices or sounds
❏ defies me by doing a forbidden activity
❏ destroys the property or work of others
❏ harms others
❏ avoids by moving into a "special place"
❏ runs away within the school or home
❏ refuses to comply with a schedule
❏ takes a long time to respond to me
❏ refuses to stay in an assigned space
❏ disturbs others with his/her movements
❏ steals belongings of others
❏ refuses to share
❏ misrepresents my actions to others
❏ overreacts to situations by crying
❏ does not eat, or eats little
❏ does not sleep, or sleeps little
❏ does not talk, or talks in single words
❏ uses baby talk or gibberish
❏ gives up too easily
❏ reacts to activities by saying "I can't"
❏ allows others to take advantage
❏ stops toileting or starts bed wetting
❏ becomes overly concerned with hygiene
❏ refuses medications
❏ refuses to go home after school
❏ spends excessive time watching TV
❏ spends excessive time using the Internet
❏ has only a single friend
❏ does not interact with family members

WHO IS DISTURBED BY THIS/THESE BEHAVIOR(S)?

❑ me
❑ everyone in the home
❑ everyone in the class
❑ others in the community

❑ other family members
❑ some peers in the class
❑ others in the school

SCHOOL

❑ classroom
❑ hallway
❑ gymnasium
❑ cafeteria
❑ bus
❑ assembly room/auditorium
❑ lab classroom
❑ resource room (art, music)
❑ administrative offices
❑ therapeutic or counseling area
other: _____

HOME/COMMUNITY

❑ kitchen
❑ bedroom
❑ living room
❑ rec center or other activity area
❑ family room
❑ dining area
❑ yard
❑ garage/driveway
❑ shopping area (mall, market, etc.)
❑ place of worship
other: _____

❑ yelling
❑ taking points
❑ refusing to take the individual to events
❑ restraining physically
❑ calling a behavioral specialist
❑ calling a pediatrician
❑ calling a school administrator
❑ calling a religious counselor
Other:

❑ removing privileges
❑ spanking
❑ restricting physical space
❑ calling the police
❑ time-out
❑ calling mental health professional
❑ leaving them alone
❑ demanding an apology

USING THE BEHAVIOR CHECKLIST

When teachers, counselors, coaches, family members, and others who are regular observers of the behavior of a child or adolescent use such a checklist for recording their observations, it helps define exactly what is "disturbing" behavior, and how the observer "qualifies" the observations. The results of such checklists may be evaluated by a trained professional to answer questions such as:

• Do the behaviors usually occur within a specific time period or on the same day?
• Are the same individuals involved when the behavior(s) occur?
• What was going on immediately prior to the disturbing behavior?
• How do the responses of others influence the individual?
• Does any specific intervention work to eliminate or reduce the disturbing behavior?
• Is there a consistent behavior management system in place in the classroom or home?
• Is the disturbing behavior new or recent?
• Can the individual adjust or adapt behavior to acquire a privilege or reward?
• When, if ever, does the individual show appropriate behavior?
• Is there a particular person who seems able to communicate effectively with the individual? Will the individual produce appropriate behavior for them?
• Is the individual medicated?

After such questions are answered, an individualized treatment plan may be designed. Consider the following case study to illustrate how the checklist may be used to develop a treatment plan.

CASE STUDY: CARLOS

Carlos is a 13-year-old adolescent who recently joined the recreation basketball team coached by Mr. Abbott. Following several practices, Mr. Abbott recognizes that Carlos becomes very angry and hostile during competition.

In fact, during a parent conference he learned that Carlos has attended a special school for students with emotional disabilities. With the parent's permission, Mr. Abbott completed the behavior checklist.

The results are as follows:

Coach Abbott's Checklist Results: Carlos's Behavior

1. Who is causing the problem? Carlos
2. What is the problem? Carlos' makes threats of harm to others and uses disrespectful language. This occurs during competitive situations in which Carlos feels unsuccessful. Carlos reports that the others tease him, which makes him angry.
3. Setting: Recreation Center
4. Who is disturbed by these behaviors: Teammates, parents, and coach (me).
1. My actions: Threatening to send Carlos home or remove him from the team.

Carlos's mom shared the results with Carlos's educational team at school including his teacher, therapist, and physical education teacher. The physical education teacher recognized the behaviors and provided suggestions for a treatment plan. The plan that Carlos's mom shared with the coach follows:

Carlos's Plan for Recreation Basketball:

1. Carlos is an adolescent with an emotional disability who needs a structured and safe environment with clearly understood and consistent rules.
2. Structure: A five-level system should be used to allow Carlos to participate at varying degrees of competition.
Level 1: Students may shoot baskets independently with only verbal feedback from staff.
Level 2: Students may compete one-on-one with a staff member.
Level 3: Students may compete one-on-one with a peer who he selects.
Level 4: Students may compete in a small group of selected peers.
Level 5: Unlimited competition.
3. Clear Rules: All members of the team must abide by Conduct Rules which include:
A. Use respectful language.
B. Keep comments positive.
C. Touch the ball not other players.
D. Finish all games by shaking at least one opponent's hand.
E. Sit yourself out if you feel angry.

---

4. Limits:

A. One successful practice is needed to be promoted to the next level.

B. A behavior "strike" is earned for breaking a conduct rule.

C. Three strikes during one practice or game results in a demotion by one level.

D. A threat or fight is automatic demotion to level one.

E. Only students on level five may compete in games with other teams.

5. Safe Environment:

A. All members of the team need to understand Carlos's disability.

B. All members of the team need to be held to high standards of conduct and all are subject to the same consequences.

C. Sportsmanship and cooperation must be encouraged, modeled, and re-warded.

The plan was explained to parents and players at a special meeting. The plan did not specifically identify Carlos or his behavioral disorder. During the season, Carlos was the most frequently demoted player, but others occasionally dropped below level five. Carlos made it through the season without being removed from the team, and was eligible to play in six out of 10 games. Coach Abbott considered this a success since he was ready to throw Carlos off the team after the second practice.

Treatment Models

Medical Model

The medical model addresses emotional and behavioral disorders with medication prescribed by a psychiatrist. There is considerable controversy regarding the use of medications, especially Ritalin, to alter children's behavior. This discussion will assume that the child has a neurological or psychological condition that is treatable using medication. Many people with emotional disabilities and challenging behaviors use medication to assist with:

1. Leveling mood swings
2. Managing anger
3. Coping with depression
4. Coping with hallucinations
5. Controlling obsessive thoughts or compulsive actions

Implications for Teachers, Coaches, and Youth Leaders

Teachers, coaches, and youth leaders need to keep the following in mind when working with persons using medication for psychological and/or behavioral reasons:

1. Many children and adolescents participate in leisure and recreation activities while using prescription medication to help them with an emotional and/or behavioral disability.

2. The use of medications is confidential. Policies and procedures need to be developed and followed protecting the person's confidentiality.

3. The administration and handling of medications needs to be taken seriously. Policies and procedures need to be developed and followed if staff members assume responsibility to administer medication. This includes medication administration/handling training from a qualified agency.

4. Recognize that sharing, loaning, or distributing medication to any other person other than the person for whom the medication is prescribed is illegal and dangerous. The practice of abusing prescription medication to become intoxicated or "high" is an alarming trend among children and adolescents with potentially fatal consequences.

5. A person's behavior may be dramatically different depending on the medication levels in their blood at the time you see them. Blood-levels may be affected by starting or ending a new medication, taking the wrong dosage amount, or skipping doses.

Counseling Model

The counseling model addresses emotional and behavioral disorders through a therapeutic relationship between a client and a therapist. People with emotional disabilities often receive medication prescribed by a psychiatrist as well as mental health counseling provided by a therapist. Children and adolescents may receive therapy provided by the school, church, private practitioner, or social service agency.

There are many therapeutic approaches and counseling theories available to assist people with emotional disabilities and behavioral problems. While "therapy" may conjure thoughts of psychoanalytic healing from a "shrink," the types of therapy children and adolescents experience is likely very different. In fact, many therapists reject the medical model in which people are considered sick and in need of healing. Instead, therapists rely on the development of a trusting relationship in which the client can work toward individualized goals. In this way, counseling is more like education than medical treatment. Some common counseling goals include helping the client to:

1. Define goals and develop plans to reach them
2. Realize self-awareness
3. Develop healthy coping mechanisms
4. Establish new behavioral patterns and rewards for reaching goals
5. Role-play responses in challenging social situations
6. Desensitize clients to anxiety-producing situations or phobias
7. Confront clients when they are being dishonest with themselves
8. Manage anger

Implications for Teachers, Coaches, and Youth Leaders

Teachers, coaches, and youth leaders need to keep the following in mind when working with persons receiving professional counseling:

1. The terms "Therapy" and "Counseling" are often used interchangeably. Many children and adolescents with emotional disabilities receive therapy from a professional counselor.
2. The therapist is an important person to give and receive information regarding the person's emotional and social well-being.
3. Knowledge that a person sees a therapist is to be kept confidential.
4. The relationship and work between a therapist and client is confidential and should not be discussed without approval of the therapist.
5. Special behavioral plans and strategies should be shared with the therapist directly or through the family.

Educational Model

Developmentally Appropriate Curriculum

All students experience the social demands and opportunities of the structured school day. When children and adolescents engage in recreational and leisure activities within their communities, these activities are often offered in environments that are school-like in design, such as recreational centers, classes, camps, teams, or structured groups. Since the academic program for an individual with special needs in the area of emotional and behavioral development is designed to recognize individual needs, set individual goals, provide assistance for the individual to meet those goals, and to assess the effectiveness of the treatment plan individually, it stands to reason that the design for providing recreational or leisure experiences should be provided with a similar structure.

Curricular Implications

The structure of the academic program is embodied in the curriculum, which includes both the scope (variety of activities) and sequence (order of activities).

Curriculum is designed to be a comprehensive and sequential set of learning activities to teach concepts. Curriculum provides structure for both the instructor and the learner. Besides being critical to effective instruction, curriculum design affects student motivation. The order in which skills are taught, and the activities are practiced help the student to understand the purpose for what they are doing. Without this connection and understanding, students may become bored and disinterested. This establishes an environment that creates opportunities for students with behavioral challenges to act-out.

In the classroom, curriculum is demonstrated by the manner in which lessons are connected to units of instruction. In leisure, recreation, and sport, curriculum is demonstrated by the manner in which practice sessions and activities are organized to help the participants realize the goals of the program. Leisure and recreation goals include increasing physical fitness, winning a league championship, or developing social skills.

Curricular Examples

The Thematic Curriculum

One of the ways curriculum may be organized and presented is called the thematic approach. Thematic curriculums are particularly helpful in creating motivational and meaningful learning environments that help students with emotional disabilities succeed.

Thematic curriculum uses a central idea, or theme, to unite all aspects of learning for a given period of time. It connects the learner to the content considering a variety of personalities and learning styles. Themes may be of various lengths of time, from a day-to-day or weekly theme (often used with young children), to monthly or quarterly themes (which may be used with intermediate to secondary grades). Themes may include concepts such as money, entertainment, sports, travel, careers, or animals. Teachers (or teaching teams) can plan their content area instruction around the central concept, individualizing the instruction for motivational levels of students, attention levels of students, maturity of students, and personal interests of students (Lewis, 1993).

Case Study: *Risk and Adventure Theme at Summer Camp*

A summer camp serves a variety of children and adolescents, some of whom have emotional and behavioral disorders. Last year the camp counselors offered daily activities randomly, usually based on whatever the majority wanted. Some of the students reported that they grew bored with the activities after one week, and began asking to go home. By the fourth week, morale was low around camp. Even the best behaved students were beginning to talk back and challenge the authority of the staff.

A consultant was hired to help re-design the camp activities for the next year. The consultant helped the staff develop a thematic curriculum lasting four weeks. The theme was Risk and Adventure. Each day was structured so that the events and activities built upon the days before, and led to a grand finale during the last week.

Thematic Unit Plan: Risk and Adventure

Theme: Risk and Adventure
Values: Trust, Teamwork, Cooperation
Motto: Challenge By Choice
Conclusion: XGames Field Day
Scope and Sequence of Activities:
Week 1: Partner Trust, Group Trust, Cooperation Games, Water Survival
Week 2: Problem Solving, Movement Games, Group Initiatives
Week 3: Obstacle Courses, Confidence Courses, Rock Climbing, Rappelling
Week 4: Low Ropes Course, High Ropes Course, Survival

The following activity called "Trust Fall" is an example of one lesson in the thematic curriculum.

Thematic Activity: Risk and Adventure

Name of Activity: Trust Fall
Procedure: A peer stands on a platform five feet off the ground. He turns his back on his peers on the ground who are standing face to face in two parallel lines joined by interlocking hands and forearms. The group's interlocked forearms form a cushion onto which the student will be caught after he falls backward from the platform.
This activity is a part of the Risk and Adventure theme. Students who complete this activity receive a "certificate of trust." This activity is part of several progressive and related activities that are connected to a central theme. It takes some students weeks to successfully complete the trust fall.

Consider the implications of offering this type of activity during the prior year, when activities were offered randomly without a thematic connection. Few campers would even participate, much less be inspired or motivated by it. The thematic curriculum is a powerful way to organize and structure learning environments for all students, but particularly for people with emotional and behavioral challenges.

This particular thematic approach ties together cognitive, motor, and affective skills. For each domain it affords students the chance to progress from the basic demonstration of skills to more advanced and complex mastery of academics, movement, socialization, and emotional development. The thematic approach allows teachers the scope of curriculum that is ideal, while allowing for grouping based on skill and social development. Thematic learning gives the learner some autonomy, as well as making the experience of learning collaborative and cooperative. Because thematic curriculum connects content and skills, it allows for movement in learning and more socialized instruction.

The Alternative Curriculum

As more students with emotional challenges are included in regular physical education and recreation programs, the need grows for changes in curriculum. There is a general shift in curricular content from traditional competitive sports units to alternative activities including cooperatives, initiatives, adventure activities, and lifetime recreation.

Cooperatives include activities that require teamwork to accomplish a task or overcome a challenge. Initiatives require a group of students to work together to solve a problem or overcome an obstacle. Adventure activities include indoor and outdoor rock climbing, as well as hiking, canoeing, rappelling, and mountain biking. Lifetime recreation pursuits include skating, bowling, biking, golfing, and a variety of activities that students may choose to continue through their adulthood.

Competition with Choices

It would be unfair to many students to eliminate competitive sports from physical education and recreation programs. Instead, many programs are offering choices to students during their traditionally "competitive" units like soccer and basketball. Students would have the choice of competing with peers, or playing the same activity on a recreational "fun" level. For example, some students may elect to play "HORSE" while others play a game of five-on-five basketball. Students with emotional challenges frequently choose the alternatives if they know they have difficulty with competitive environments. Students that choose to compete, but fail to follow game and conduct rules, may be removed from competition and still have options for participation.

Developmentally Appropriate Instruction

While the following instructional factors are important for all students, they are critical for students with emotional disabilities and challenging behaviors. Each of the following factors influences the degree to which these children and adolescents will be successful.

Frequency

Frequency refers to the number of times per week the activity is held. Recreation sports typically meet once per week for practice and once per week for games. Physical education classes in school range from once per week to five days per week. Some summer programs are residential in nature, meeting 24 hours per day, seven days per week. The most appropriate frequency is dependent upon each individual. While some may benefit from the repetition and practice of daily meetings, others may be stressed out by the constant demands.

Intensity

Intensity refers to the difficulty of the tasks to be performed. Tasks may be presented at the practice, instructional, or frustration levels. Practice-level activities may be performed independently with a high degree of success. Instructional levels require the assistance of teacher or coach for successful mastery of new or more challenging tasks. Frustration-level tasks are too challenging for an individual's state of readiness. It is the responsibility of the staff members to ensure that students do not reach the frustration level. Moving the student to a more appropriate group or adapting the task to meet the student's developmental needs may accomplish this.

Duration

Duration refers to the length of time in minutes or hours that an activity lasts. Many students with conduct disorders have short attention spans, and duration becomes an important factor in programming for their success. Younger children and those with short attention spans may require activities presented in 15-20 minute waves. Older students with longer attention spans may be able to focus for more than an hour.

Mode

Mode refers to the number of senses involved during instruction. Multi-sensory instruction involving hearing, seeing, and touching is preferred. Practically speaking, it is better to provide a visual model and allow hands-on practice than to lecture or provide lengthy verbal instructions.

Peer Group

Peer group refers to the nature of the students involved in the activity. Inclusive peer groups include both disabled and non-disabled people. Self-contained groups include people with similar abilities and/or disabilities. Some recreation baseball programs include players with various disabilities, and some have developed special leagues for players with disabilities. The selection of inclusive or self-contained peer groups is an individualized decision. Usually people have very strong feelings about where they belong. It is most challenging when those strong feelings are toward the group that is least developmentally appropriate.

Teaching/Coaching Styles

Teachers who "bark" directions, position students in lines for skill drills, and expect intrinsic motivation are likely to experience trouble with students who have emotional challenges. Teachers who are student-centered and present activities with respect to individual differences will be more successful motivating students and keeping students on task.

Command

The command-style teacher controls students in an authoritative manner. This is a teacher-centered style in which the teacher governs all aspects of student participation. Command-style teachers are highly structured and depend on student compliance. These teachers act like drill instructors.

Directive

The directive-style teacher provides instructions to students, usually with a demonstration. Students are then offered opportunities to practice the skill during drills and lead-up games. Directive teachers teach while students practice drills and play the game. These teachers are most like coaches.

Exploratory

The exploratory-style teacher provides open-ended challenges to students in an effort to stimulate creative movement. Students are challenged to "throw the ball higher" or "hang with different body parts." Exploratory style teachers provide movement challenges and let students develop individualized responses. These teachers challenge, entertain, and cheerlead.

Guided Discovery

The guided discovery-style teacher provides convergent challenges that start broad and gradually focus the learner on the desired outcome. For example, the teacher may begin by asking students to "make the ball go over the net." After practice the next challenge would be to "use your hands to make the ball go over the net." Next, "use your hands to strike the ball over the net." This progression would eventually lead the player to demonstrate the overhand volleyball serve. These teachers lead students toward skill-specific performance.

Student Centered

The student centered-style teacher provides activities that promote individualized student achievement. For this teacher a basketball unit may be used to assist students in developing thinking skills, social skills, physical fitness, or motor skills. However, the execution of basketball skills is not considered important unless that is the goal of the student. These teachers place the needs of individuals over the mastery of sport-specific skills. Personal choice is a major part of the instructional climate.

Instructional Strategies

IPI Inclusion Model

The Individual, Preparatory, Inclusive (IPI) instructional model provides a progressive framework for teaching students with special needs and emotional disabilities when they are grouped in the same class with their non-disabled peers. At any given point in a lesson, students with special needs should be engaged in one of the three levels of participation. Students without disabilities who are the majority of the class, and are engaged in non-adaptive activities are referred to as the main body of the class.

At the individual level the student participates in a meaningful activity related to the objectives of the lesson that can be demonstrated individually with either direct teacher support, or indirect teacher support. This affords students the opportunity to experience success in a non-threatening environment.

At the preparatory level students participate in realistic "practice" that focuses on a skill that will be used when he or she is included with the main body of the class. This "practice" can be demonstrated individually or with a peer group with either direct teacher support, or indirect teacher support. Preparatory activities "prepare" the student for the physical, cognitive, and social demands of the inclusive activity. The preparatory activity provides an opportunity for a developmentally appropriate task, or piece of the bigger game, to be practiced and refined in the safe, controlled setting. When the student is integrated into the main body of the class, he or she will approach their task with greater competence and confidence, having practiced it repeatedly.

At the inclusive level, students participate in realistic "game-play," incorporating a skill that was mastered at the preparatory level of participation. The purpose of the inclusive activity is to provide the opportunity for the student to demonstrate a newly mastered adaptive skill in a competitive game with the main body of the class.

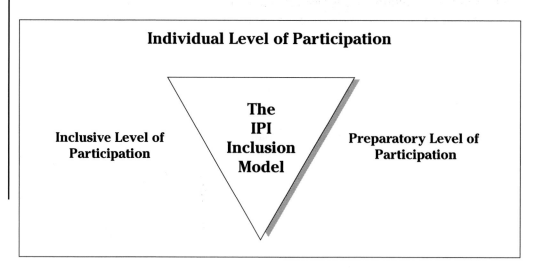

Individual Level of Participation

Inclusive Level of Participation

The IPI Inclusion Model

Preparatory Level of Participation

Progressive Competitive Levels

One of the key elements of developing success-oriented activities for students is to implement the Progressive-Competitive-Levels (PCL) strategy. PCL is simply presenting any sport or activity as a series of levels—each progressively more challenging than the last. The highest level of play should be regulation game play. Chapter four provides more detailed information on the PCL Strategy.

Primary Competitive Adaptations

The three primary competitive adaptations used when working with students who are emotionally challenged in physical education include modifications to objects, space, and time. In student-friendly terms, these concepts are called hot, crease, and clock. Students would then elect the adaptation of their choice by requesting to use a hot object, or be a crease player, or clock player. Chapter four provides more detailed information on the PCA strategy.

Alternative Rules and Scoring

Traditional rules for competitive sports are not designed to be forgiving for students with fragile egos. It is best to establish the policy of adapting the rules and the scoring practices to best serve the students at their developmental levels. Consider the embarrassment associated with striking out in front of all of your peers and the staff during a baseball game, the frustration of serving every volleyball out of bounds, or the hopeless feeling of never scoring a point in a basketball game. Teachers who modify games for student success facilitate a positive play environment that prevents many of the problems that manifest from failure.

During baseball, consider not allowing students to earn a third strike. Instead, students receiving two strikes must toss the ball to themselves. If two strikes are earned by tossing, then the student may use a batting "tee" to hit.

During volleyball, allow students to choose the distance from the net for serving. There is no rule carved in stone that requires students to serve from behind the regulation service line. Students will accept the rule changes as long as staff presents them positively.

During basketball, consider allowing students to score one point for hitting the rim. They may also score two points for a basket. Some students will not choose this option, but some will be thrilled to finally contribute to the team's score.

Ability Grouping

Staff needs to recognize the potential for disaster with traditional "team captain"- type grouping. Inevitably the same students are consistently picked last by the "popular" peers. When students are included with emotional problems and challenging behaviors, the staff has the responsibility to prevent potential problems before they occur. One of the best preventive strategies is to work with the students in a process called "ability grouping." This strategy involves students pairing with a partner who has basically the same athletic ability. The partners then separate and wear opposite color jerseys. This technique ensures two equitable teams. Note that players who wish to be on the same team should not partner, because partners separate. Also note that the least "popular" student may still be left without a partner if the number of students is odd. One staff person should partner with that student. The staff partner not only cushions the reality of not being liked, but the student is likely to need the attention and directions of the staff to keep him or her on task.

Engaged Staff

Staff should be actively involved in every aspect of the activity. Staff should greet the students when they enter, work with the students during the lesson introduction and distribution of equipment, assist the students with ability grouping, provide constant verbal feedback during the lesson, and assist the students during the transition to their next activity. Staff should participate actively, and play-officiate during competitive activities. As emotional "fires" ignite during the lesson, the engaged staff members will recognize them, and intervene before they flare out of control.

Indoor v. Outdoor

Students with emotional difficulties require collaboration and communication between staff members. Outside activities present communication challenges. Programs with radios may choose to take students out of the building, provided that support staff is monitoring the other radio in case of emergency. A second factor related to inside activity is that students with emotional challenges frequently have low tolerance for weather extremes. Playing in the cold, hot, or even wind can provide enough reason to refuse participation.

The Cycle of Change

The cycle of change refers to the predictable pattern that occurs when different routines and alternative ideas are presented to students. There will likely be initial resistance to give the new way a try. Following the initial resistance there will be cautious acceptance. Ultimately students will reach genuine acceptance of change.

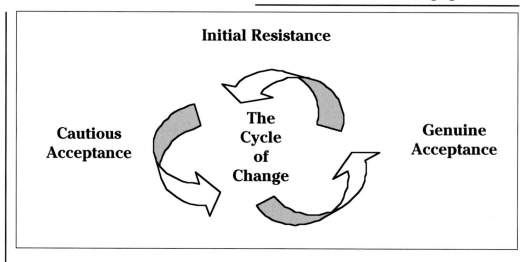

Working Through Student Resistance

The main factor that determines how new concepts are received by students is the manner in which they are presented by the staff. All staff members need to be consistent and positive when communicating rules and procedures. A second factor is to allow students to make choices regarding their participation. For example, a student says, "Why does Josh get to serve the easy way?" An appropriate response would be, "It is an easier way, and anyone can choose to use that technique." Lastly, students will inevitably challenge the new rules. Staff needs to be prepared to set limits and provide choices. The student that refuses to bat from a tee because that is "the baby way," should hear, "You can hit from the tee or you can give your turn to a teammate, but no one gets a pitch after two strikes."

Again, the key to limiting student resistance to these alternative concepts is positive presentation by the staff. If the students do not to buy into the alternative rules, it is because the staff has failed to sell them.

Behavioral Model

Behavior Modification Principles

Behavioral psychology maintains that there are four responses that shape or influence human behavior. Teachers, coaches, and youth leaders need to understand these four responses and their implications on children and adolescents with emotional disabilities and behavior problems.

Four Responses to Behavior

Punishment

Punishment is the immediate application of an unpleasant and/or painful action in response to a behavior. Examples range from privilege removal like detention to pain infliction like paddling. Perhaps the most troubling aspect of punishment is, to the untrained observer, it appears to be effective. The behavior, however, is only stopped in the presence of the punisher. This may serve to provide discipline in a specific class, or peace at the dinner table, but it does little to promote internally motivated positive behaviors and social skills.

Negative Reinforcement

Negative reinforcement is not the same as punishment. It includes the presence of a looming threat that something negative will happen if a specific behavior is demonstrated. The negative thing may be unpleasant, but unlike punishment does not threaten physical pain. For example, a company successfully marketed a new brand of diapers based on the power of negative reinforcement. This diaper included bright blue stars on the fabric. The toddlers associated the stars with being a "big boy" or "big girl." The stars, however, disappeared when the fabric became wet. In this example the looming threat was the loss of the stars on the diaper. Many behavioral strategies are founded on the principle of negative reinforcement.

Absent Reinforcement

Absent reinforcement is "ignoring" the behavior as if it did not occur. This is only appropriate when the behavior is not a threat to anyone and is not disruptive to learning. Annoying behaviors like tapping pencils or whistling may be appropriately addressed by this strategy. These behaviors are often demonstrated with the purpose of getting attention from others. Ignoring works best when praise is immediately provided for demonstrating a positive behavior. In this way the person is likely to repeat the behavior that earned the attention.

Positive Reinforcement

Positive reinforcement is the application of a reward following desirable behavior. **Teachers and coaches who are successful working with people with emotional disabilities reinforce good behaviors more than ignore or punish bad behaviors.** There are three categories of reinforcers that are appropriate for different developmental levels. It is helpful to reflect on the fact that all people are motivated to act and work by various rewards that are meaningful to them as individuals.

Social Reinforcers

Social reinforcers are the most desirable reinforcers in that they reflect a higher developmental level of emotional maturity. Social reinforcers are rewards that provide quality time with peers and adults, privileges, and responsibilities. Students who desire social reinforcers are motivated intrinsically by pride in accomplishment. Examples include earning the privilege of eating lunch with staff members, earning a special "staff assistant" responsibility, or earning a social field trip with peers.

Tangible Reinforcers

Tangible reinforcers are next most desirable in that they reflect a moderate developmental level of emotional maturity. Tangible reinforcers are rewards that can be physically held, and seen. Students who seek tangibles are motivated extrinsically by the satisfaction of earning things like prizes, toys, and certificates.

Edible Reinforcers

Edibles are the least desirable reinforcers in that they appeal to the most primitive of motivations—to eat. Providing edibles is often necessary to provide a basic foundation of earning and success for the most disabled children. Edibles typically include small candies, crackers, and pretzels. Obviously it is most prudent to provide nutritious foods so the reward does not bring with it extra calories and sugars. Staff members should begin transitioning from edibles to tangibles as soon as the child is developmentally ready. The key is to market the tangible reinforcers as a more attractive reward than the edibles.

Behavioral Strategies

Preventive Strategies

All misbehavior is costly in terms of instructor time and energy. It is in the service provider's best interest to focus on preventing behavior problems before they occur. Most behavior problems experienced by staff members could have been prevented. The following factors are significant in the prevention of behavior problems.

Developmentally Appropriate Instruction

As discussed in the curriculum section of this chapter, there is no substitute for providing developmentally appropriate instruction that is meaningful, interesting, challenging, and motivating to the student. Teachers, coaches, and youth leaders will eliminate a significant number of behavior problems by providing well-planned lessons.

Structure and Routine

Students who understand what to expect in the learning environment are more likely to follow rules and meet teacher expectations. This is best accomplished by including daily routines. This means that there should be a defined beginning, middle, and end to the activity. Staff members should emphasize the routines associated with transitioning students from one area to the other. An activity without structure and routines provides fertile ground for misbehavior.

Clear Rules

Rules need to be clearly communicated and understood by the participants. Rules are often posted and forgotten. When working with children and adolescents with behavior disorders it is critical that rules be posted, discussed, and practiced through role plays. Rules should be phrased in the positive context so staff members are reinforcing students for doing the right things instead of punishing them for doing the wrong things. For example, the rule "Do not hit others" should read, "Keep your hands to yourself."

Consequence Sequence

Just as participants need to understand the rules, they need to understand the consequence sequence in the program. Students with behavioral challenges are masters at manipulating poorly enforced or inconsistent consequence structures. It is common for students to become emotionally escalated when they feel they have been treated unfairly, which is frequently a result of a breakdown in the consequence system. For example, Michael recognizes that he was asked to leave class for the same behavior that a peer demonstrated yesterday without leaving class. Michael will likely challenge the staff member, creating the potential for a behavioral crisis.

Create Leverage with Reinforcers

Teachers and coaches may find that children and adolescents with emotional disabilities do not respond the same way to behavior management strategies as their non-disabled peers. The coach who controls behavior by raising his voice, for example, may find that strategy ineffective with players who have conduct disorders. Many students with emotional disabilities have suffered traumatic experiences including physical, psychological, and sexual abuse. Given their histories of abuse, one may ask what a teacher or coach could ever do to a child that would "keep them in line." The more appropriate question is what can the teacher or coach provide for the student in terms of needs and wants—reinforcers. Leverage is the power of influence created when a student is motivated by a specific reinforcement.

Establish a Confident Presence

It is important to present oneself as a confident leader who is in control of the learning environment. This is best accomplished by thoughtful consideration of the factors listed above. Students with emotional disabilities will recognize disorganization, unpreparedness, lack of rules, inconsistent consequences, and absence of leverage as weakness. These students will exploit the weaknesses in the program and take advantage by acting out. The untrained instructor will perceive these students as unruly failures, when it is in fact the instructor who failed the students

Supportive Strategies

Supportive strategies are used when students begin to demonstrate anxiety, agitation, or disruption. These strategies are designed to stop inappropriate behaviors during their early stage. A key to providing supportive strategies is that individual students are not directly confronted about the potential misbehavior. Consider the following strategies for stopping misbehavior before it starts.

Surface Management Strategies

Antiseptic Bouncing—asking a student to perform an errand to get him or her away from a negative peer interaction like teasing. It is important to address the teasing before the student returns.

Planned Ignoring—ignoring a behavior that is only annoying to the teacher tells the student that behavior will not result in getting teacher attention. It is important to provide attention to the student immediately after demonstrating an appropriate behavior.

Remove the Seductive Object—remove or hide objects in the learning environment that distract student attention. Consider players on a recreation basketball team who play with the ball in their hands instead of listening to the coach's direction. A routine of placing the ball between players' feet or turning it in to the storage rack would be appropriate ways to remove the seductive object.

Proximity Control—adults who move close to students who are talking, passing notes, or giggling will find that the disruptive behavior stops. Staff members need to stay on the move to position themselves strategically next to students who are beginning to be disruptive.

Signal Interference—instructors who have a signal, such as turning off the light to communicate "quiet time" are using signal interference. This works best when students recognize the signal as a routine part of the program.

Token Economies

Token economies are structured earning plans for students. Students typically use point sheets to monitor their progress following class rules and working toward personal goals. The points earned then translate into tokens for buying power and/or levels for privilege power.

Tokens may be poker chips, phony dollars, or even non-negotiable checks. Students use the tokens to purchase goods and services in the class store or school store. The goods and services should be age-appropriate to be most motivating.

The levels provide privileges for students and are earned by accumulating daily points. The lowest levels should be restrictive, while the higher levels provide progressively more social privileges. Level one may require that staff members escort students, for example. Level five may afford the student the privilege of ordering carryout food for lunch.

Body Language

Teachers, coaches, and youth leaders need to be mindful of their body language when working with children and adolescents with emotional disabilities. While being supportive, it is important to make eye contact so the student understands your concern. Your eyes, facial expression, and gestures are often the major means of communicating your intent. It is therefore important to recognize what non-verbal signals your face and eyes communicate. Remember that students perceive your non-verbal messages louder than your words. It is also important to respect students' personal space. As a rule, keep more than an arm or leg distance between you and the student. People with emotional challenges are often more sensitive to violations of their personal space than non-disabled peers. Getting too close may be perceived as a threat.

Paraverbal Communication

Paraverbals are "how we say what we say." They include tone (emotion), volume (loudness), and cadence (speed). Like body language, more is communicated by how we say something than what we say. Try the following experiment to demonstrate the power of paraverbals.

Experiment 1: Use an angry tone, loud volume, and fast cadence to inform a student that you will have to call his or her parent to inform them of how good his or her behavior is.

Experiment 2: Use a happy and proud tone, soft volume, and slow cadence to inform a student that you can't believe he or she scored the *lowest* on a test.

More times than not, the student will respond to the paraverbal intent instead of the content of the words.

Effective Praise

Providing consistent praise to students results in consistently appropriate behaviors—especially when the praise is behaviorally focused. It is important to not offer blanket praise such as, "Good job, Nate." Students with behavioral problems need specific feedback about what they do wrong or right. The following steps are important in providing effective praise:

1. Personalize it with the student's name.
2. Be genuine with a deserved compliment.
3. Be specific when describing the good behavior.
4. Be age appropriate when praising with paraverbals, gestures, and words.

"Nate, thanks for being the first person to remember to put your basketball between your feet when the whistle blew!"

I Statements

Adults that address behaviors by starting with "you" have already put the student in the defensive position. Consider the staff member who needs to address Jen's giggling during instructions. The staff member addresses Jen in front of her peers, "You need to stop laughing." Jen may feel threatened and embarrassed and try to protect her ego by talking back to the teacher. A better strategy would be to use "I statements" to indirectly address the behavior. Consider the following examples:

- I am feeling like I am losing your attention, so I will give directions quickly.
- I think some of us are getting silly, so I will wait until we get it together.
- I would be embarrassed if parents were watching our class right now.

These are even more effective when combined with proximity control.

The Columbo

Like "I Statements," the Columbo is a verbal strategy for indirectly addressing misbehavior. The instructor simply states a question to which the students know the answer in an attempt to subtly remind them of the expectation. The following examples would be appropriate if a group of adolescents were throwing food at each other in the cafeteria.

- "Help me to remember the rule about cleaning the tables before we leave?"
- "I keep trying to figure out how these crumbs got on the floor?"
- "Could any of you remind me of the consequence for food fights?"

The attractive part of this technique is that it empowers students to adjust behavior without judgment or embarrassment. It also encourages students to verbalize rules and consequences in a non-threatening way.

Corrective Strategies

Corrective strategies are used when students demonstrate behaviors that need to be directly addressed. These strategies are designed to address behavior directly and provide consequences. A key to providing corrective strategies is that consistency is important. Consider the following strategies for directly addressing misbehavior.

Self-Control

It is critical for staff members who work with children and adolescents with emotional disabilities and conduct disorders to be emotionally mature and professional. This may be easier said than done considering that many of these students are masters at finding staff members' "emotional hot buttons." Hot buttons are those words that cause one to get emotional, angry, and/or embarrassed. An obese staff member may become embarrassed and angry when a student calls him "fat." The student successfully pushed his hot button. It is not uncommon for students to name-call, curse, tease, and even threaten staff members in an attempt to get them upset. When this happens, the staff member's only recourse is to defer to a colleague who is able to work with the student calmly and rationally. The following guidelines are important when working with emotionally challenged children and adolescents:
1. Remaining calm and rational when setting limits
2. Desensitizing self to "hot buttons"
3. Remember that curse words are just words
4. Do not take insults or threats personally

RIOR Progression

RIOR is a four-step progression for directly addressing misbehavior. The key to using a system like RIOR is that it provides consistency for applying consequences to students.

Recognize Behavior—the teacher needs to communicate to the student that he or she recognizes the inappropriate behavior. Often-times this is when a limit is set. Example: "Josh, I asked you to sit down and you are still walking around. Sit down or take a minute."

In-Area Minute—this is a non-punitive place nearby the learning area and may be in sight of peers. By taking a minute, the student must leave his or her space, and successfully sit without further disruption for approximately a minute in a designated space. The teacher needs to provide an activity that will keep the group focused so he can work with the student. The teacher asks the student to accept responsibility for the behavior. If a point sheet is used, then the student would adjust the points to reflect the misbehavior. The teacher then offers support to keep the behavior from happening again. Finally the teacher asks for a commitment to do the right thing upon returning.

When the minute protocol is used positively and is a routine in the class, peers do not view it as a "big deal." The key is to communicate that the minute is a way the teacher can help the student.

Out-of-Area Minute—If a student is unsuccessful with the in-area minute or repeats a second disruptive behavior after taking an in-area minute then he or she is directed to take an out-of-area minute. This area needs to be close to the learning area but out of sight of peers. The same process is used to counsel the student, however, the out-of-class minute is understood as "strike two."

Referral to Intervention Area—Referral to the intervention area happens if the student is unsuccessful with the out-of-area minute, repeats a third behavior after the out-of-area minute, or demonstrates some extreme behavior that warrants immediate removal from class. The student is usually escorted to a room or office where he or she can work through the difficulty with a person trained in therapeutic behavioral counseling.

RAPP Processing

The processing that occurs in the Intervention Area is similar to the "minute processing." The Acronym RAPP may be used to communicate consistency in the steps for successful processing.

1. Recognize the behavior by explaining what was inappropriate or disruptive
2. Accept responsibility by adjusting points, apologizing, or some other retribution
3. Provide alternative solutions to prevent the behavior next time
4. Positively transition back into class with the teacher

Brief Limit Setting

Limit setting is a procedure for communicating behavioral boundaries and the consequences for crossing those boundaries. Example include:

- "Sit down on the bench with the team or sit down with me instead of playing."
- "Keep your hands to yourself or move to the end of the line."
- "Keep your comments positive or visit the penalty box."

Comprehensive Limit Setting

Comprehensive limit setting is a verbal process that involves one-on-one work with a staff member. The steps are as follows:

- Explain which behavior is inappropriate. "Tavon, headphones are not to be worn in the gym."
- Explain why the behavior is inappropriate. "It is difficult to hear directions from the coaches with headphones on."
- Give reasonable choices with consequences. "You may participate in the game if you place your Walkman and headphones in your gym bag. If you choose to keep wearing them, I will not be able to invite you to play in the game, and I will ask your parents to keep your Walkman at home."
- Allow time. Immediate demand makes this an ultimatum. Allow one to two minutes before following through. "I will give you a minute to think about it—we really need you in the game, so I hope you make the right choice."
- Follow through with consequences depending on the student's choice. "I see you put them away...great! Let's get going."

"I see that you have chosen to not play in the game. I will explain to your parents when they pick you up."

Non-Violent Physical Restraint

In some extreme cases, students with emotional disabilities may become violent and threaten the safety of others. If a program serves students with conduct disorders it is best to be prepared for this type of situation by providing staff members with specialized training in non-violent physical restraint. This process involves therapeutically holding onto a person to keep him or her safe. The following factors need to be considered to protect the staff members and organization concerning liability:

1. All staff members participating in the restraint need to be certified by a sanctioned organization or agency. (See Resources)
2. Parents should be required to sign a form giving permission for trained staff to restrain their child.
3. All procedures should be in writing to ensure consistent practice, training, and evaluation of the restraint process.
4. Students should not be locked in any room during the crisis without the supervision of a licensed mental health professional.

The Crisis Plan

If one expects the unexpected, the unexpected will never come. This is the principle that supports the development of a behavioral crisis plan. The behavioral crisis plan is a procedure for keeping all students and staff members safe if a student becomes violent and unsafe.

1. Signal and Communication (Staff v. Team Calls)—There needs to be a means of communicating the time and place of the crisis. An overhead intercom system is the most common means of activating the crisis plan. For programs that operate outdoors, two-way radios or wireless phones may be used.
2. Removal of peers—The crisis frequently de-escalates after the upset student's peers are out of sight. Even if this is not the case, the peers are removed to keep them safe.
3. The Crisis Team Leader—One person needs to take control of the situation and provide directions to the student and the staff members. This provides centralized communication for staff, and the student in crisis.

4. Removal of escalated student—The student needs to get to the intervention area for de-escalation and verbal RAPP processing. Every opportunity should be provided for the student to walk independently. A two-person escort may be used if the student is mildly combative. A six- or seven-person carry may be required if the student is extremely combative.

5. Crisis Intervention Processing—Once in the intervention area, the student should be allowed to de-escalate emotionally, mentally, and physiologically. This process could take from ten minutes to several hours. Once the student is able to talk rationally and commit to being safe, he or she may begin the RAPP processing with an intervention counselor.

VERBAL ESCALATION

STUDENT ACTION	STAFF RESPONSE
Questioning	Answer if rational. Re-direct if irrational
Refusing	Set brief limits
Yelling	Allow venting, then set brief limits
Threatening	Remove others, then activate crisis plan
Apologizing	RAPP processing

PHYSICAL ESCALATION

STUDENT ACTION	STAFF RESPONSE
Agitation	Supportive
Posturing	Corrective
Acting Out	Activate Crisis Plan
Apologizing	RAPP Processing

Selecting Appropriate Leisure and Recreation Opportunities

The following rating scales are designed to assist a parent or guardian to decide whether a leisure and/or recreation program may be developmentally appropriate for his or her child or adolescent.

Rate each characteristic on a scale of 0 to 3. Lower scores mean less appropriate environments. Higher scores mean more appropriate environments. A combined average of 1.5 or less for all three areas reflects a program that is not likely to meet the developmental needs of children and adolescents with emotional disabilities and behavioral challenges.

Rating Curricular Appropriateness

0=Do not agree   1=Somewhat agree   2=Mostly agree   3=Fully agree

    A plan of activities (or schedule) is available for review
    Plan shows scope or categories and variety of activities
    Plan shows progressive sequence for activities
    Activities include a theme (i.e., sport, value, concept…)
    Activities include non-competitive alternatives

Rating Instructional Appropriateness

0=Do not agree   1=Somewhat agree   2=Mostly agree   3=Fully agree

    Meets with a frequency appropriate for my child
    The duration of time is appropriate for my child
    The intensity of the activity is appropriate for my child
    Instruction is multi-sensory (seeing, touching, hearing)
    The peer group is appropriate for my child
    The teaching/coaching style is appropriate for my child
    Degree of staff engagement is appropriate for my child
    Instruction includes adapted rules and scoring alternatives
    Participants are grouped by ability in a thoughtful manner
    The physical climate is appropriate for my child
    Instruction supports inclusion with non-disabled peers
    Instruction includes alternatives to regulation game-play

Rating Behavioral Appropriateness

0=Do not agree   1=Somewhat agree   2=Mostly agree   3=Fully agree

Emphasis is on positive reinforcement of appropriate behavior
Emphasis is on preventing behavior problems
My child is motivated by the reinforcement offered
My child may self-monitor using a point sheet
My child understands the consequence progression
My child understands the daily routine
My child understands the rules
My child has choices
Staff members use time-out therapeutically
Staff members avoid power struggles therapeutically
Staff members use limit setting therapeutically
Staff members use leverage therapeutically (i.e. tokens or levels)
Staff members have a non-violent crisis intervention plan
Staff members are trained in therapeutic physical restraint
Staff members are able to react calmly during a crisis

References

Achenbach, T.M. (1966). The classification of children's psychiatric symptoms: A factor analytic study. *Psychological Monographs: General and Applied, 615,* 1-37.

Achenbach, T.M., & Edelbrock, C.S. (1980). *Child behavior checklist- Teacher's report form.* Burlington: University of Vermont, Center for Children, Youth, and Families.

Achenbach, T.M., & Edelbrock, C.S. (1981). Behavioral problems and competencies reported by parents of normal and disturbed children aged 4 through 16. *Monographs of the Society for Research in Child Development, 46,* (Series no. 188).

Ackerson. L. (1942). *Children's behavior problems.* Chicago: University of Chicago Press.

Algozzine, B., & Lockavitch, J.F. (1998). Effects of failure-free reading program on students at-risk for reading failure. *Special Services for Schools, 13,* 95-105.

Audette, B., & Algozzine, B. (1997). Re-inventing government? Let's reinvent special education. *Journal of Learning Disabilities, 30,* 378-383.

Bullis, M., & Davis, C. (1996). Further examination of job-related social skills measures for adolescents and young adults with emotional and behavioral disorders. *Behavioral Disorders, 21,(2),* 160-171.

Carnegie Council on Adolescent Development. (1994). *Consultation on afterschool programs.* Washington, D.C.: author.

Clark, C.S. (1993). TV violence. CQ *Researcher, 3,(12),* 167-187.

Coleman, M., & Churchill, S. (1997). Challenges to family involvement. *Childhood Education, 73, (3),* 144-148.

Curwin, R.L., & Mendler, A.N. (1999). Zero tolerance for zero tolerance. *Phi Delta Kappan, 81,(2),* 119-120.

Doughty, J.E. (1997). The effect of a social skills curriculum on student performance. Paper presented at the Third Annual Research Colloquium. Carrollton, GA.

Duke, D.L., & Griesdorn, J. (1999). Considerations in the design of alternative schools. *Clearing House, 73,(2),* 89-92.

Epstein, J.L. (1984). *Single parents and the schools: The effect of marital status on parent and teacher evaluations.* Baltimore, MD: The Johns Hopkins University, Center for the Social Organization of Schools.

Finn, P. (1980). Developing critical television viewing skills. *Educational Forum, 44,* 473-482.

Funk, J.B. (1993). Reevaluating the impact of video games. *Clinical Pediatrics, 32,* 86-90.

Gresham, F.M. (1997). Social competence and students with behavior disorders: Where we've been, where we are, and where we should go. *Education and Treatment of Children, 20,(3),* 233-249.

Gresham, F.M. (1998). Social skills training: Should we raze, remodel or rebuild? *Behavior Disorders, 24,(1),* 19-25.

Hansen, D.J., Nangle, D.W., Douglas, W., & Meyer, K.A. (1998). Enhancing the effectiveness of social skills interventions with adolescents. *Education and Treatment of Children, 21,(4),* 489-513.

Hewitt, L.E., & Jenkins, R.L. (1946). *Fundamental patterns of maladjustment: The dynamics of their origin.* Springfield, IL: State of Illinois.

Johns, B.H. et al. (1996). *Best practices for managing adolescents with emotional/behavioral disorders within the school environment.* Reston, VA: Council for Exceptional Children.

Kamps, D., Ellis, C., Mancina, C., & Greene, L. (1995). Peer-inclusive social skills groups for young children with behavioral risks. *Preventing School Failure, 39,* 10-15.

Lewis, M.E.B. (1993). *Thematic Methods and Strategies for Students with Learning Disabilities.* San Diego, CA: Singular Publishing Group.

Mathur, S.R., & Rutherford, R.B., Jr. (1996). Is social skills training effective for students with emotional or behavioral disorders? *Behavior Disorders, 22,(1),* 21-28.

McConaughy, S.H., Kay, P.J., & Fitzgerald, M. (1998). Preventing SED through parent-teacher action research and social skills instruction: First-year outcomes. *Journal of Emotional and Behavioral Disorders, 6,* 81-93.

Melloy, K.J., Davis, C.A., Wehby, J.H., Murry, F.R., & Leiber, J. (1998). *Developing social competence in children and youth with challenging behaviors.* Reston, VA: Council for Exceptional Children.

Moore, R.J., et al. (1995). The effects of social skill instruction and self-monitoring ongame-related behaviors of adolescents with emotional or behavioral disorders. *Behavior Disorders, 20,(4),* 253-266.

Nelson, C., & Pearson, C. (1991). *Integrating services for children and youth with emotional and behavioral disorders.* Reston, VA: Council for Exceptional Children.

Neuman, S.B. (1982). Television viewing and leisure reading: A qualitative analysis. Paper presented at the annual meeting of the American Educational Research Association, New York, March, 1982.

Peterson, R. (1961). Behavior problems of middle childhood. *Journal of consulting psychology, 25,* 205-9.

Posner, J.K., & Vendell, D.L. (1994). Low-income children's after-school care: Are there beneficial effects of after-school programs? *Child Development, 65,(2),* 440-456.

Prater, M.A., Bruhl, S., & Serna, L.A. (1998). Acquiring social skills through cooperative learning and teacher-directed instruction. *Remedial and Special Education, 19,(3),* 160-172.

Reganick, K. (1995). *Using adventure-based cooperation training to develop job related social skills for adolescents with severe behavioral and emotional problems.* Tampa, FL: Nova Southeastern University. (Ed.D. practicum paper.)

Rich, D. (1985). The forgotten factor in school success: The family. A policymaker's guide. Washington, D.C.: The Home & School Institute, Inc.

Rinne, C.H. (1998). Motivating students is a percentage game. *Phi Delta Kappan, 79,(8),* 620-624.

Rockwell, S., Cuccio, S., Kirtley, B., & Smith, G. (1998). *Developing personal and interpersonal responsibility in children and youth with emotional/behavioral disorders.* Reston, VA: Council for Exceptional Children.

Safran, S.P. (1995). Peers' perceptions of emotional and behavioral disorders: What are students thinking? *Journal of Emotional and Behavioral Disorders, 3,(2),* 66-75.

Scherbert, T.G. (1996). *Language intervention strategies for improving communication skills of students with severe emotional disabilities in a public elementary school.* Tampa, FL: Nova Southeastern University (Ed. D. practicum paper).

Von Isser, A., Quay, H.C., & Love, C.T. (1980). Interrelationships among three measures of deviant behavior. *Exceptional Children, 46,* 272-276.

White-Hood, M. Managing schools better: Educating from the heart! *Schools in the Middle, 7,(2),* 40-42.

Williams, P.A., Haertel, E.H., Haertel, G.D., & Walberg, H.J. (1982). The impact of leisure-time television on school learning: A research synthesis. *American Educational Research Journal, 19,* 19-50.

Wood, F. (1982). Defining disturbing, disordered, and disturbed behavior. In F. Wood, & K. Laken (Eds.), *Disturbing, disordered or disturbed?* Reston, VA: Council for Exceptional Children.

Wood, F., & Smith, C. (1985). Assessment of emotionally disturbed/behaviorally disordered students. *Diagnostique, 10,* 40-51.

Zionts, P. (1996). *Teaching disturbed and disturbing students: An integrative approach* (2nd ed.). Austin, TX: Pro-Ed.

Implications for Education and Community Providers

Buzz Williams

Introduction

Mr. Harvey is a first-year middle-school physical education teacher who co-teaches after-school activities with Ms. Roberts, an experienced recreation leader with a successful history working with the school's most challenging adolescents. Mr. Harvey is overwhelmed after his first week of teaching, and has observed his most challenging students working appropriately for Ms. Roberts.

"Ms. Roberts, I don't know how you do it. Jasper and George are so polite to you, and they do whatever you ask them to do without arguing."

"Well, it isn't always that way. There are tough times, too. I have known George and Jasper since last year—we have a history. In the beginning it was rough, and they weren't so polite."

"I hear people say that all the time...it comes with experience...you have to know the kids...but what does all that mean for me right now? I need help today!"

"Is it just George and Jasper?"

"No. Both of my special-education sections are having trouble. I didn't even know there were "special education sections." I thought that meant the students had learning disabilities. They fight with each other, and use the worst language! They even argue with me and other teachers. They pretty much do whatever they want. School sure has changed."

"I don't know if school has changed, but the students in those sections probably behave differently than you or your classmates did in school. The students in those sections have emotional disabilities. You will need some skills and strategies that you might not have learned in college. Most people become skilled with on-the-job training—and working with an experienced mentor. It all starts with understanding the students and the implications of their disabilities."

This chapter examines the implications for educators and community providers when implementing sport, recreation, and leisure programs for people with emotional disabilities and challenging behaviors. An operational definition of "at-risk" students is offered, followed by a brief discussion of the origins of emotional disabilities and the growing need for appropriate services. The chapter then describes the manifestations of various emotional disabilities—that is, the observable behaviors that present challenges to service providers. Prevention strategies are included to assist educators and community providers with a foundation for avoiding behavioral problems. Despite the best preventive measures, some inappropriate behaviors will occur. The section on interventions will address the most appropriate staff responses and skills necessary to calm students, stop or redirect inappropriate behaviors, and start appropriate ones.

"At-Risk" Implications

At-Risk Defined

The term, "at-risk," is used frequently in educational literature. Students may be at-risk for failing school, becoming pregnant, abusing drugs, getting arrested, or running away from home. Some students are at-risk for more than one of the above. Many of these students have in common a learning and/or emotional disability. For many, their disability has been clinically diagnosed and they receive special education services. For others, their disability has yet to be identified and they struggle to meet the same daily demands as their non-disabled peers. It is our goal to interact therapeutically and positively with these people. Participation in sport, recreation, and leisure activities is often one aspect of life in which at-risk populations experience success. Many intervention agencies and organizations, such as the YMCA and Outward Bound, have demonstrated the ability to turn people's lives around through sport, recreation, and leisure. It is therefore critical for educators and providers to work therapeutically with challenging students and clients. These people cannot afford to be at-risk of losing opportunities to play and recreate—which are often the life-lines to which people cling in times of trouble.

Biological Origins

It is often difficult and frustrating for the lay person to understand why these "emotionally disturbed" people cannot simply react and cope in rational ways. Inexperienced staff members often ask whether there is some biological or medical reason for students' inappropriate behaviors. This question stimulates the nature vs. nurture debate. That is, is it biology or are these behaviors learned as products of their environment? Clearly there is evidence that some aspects of people with emotional disabilities is biological—specifically neurological. One will receive different interventions depending on the background of the professional involved. If the person is a psychiatrist, he or she is likely to treat the problem medically. Oftentimes people diagnosed with emotional disabilities are prescribed medications to facilitate a more balanced emotional and mental state. It is very clear to anyone who has observed a student whose medication dosage is incorrect, that there is some merit to the "biology" side of the debate.

Another biology-type observation involves students with traumatic brain injuries. Consider the case of Jason, for example. Jason was a normal 13-year—old adolescent in the seventh grade. He had average intelligence and earned a 'B" average in school. Teachers described Jason as a polite student with a lot of friends. Over the summer Jason crashed while riding a dirtbike and suffered frontal lobe damage to his brain. After a six-month hospitalization, Jason returned to school. Staff noticed a very different personality. Jason was confrontational, angry, and challenged authority. He alienated his former friends, and began socializing with a negative peer group. The summer following the accident there was enough documentation to clinically diagnose Jason with oppositional-defiant disorder (ODD).

The above examples illustrate that biological origins for emotional and behavioral disabilities do exist. That is not to say that all behavioral and emotional disabilities are medical in nature. The social environment in which people develop also contributes much to emotional stability and personality development.

Social Origins

Theorists, such as Erik Erikson, have developed psychosocial models of human development which describe how social experiences as infants and children lay the foundation for personality development and emotional well being for life. We know, for example, that the touch and attention of a primary caregiver gives infants a sense of security. This facilitates an attachment necessary for normal emotional development. Consider the implications for an infant born to a drug-addicted mother who is neglectful of the baby's needs. In other cases the child may have a loving caregiver, but suffer physical, sexual, mental, or emotional abuse. Many children who have emotional and behavioral disabilities have family histories of abuse and neglect.

A growing number of children live in impoverished communities where they attempt to play in the midst of the drug culture. These children while in their most impressionable years experience traumatic events, like gun-involved murders, in their neighborhoods. An increasing number of children growing up in combat-like areas present the same symptoms with Post-Traumatic-Stress-Disorder (PTSD).

Still others find themselves in middle-class neighborhoods struggling with the stressors of parental divorce or separation. Whether living with the guilt leading to the separation, the hostility of the actual split, or the emotional tug-of-war associated with visitation, a divorce takes a tremendous emotional toll on the children. Given the extraordinary divorce rate in America, it is clear that each generation is subject to more divorce-related stress than the previous one.

Father absence is another significant contributor to the emotional instability of many children. It is common for half of all children in schools today to spend at least part of their childhood without a male living in the same house. The implications of children growing up in single-parent households include less supervision, less financial support, and less modeling of appropriate social interaction.

Social learning pioneers like Albert Bandura have documented the effects of social modeling on children. That is, children will copy the behaviors that they observe. Any person who has spent a few hours with a toddler will draw the same conclusions regarding the effect behavioral modeling has on children. One would have to then consider the implications of children spending their unsupervised time watching television, listening to music, or playing video games. Again, the key here is "unsupervised." Given any of the above circumstances, or combination thereof, there will be substantial probability that a child will develop some emotional or behavioral difficulty.

Social Trends

The behaviors that educators and community providers face today are significantly more challenging than they were 50 years ago. With each generation the frequency and intensity of inappropriate behavior increases. Talk to a teacher who started working with children in the 1950s. You will learn of few cases of classroom disruption, student violence, and challenge of authority. With each decade new political and social changes have occurred which have negatively impacted the social fabric of American youth.

The implications to educators and community providers is that there will be increasing incidents of physical assaults to peers and staff, inappropriate and offensive language, opposition and defiance of authority, and a general refusal to follow directions or conform to rules. Whether biologically and/or socially based, this is the reality that faces us in the classrooms, gymnasiums, and playing fields across the country. Our purpose here is to offer some perspective on the scope of the challenge of working with people with emotional disabilities and behavioral challenges. With this accomplished we will move forward with our discussion of the implications for working with behaviorally challenged population and the strategies and skills that are most effective. The next section describes behaviors that are often demonstrated by students with a variety of emotional and behavioral challenges.

Manifestations

Chapter two describes the characteristics of students with emotional problems and challenging behaviors as they are presented in the DSM-IV. The following section will describe the most common behaviors that are manifested by the diagnoses presented in chapter two. The behaviors include active and passive aggression, verbal escalation, manipulation, bullying and intimidation, teasing and harassment, social withdrawal, irrational anxiety, and power struggling. The issues involving trust and cooperation, as well as body image are also explored.

Active Aggression

The student that demonstrates **active aggression** seeks to have his or her needs met with either verbal or physical acting-out behaviors. The actively aggressive student may be verbally assaultive—usually in the form of harassment, intimidation, or threats. Physical aggression may include "posturing," hitting, kicking, pulling hair, choking, spitting, and/or destruction of property. Some students may demonstrate these behaviors against themselves, which is called self-injurious behavior (SIB). These behaviors do not happen instantly without warning. They usually are the result of a **behavioral escalation** in which the engaged staff have failed to recognize the earlier stages and offer therapeutic responses. Behavioral escalation is the sequential emotional progression from a calm state to a physically assaultive state, and includes a return to the calm state. Behavioral escalation as defined by the National Crisis Prevention Institute (CPI) includes four stages: anxiety, defensive, acting out, and tension reduction. **Verbal escalation** is the sequential emotional progression from a calm state to a verbally assaultive state, and back to the calm state. Verbal escalation as defined by CPI includes five stages and includes: questioning, refusal, release, intimidation, and therapeutic rapport.

Example 8-1: Active Aggression

Josh is a 15-year-old boy who is emotionally disturbed. His camp counselor, Mr. Jones, acknowledges Josh's excellent behavior during the week, and invites him to attend the Friday swimming trip. Josh's smile disappears, as he stares blankly at Mr. Jones. Mr. Jones informs Josh that all of his friends are going, and adds that it would be pretty boring to just hang around. Josh replies, "Swimming sucks," and turns to walk away. Mr. Jones, clearly upset by Josh's language, approaches Josh and holds onto his arm. Josh swings his arm angrily away and shouts, "Keep your damned hands to yourself!" Mr. Jones runs to get in front of Josh and stands in his path. Josh continues to walk and kicks Mr. Jones in the shin as he approaches. Josh runs into his building and slams the door shut.

Implication

A thorough understanding of, and experience with, the behavioral and verbal escalation cycles are critical in the prevention of aggressive acting-out behaviors. CPI training will also prepare staff for providing therapeutic intervention when necessary as well. For each student action there are appropriate staff responses. These responses need to be learned, rehearsed, and role played to be effective. Staff skills are refined by using them in real-life situations like the one described above. It is critical that staff be supervised and mentored by people experienced in working with actively aggressive students. A debrief following each intervention should highlight staff strengths and areas needing improvement.

Passive Aggression

The student demonstrating **passive aggression** seeks to get his or her needs met by covert means. The passively aggressive students may demonstrate social withdrawal, manipulative tactics, and/or non-verbal gestures. Typically these students are clever, sneaky, and persuasive with peers and staff. The unique characteristic of passive aggression is that it is carried out without confrontation. Students who use sneaky and manipulative tactics to get their way create tension and anxiety for all involved. Passively aggressive students will target actively aggressive peers and "set them up" in anxiety-producing situations to evoke a behavioral episode. The passive-aggressive student takes silent pleasure in disrupting the environment.

Example 8-2: Passive Aggression

Elise is a nine-year-old girl with passive-aggressive tendencies. She is attracted to Tevon, and is in competition with Vonda for his attention. During lunch, Elise "cuts" in line to stand next to Tevon. She then looks back and smiles at Vonda, who knows what she did. Vonda is clearly upset and informs the teacher, who confronts Elise. Elise shows no emotion and explains that Tevon was holding her place. At this point, Vonda is raising her voice and has moved up in line to confront Elise. The teacher diverts attention to Vonda to keep her calm. As the teacher escorts Vonda back in line, Elise winks at her. Vonda then pushes the teacher to get to Elise. Vonda is escorted out of the cafeteria and Elise enjoys her lunch with all of Tevon's attention.

Implication

Staff need to identify students who are likely to demonstrate passive aggressive acts. It is also important to recognize the early stages of passive aggression so that the student may be re-directed. Staff need to communicate with the student to understand what he or she was attempting to accomplish. If the goal is appropriate, staff should explain a more assertive strategy. An astute staff person would recognize that Elise wanted to sit with Tevon. The next step would be to coach her with assertively asking him to save a place for her at the table.

Manipulation

Manipulation, in the context of student behavior, is the practice of taking advantage of a set of circumstances to get one's way by circumventing established rules and policies. Students may manipulate using one staff person or they may involve more than one to capitalize on breakdowns in communication and consistency. The key for students is to identify and exploit either a weakness in an individual or a flaw in the system. Here are common examples.

Staff Splitting

One of the most common manipulative tactics is staff splitting. This is when a student shares conflicting information with two or more staff members with the goal of creating opposing viewpoints. Ultimately, one of the staff sides will align more with that of the student, and the student will filter all requests to that side.

Example 8-3: Staff Splitting

Jermaine wants to wear his hat during school. The school policy states that hats are not to be worn in school. Jermaine enters the building on Monday through the front doors, and is stopped by Ms. Blake who directs him to remove the hat before he enters. Tuesday Jermaine enters through the rear of the building and walks right past Mr. Dunlop, who believes students can wear hats until they visit their lockers. Ms. Blake notices Jermaine wearing his hat and directs him to remove it. Jermaine responds that Mr. Dunlop gave him permission until he went to his locker. Jermaine has recognized an inconsistency among staff and has effectively split Ms. Blake and Mr. Dunlop. Jermaine was successful manipulating the situation to serve his interest.

Implication

Given the above circumstances, Jermaine has set up Ms. Blake to make a difficult decision. If she persists with the direction he is likely to escalate emotionally. Jermaine will "play out" the inconsistency as unfair treatment. He is likely to perceive Ms. Blake's direction as a personal attack, and will be ready to defend his position both verbally and physically. Ms. Blake needs to recognize the attempt to "split staff," and acknowledge Jermaine's concern. She should inform Jermaine that he has helped her to see that staff have different interpretations of the same rule. Ms. Blake should not pursue removing his hat, as this would provide a forum for escalation. Instead, she should inform Jermaine that she will meet with Mr. Dunlop after school to come to an agreement. Ms. Blake and Mr. Dunlop should discuss the problem in a staff-only meeting, come to an agreement, and communicate their decision to Jermaine together. This communicates effective staff communication and "teamwork" that is difficult to split.

Pushing Buttons

The practice of pushing buttons involves a student who recognizes a particular vulnerability in a staff person, and then attacks that vulnerability when it is in his or her best interest. All people have sensitivities that make them emotionally vulnerable. Typically students attack a staff person's physical appearance and/or character. It is extremely difficult to appear unaffected when the student finds and pushes a "sensitive button."

Example 8-4: Pushing Buttons

Janice is anxious about her softball game today. She really wanted to be the starting pitcher, but the coach chose another player instead. After the coach assigned her to right field, she refused to play and remained on the bench. The coach encouraged her to take the field, "Come on Janice, the game is about to start and we need you!" Janice stood on the bench and screamed, "Somebody better play right field or else Coach might have another heart attack and die on us!" The coach, clearly embarrassed, threw Janice off the team.

Implication

The implication is that staff need to become aware of their buttons and be consciously ready for the attack when it happens. This awareness takes away the element of surprise and makes it easier to address the student calmly and rationally.

The coach needed to recognize that Janice had a history of saying hurtful things when she does not get her way. He needed to be aware that his recent heart attack was likely ammunition for Janice's next attack. As such he should have been prepared. This awareness would have allowed him to depersonalize Janice's comment. An appropriate response would include setting the following limit: "Janice, you can play right field or you can sit on the bench—those are your choices. You have five minutes to think about it and then let me know your decision."

Blackmail

Students will observe and gather information about staff that they may use against them at a later time. A student who wishes to get his or her way will often use this information as leverage to coerce staff into giving in—this is blackmail. Oftentimes the student perceives the information to be more valuable than it is. Occasionally students learn of information that is significant and might result in unpleasant consequences if discovered. These are the most difficult situations to diffuse.

Example 8-5

Jarad learned that Ms. Bennett, his science teacher, was a lesbian. Although true, this was not widely known among staff or students. One day Ms. Bennett asked Jarad to stay after class to discuss missed homework. She informed him that he could complete the work during lunch detention or receive zero credit for the assignments. Jarad informed Ms. Bennett that he had a third choice. "How about you forget about my missing homework and I'll forget about you being gay." Ms. Bennett asked, "What are you talking about?" Jarad answered, "I know you're gay, and I know you want to keep it a secret. You don't give me homework, and I won't tell anybody." Ms. Bennett just sat in silence, thinking about what was happening.

Implication

Staff should not go along with any blackmail agreement for any reason. Students will need to be confronted with their attempt to manipulate. The staff who is threatened needs to assess the nature of the threat as either valid or invalid. If the threat has no merit, then the student should be given a specific direction or limit. In the above example the teacher should not comment on the accusation. Instead she should set a limit such as, "I'm letting you know that you have two choices—either finish during lunch detention or earn zeros." The teacher might add, "If you would like to discuss a third option we can do this with the principal and your parents."

If the threat does have merit then the staff person needs to meet with a supervisor to discuss personal and/or professional consequences should the information become public. Situations will be handled individually, regarding the staff, but the universal rule is to not negotiate blackmail threats of any kind with students.

Bullying

Bullying and intimidation both describe an attempt to use force and the threat of aggression to instill fear in others. Bullying, for our purposes, is described as threats and assault initiated from students against other students. Likewise, intimidation is initiated from the student toward the staff.

People often question the origins of the aggression in an attempt to provide interventions. Some may believe a student to have a psychological challenge requiring medication prescribed by a psychiatrist. Others may believe the problem to be more environmental. That is, the student learned the behaviors at home or in the community. The truth usually lies somewhere in between. It is true that many students diagnosed with emotional disabilities receive medication as a part of their therapy. It is also true that many demonstrate behaviors that are modeled and reinforced in their families. Not all students who bully or intimidate others have emotional disabilities. Nonetheless, the prevention and interventions are the same for any student that uses bullying or intimidation tactics.

Example 8-6: Bullying

Keisha is a 7th grade student who is bigger and stronger than many of her peers in physical education class. During the first week in the locker room, Keisha told the other three girls to find a new bench on which to change their clothes. Sarah challenged Keisha by explaining that the lockers were assigned, and they really did not have a choice. Keisha responded, "Well I guess you'll have to wait until I'm done with the bench then, won't you!" As Sarah turned to leave the locker area, Keisha pushed her down to the floor and told her she would get more if she told the teacher. Another student who witnessed the incident reported it to the teacher.

Implications

Working through difficulties with bullies requires three levels of intervention—environmental, victim-oriented, and bully-oriented. Environmental interventions begin with staff supervision. Staff need to be present and observant in places when students are most at risk to bullying-type behaviors. Locker areas, stairwells, and lunch rooms are commonly such environments. Secondly, trusting relationships need to be established with students so they can disclose information confidentially. Thirdly, staff need to clearly communicate their expectations of a safe and respectful class climate. Horseplay, name-calling, and teasing are all antecedent behaviors that create a negative environment. Students with emotional disabilities need very structured environments with a zero-tolerance policy regarding social skills.

Victims need to be educated about which of their behaviors make them vulnerable to bullies. As part of the process, victims need to confront the bully, with staff support. Staff need to empower the victim(s) to be assertive and responsible for their safety and welfare. Victims also need to understand how to support each other in confronting a bully. It should be recognized that bullies will not victimize students who are able and willing to ask for help.

Once a student is suspected or identified as demonstrating bullying behaviors, he or she needs to be addressed privately by staff. In this meeting staff need to state exactly which behaviors are unacceptable, and the corresponding consequences. Recognize that bullies are attempting to seek attention, gain peer approval, and/or feel powerful. It is very likely that students who bully have learned to get these things by pushing others around. Staff need to provide appropriate alternatives so that these students re-learn new ways to get their needs met.

In example 8-6, an ideal resolution may include the following plan. At least one teacher is assigned duty whenever students are in the locker room. Sarah and her two friends confront Keisha in a meeting with the teacher to let her know they will not accept her threats to keep the bench to herself. Keisha agrees to share the bench with the other girls, and in return earns the privilege of helping the teacher in the equipment room before and after class. Keisha's job depends on demonstrating appropriate social skills with her peers.

Intimidation

Intimidation is defined similar to bullying, only the threats are directed from the student to the staff. At first this may seem ridiculous, but it is a pervasive problem within programs that include adolescents with emotional disabilities—especially when the program employs young and/or inexperienced staff. Intimidation may be overt, such as directly threatening to assault a staff member, or covert as in brushing a staff person aside with a shoulder as a student passes. All students test staff members in some capacity. When this test involves intimidation, the staff person must respond in a timely and effective manner, or he or she will be targeted by students as a push-over.

Example 8-7: Intimidation

Mr. Russell is a new instructor for a high ropes course at an outdoor learning center. He is co-leading a group of students from a residential treatment center for adolescents with emotional disabilities. His partner, Ms. Andrews, is an experienced leader who has worked effectively with groups such as this for years. When the students arrive they are separated into two groups for equipment distribution. Larry, a particularly loud and abrasive student, orders Mr. Russell to give him the first helmet. Mr. Russell concedes. As Mr. Russell prepares to hand out harnesses, Larry approaches and holds out his hand. Mr. Russell asks Larry to return to his place in the group, and Larry snatches the harness from Mr. Russell's hand. Mr. Russell comments, "That wasn't cool!," but allows Larry to keep the harness. When Mr. Russell began to explain the safety rules for the first obstacle, Larry interrupted, "Can we just get on with this, man. We're tired of hearing you talk!" Several other students agreed and the group soon became unruly. Although the staff from the residential treatment center calmed the students, Mr. Russell never fully regained leadership of the group. At mid-day, Larry was transferred to Ms. Andrews' group and finished the day successfully.

Implications

The skill-level and assertive responses from staff mean more than gender or physical size when intervening with a student who attempts to intimidate. Recognize that students will not intimidate overtly at first. The intimidation usually begins with verbal challenges and indirect opposition to directions. Staff who address these in a fair and firm manner communicate control of the situation. Staff also need a complete understanding of the resources they have to intervene if needed. They also need to know the consequence sequence for students who challenge their authority. The most difficult skill—actually more of an art than a skill is to communicate the limits to the student in a non-confrontational manner. When Larry first demanded he receive the first helmet, Mr. Russell needed to communicate that there was a system in place (and there should have been). It may have sounded like, "It looks like you are anxious to get started...I am handing out equipment around the group circle. You will be the fifth person to get a helmet...there is enough so everybody will get their own." If Larry persists, Mr. Russell would need to provide a directive such as, "Hold on there, sir. I can give this helmet to you fifth, or I can give it to you last after you chill out with your staff."

The phrases, tone, volume, stance, and non-verbal gestures all play a critical role in the success of the staff setting the behavioral limits. The keys for staff are to be fair and firm, and to have an orderly and predictable environment to decrease opportunities for students to challenge. Given the opportunity, staff need a sequence of consequences and the resources to follow through when necessary.

Teasing and Harassment

One phenomenon common to most programs serving students with emotional disabilities is inappropriate teasing. Teasing may be verbal or non-verbal, and is defined as communicating with another person with the intent to hurt their feelings and or gain a superior position in a series of "put-downs." Teasing evolves into harassment when one student does not participate in the dialogue, and the negativity becomes one-sided. Teasing builds a foundation for an inevitable confrontation. This confrontation may take days or weeks to develop, but each episode of teasing adds to peer-on-peer tension.

Many adolescents engage in verbal battles of wit and humor. These battles have been referred to as "put-downs," "cut-downs," and "ragging." These may be one line comments such as, "Yo, your breath is kickin' awful...buy a toothbrush!" Others may be condescending and rhetorical, "Look at those shoes...Did your mommy dress you this morning?" In an effort to save face most students will respond with an even more personal attack like, "At least I don't need food stamps to buy lunch." If left unchallenged, these insults will lead to one student pushing the other's button. For many this button involves a significant other that is taboo and "not fair play." When the duel reaches its peak, one student will cross the line with "Your Mother...or Your sister...or Your Father..." Hence we have the inevitable fight.

Example 8-8: Teasing

Mark is eating his lunch with a few friends. Terrell is sitting at a table next to Mark. Mark believes Terrel is staring at him and asks, "What are you looking at?" Terrel answers, "I'm surprised you could tell wearing them Dollar-Store glasses!" Mark follows with, "Maybe if you had a pair you could pass the social studies test you failed last period." By now students from several tables are listening and cheering for their respective friends in the battle of the put-downs. Terrell fires back, "At least I could read the questions without the teacher's help." Mark waits for the laughter to fade and adds, "So your mommy bought you Hooked-On-Phonics, huh!" Terrel, feeling his edge slip crosses the line, "At least I know where my mother is." Mark jumps up from the table and charges at Terrel.

Implications

Because every teasing incident does not escalate into a crisis, some misinformed staff do not treat teasing as a serious offense. Teasing needs to be recognized as a significant contributor to many peer-to-peer conflicts. It is best to adopt a zero-tolerance policy regarding teasing. Teasing usually starts out at a low level which is easy to diffuse. Students need to be re-directed to change their focus from each other to a productive task. Many students spend their non-supervised hours engaged in this form of social interaction. It is helpful to identify appropriate topics and role-play how to talk in a socially appropriate and cooperative manner. Many students need very specific instructions on how to communicate with peers in a responsible way. It is counterproductive to assume that students have the skills to talk responsibly with each other.

Social Withdrawal

Social withdrawal is a passive aggressive action that involves partial or complete refusal to participate in activities. Students with emotional disabilities may choose to stop cooperating on multiple levels. Withdrawn students may refuse to talk, write, and/or read during class. Sometimes the refusal is limited to staff, and other times students may shut-down with peers as well. Oftentimes there is a lack of emotion and expression of feelings.

One condition noted in the DSM-IV related to social withdrawal is selective mutism, a refusal to talk in specific social settings. Commonly students choose to be mute at school, but will talk at home. In other situations, students may choose to keep their eyes closed, or directed at the floor. It is believed that for some of these students they have chosen to withdrawal as a demonstration of self-control. This is especially true when they feel that their disability has created a loss of control for them in their daily lives.

Example 8-9: Social Withdrawal

Tony has been in Mr. Roberts' physical education class for two years. Mr. Roberts has learned that Tony is socially withdrawn and will seldom participate. Tony has never spoken to Mr. Roberts. In fact, the only response Tony gives is an antagonistic smile whenever Mr. Roberts gives Tony a direction. Mr. Roberts has worked with Tony's therapist to develop strategies for Tony, but none have been successful. Mr. Roberts was surprised one day to see a signed permission slip with Tony's name, for an upcoming rock-climbing field trip. Mr. Roberts saw Tony in the hall later that day and returned the permission slip. He informed Tony that the bus could only hold 60 students, and there was no room for students who "just want to go along for the ride." As Mr. Roberts turned to walk away he heard Tony's voice for the first time, "I can climb." Mr. Roberts allowed Tony to put the permission slip back into his hand as he answered, "I can't wait to see you climb, Tony."

Implications

Social withdrawal has its roots in psychopathology. Most teachers do not have the resources to work through deep-rooted emotional issues which manifest into withdraw symptoms. It is important to recognize the symptoms when they occur. It is very difficult to depersonalize the resistance to your effort. It is particularly disheartening to have worked hard on a particular activity, only to have a student balk at it. It is even more frustrating to employ sound behavioral strategies with a student, only to have him or her smile in response. It is a helpless and frustrating experience for any person who works with children. This example was included because it demonstrates the most significant principle when working with withdrawn students—always keep the door of opportunity open. Some day a student may come out of his or her shell, even if for only a brief period of time, and it would be tragic if the opportunity was missed because of a door that was closed by a staff person who let ego get in the way.

Anxiety Disorders

Students with emotional disabilities may exhibit symptoms of one or more conditions grouped under the title, anxiety disorders. Anxiety disorders are conditions that cause emotional distress and limit a person's daily functioning to some degree. Our discussion of anxiety disorders includes Panic disorder, Agoraphobia, Obsessive Compulsive Disorder (OCD), and Post Traumatic Stress Disorder (PTSD).

Panic Disorder

Panic disorder is characterized by the sudden onset of intense apprehension and fear, often associated with feelings of impending doom. Physical symptoms include shortness of breath, heart palpitations, chest pain, and a general fear of "going crazy."

Agoraphobia

Agoraphobia is characterized by anxiety about, or avoidance of, places or situations from which escape might be difficult or embarrassing. It is commonly associated with a fear of leaving the safety of one's home. There is also fear that help may not be available if a panic attack occurs. People who have Agoraphobia often experience panic attacks when they are placed in anxiety-producing situations. The following example illustrates how these conditions relate to each other.

Example 8-10: Panic Disorder/Agoraphobia

Carrie is a seventh grade student who is very anxious about playing soccer with her peers during after school recreation time. Carrie's soccer skills are not as developed as those of her peers and she has asked to sit on the bench instead of playing. Ms. Parker has worked with Carrie and has seen her experience a panic attack. She also knows that Carrie wants to participate, but has learned to "avoid" the anxiety of game-play—she usually just sits out or complains of being sick. Ms. Parker offered Carrie several adaptive choices for participation. She offered her the chance to play as a clock player, crease player, or hot ball player (see chapter 4 for descriptions). After explaining the adaptations, Carrie chose to be a hot ball player. Carrie still seemed anxious when players were near her, but she remained on the field. When Carrie's father arrived to pick up Carrie, she boasted of playing in a "real" soccer game. Carrie asked her father to come early next time to watch her play.

Implications

Educators and community service providers occasionally find themselves working with students who avoid participation. It is important to remember that students may opt out of activities for a variety of reasons. Before an intervention can be effective, staff need to understand the reasons behind the refusal. Even students without anxiety disorders sometimes need to sit out from an activity. Physical illness, fatigue, a disagreement with a peer, or anger over an officiating call are typical reasons for taking a break from playing. Some students, however, have a pattern of not participating. Perhaps a student only shuts down during swimming activities, or possibly during the combative team-type contact sports. Some students may not want to participate in any physical activity. If a pattern exists, it is likely that the student is experiencing anxiety associated with some aspect of the activity. The staff response needs to be empathetic and understanding. Through a series of non-threatening questions, staff can determine the source of the anxiety. For some students the source may be failing in front of peers, while for others it may be wearing clothing that displays too much of their bodies. In the example above, Carrie was anxious about having opponents run toward her to take the ball away. She was also anxious about being hit by a fast-moving ball. The intervention to use a "hot ball," then, is appropriate since it eliminates these stressors by definition.

Obsessive Compulsive Disorder

Obsessive Compulsive Disorder (OCD) is characterized by "obsessions," which are repetitive thoughts that cause anxiety and stress. "Compulsions" are the acts or rituals which are carried out to reduce the anxiety and stress produced by the obsessive thoughts.

Example 8-11: OCD

John was diagnosed with OCD when he was 12-years old. Now in high school, his OCD behaviors are manageable, although still present. John belongs to a recreation baseball league for players age 15 to 16. He tried out for the junior varsity team at high school, but his OCD behaviors were too "disruptive" according to the coach. The staff of the recreation team understood OCD, and worked with John to give him the opportunity to participate. Most of John's OCD behaviors were associated with batting. John would become stressed over getting a hit to keep his batting average over .200. In an effort to cope with the obsessive thoughts surrounding his hitting, John engaged in rituals which he believed to help him maintain his hitting average. John would need to take nine practice swings while on deck. The practice swings required a special aluminum bat that only he used. While batting, John needed to tap each of his cleats three times before each pitch. In addition, he needed to take an additional three swings before the pitcher delivered the ball. Although John's compulsive behaviors slowed the pace of the game and annoyed some of the opponents, people generally tolerated John's OCD behaviors as a necessary part of his personality.

Implications

OCD behaviors may be limited and controlled with behavior therapy and/or medication. Staff need to recognize the behaviors as products of very intense motivation and desire. Simply reprimanding or "ordering" a student to stop the OCD behaviors are ineffective. Staff need to recognize the behaviors as a coping strategy that helps the student to decrease anxiety. It is necessary to educate others about the nature of the student's OCD, and prepare them for what to expect. It is also important to set limits on those people who choose to tease or harass a player with OCD behaviors (or for any other reason as well). People with OCD know what they are doing, and they recognize that others are noticing their behavior. It is this awareness that keeps many people with OCD from engaging in social situations where others may notice their rituals. The less attention directed at the behaviors, the less stress the student experiences, and the more likely he or she will continue to participate.

Post Traumatic Stress Disorder

Post Traumatic Stress Disorder (PTSD) is characterized by the re-experiencing of a traumatic event, accompanied by increased stress created in an effort to avoid the stimuli associated with the trauma.

Example 8-12: PTSD

Shawnice is a ten-year-old girl who lives in a group home, awaiting foster care placement. Shawnice has been diagnosed with PTSD, following a hospitalization at a mental health facility. Shawnice was sexually molested and raped repeatedly over a two-year period by her mother's live-in boyfriend. As a result of the trauma Shawnice experienced, she suffers intense nightmares. She also believes that the man who assaulted her will find her and hurt her again. One of the symptoms of the PTSD is an aversion to men. Shawnice will only speak to and interact with female staff. Whenever male staff attempt to interact, Shawnice becomes very hostile and aggressive.

Implications

PTSD is a serious mental health condition that needs to be addressed with therapy. Any person that works with students with PTSD needs to understand the stimuli that trigger anxiety, and limit exposure to it. In the above example, Shawnice needs to interact with female staff whenever possible. Efforts to overcome her anxiety need to be implemented in collaboration with the therapist. Students with PTSD should be afforded choices regarding the conditions of participation. Shawnice, for example, may choose to ride a bicycle with a group of boys and girls. She may not, however, choose to sit in the same canoe with a boy. Staff without an understanding of PTSD may dismiss Shawnice's refusal in the previous example as belligerence. In fact, it is a very predictable response considering Shawnice's disorder.

Power Struggles

A power struggle refers to a verbal battle of wills between a staff and a student. Engaging in power struggles is one of the most common errors of inexperienced staff. It is counter-productive in establishing a positive learning climate, and often results in escalating students to a confrontational and aggressive state. Power struggles begin when a staff person presents a direction to a student who opposes the direction. The staff then internalizes this opposition as a challenge to his or her authority. Staff then approach the situation as a "me versus you" type dynamic.

Example 8-13: Power Struggle

Mr. Jones observed Melvin wearing his baseball cap in the hallway which is against school rules. Mr. Jones addressed Melvin, "Take your hat off... you're inside the school now." Melvin answered, "No shit!," as his friends began to laugh. Mr. Jones walked quickly to get in front of Melvin and his friends. Again he commanded, "I said off with the hat!" Melvin answered in an agitated voice, "Man I heard you...now get out of my face!" As Melvin maneuvered to walk around, Mr. Jones stepped in front of Melvin again. Mr. Jones informed Melvin, "I will get out of your face when you take off the hat." Melvin stepped up to Mr. Jones' face and said, "Make me take it off." Mr. Jones reached up to grab the hat and Melvin grabbed him by the collar. Both were locked in a wrestling-type position when staff separated the two. Mr. Jones was reprimanded by the principal for his part in the power struggle. Melvin was suspended for assaulting a teacher.

Implications

Staff that perceive that they have power over students are misguided. Students with emotional disabilities are practiced at identifying staff who are vulnerable to power struggles and they will exploit the staff every chance they get. Students who are diagnosed Oppositional Defiant Disorder (ODD) are experts at this type of manipulation of staff. ODD is characterized by a pattern of negative, disobedient, and hostile behavior. Students who are oppositional-defiant intentionally choose to not follow the directions of adults. They commonly engage in behaviors that elicit directions from staff—then they challenge the direction.

The key to avoiding power struggles is to reframe the dynamics of the student-staff relationship. It is not productive to view the staff role as one assuming a position of "power." In fact, therapeutic environments empower students to take control of their decisions, actions, and the corresponding outcomes. The staff is responsible for communicating choices and following through with consequences, but ultimately the "power" of choice belongs to the student.

In example 8-13, Mr. Jones could have easily avoided the power struggle. The first thing he needed to do was to call Melvin aside away from his friends. This allows Melvin to work with Mr. Jones without his peer audience. Mr. Jones should have reminded Melvin that school rules do not allow hats in the building. Mr. Jones should have asked Melvin if there was a reason why he was wearing the hat in the building. There is a chance that Melvin may have a reason, such as an embarrassing haircut. If this is the case then Mr. Jones needs to help Melvin with the problem, which is not the hat. If there is no reason other than defiance, Mr. Jones needs to present two options to Melvin. First the good choice. "Melvin, if you take the hat off you may keep it—and keep your eligibility to play in the big game after school." Then the bad choice. "If you choose to keep it on, I will inform the coach that you may not play in the game after school." Mr. Jones could allow Melvin some time to think about it, so the choices are not viewed as an ultimatum. Mr. Jones needs to follow through with the consequence once Melvin makes his choice. Whatever Melvin chooses, Mr. Jones was not in a position to win or lose a battle—the power was held by Melvin.

Prevention Strategies

Staff who are experienced working with people with emotional disabilities will support that it is easier to prevent behavioral problems than to intervene once they occur. The prevention of inappropriate behavior does not happen by accident. It occurs through tediously planning the educational environment, creating developmentally appropriate content, establishing consistent and fair policies and routines, researching student disabilities and psychosocial histories, and interacting with students in a therapeutic manner.

Proactive Environment

A proactive environment includes designing the physical set up of the facility to maximize learning and motivation, and to minimize distractions and off-task behavior. Staff need to consider the appropriate lighting and temperature for the activity. Equipment needs to be stored out of the way, but accessible when needed. A method for distributing and collecting equipment also needs to be considered.

Curriculum Content

There is a direct negative correlation between poor instructional content and inappropriate behaviors. When students perceive the material is boring or not relevant to their lives, the likelihood of behavioral disruptions increases. This point cannot be stressed enough. Staff need to understand the population for whom they are planning. When staff provide interesting and challenging activities for students, half of the work is finished with respect to preventing behavioral problems.

Example 8-14: Curriculum Content

Staff from an alternative high school planned a rock-climbing trip with a group of behaviorally challenged adolescents. The purpose of the trip was to build trust and establish a foundation of teamwork among peers and staff. During the three-hour activity, 90 minutes were spent teaching the students to put on their own harnesses. Many of the students had learning disabilities that impeded their ability to untangle, position, and fasten the harnesses. Several of the students became frustrated with the harnesses and quit the activity. Out of 12 students, only six were able to climb, and for only a short period of time. If the activity was planned better, the staff would have recognized the harnessing difficulties and simply provided assistance until all students were harnessed. Because the trip turned into a "harnessing" workshop, the objective of the trip was not met.

Routines, Policies, and Procedures

Students with behavioral challenges zero in on a disorganized environment. Students will determine the level of consistency and organization within a program on the first day. Students will test staff by asking to go to the bathroom. If the response is not part of an established policy or routine, this communicates an opportunity to abuse this privilege. Likewise, students will seek some method to the schedule of events or activities. If there is no schedule or calendar, this communicates disorganization, or even worse—that staff can be influenced to change the activities.

Students will test the discipline procedure to see where the staff limits are and what the consequences are. If the first few students who behave inappropriately are not addressed with consistency, students will perceive the staff to be unfair.

Staff need to brainstorm what types of questions and challenges students will present, and establish policies for them. An example would be to foresee that students will need to visit the restroom at some point. The policy could be established that one student at a time may visit the restroom, once they receive a designated pass from the teacher.

Knowledge of Student Disability and History

Staff working with students with behavioral problems need to get information regarding the student's disability and behavioral history. Parents may sign a release which affords designated individuals access to confidential student records. If records are not available, parents or guardians may be able to share information that will help staff to understand a student's history of behavioral difficulty. It would be important to learn, for example, that a student had a history of bullying younger children. It would be appropriate then, for the staff to closely supervise any interaction with younger children.

Therapeutic Staff Interaction

Student behavior occurs, for better or worse, in response to interactions with others. Negative peer interactions are often the catalysts for acting-out behaviors, including cursing, threatening, arguing, and physical fighting. The staff that work with students with emotional challenges need to be trained in how to communicate with students in a proactive, non-threatening, and professional manner. This is referred to as therapeutic staff interaction. One organization that trains professionals to interact therapeutically with students is the Crisis Prevention Institute (CPI). This training teaches people how to recognize that a student is "escalating" emotionally, as well as how to act and what to say to help the student "de-escalate" or calm down. CPI also trains professionals to stop inappropriate behaviors, and to physically escort or restrain combative students.

Intervention Strategies

While emphasis on prevention is effective in decreasing the majority of inappropriate behaviors, some behavioral problems are inevitable. Skilled providers recognize when prevention techniques have been ineffective, and employ intervention strategies. The following interventions are designed to provide students with clear, firm assistance to work through emotional difficulties. Programs that include students with emotional challenges must be prepared to carry out interventions in a therapeutic manner. Students will test the program and staff readiness by acting out behaviorally—breaking rules, cursing, threatening, fighting, and generally refusing to follow directions. These are the very behaviors that have caused them to be excluded from many other programs. This is also the point in which poorly trained staff members have failed these at-risk students. Programs that have staff who are willing and ready to employ therapeutic interventions will best serve students with emotional disabilities. The use of therapeutic interventions creates a positive and safe environment in which students may learn to work through decision making, anger management, authority issues, and other personal challenges. These are the skills that make or break a program in terms of serving students with emotional disabilities. Each of the following interventions are comprehensive strategies that require practice and refinement under qualified supervision. They are not simply concepts that can be read once and immediately used. The employment of interventions should be thought of as an "art."

Limit Setting

Limits may be thought of as the boundary for established rules in a given program. Adults recognize that most public roads have posted maximum speeds, known as the speed limit. One of the established rules for driving is to keep one's speed under the "limit." The speed limit example is also a great example of what happens when limits are not consistently enforced—many people regularly exceed the posted maximum speed when law enforcement officers are not in sight. In fact, the radar-detection industry is based upon helping drivers break the limit without being caught! Testing established limits is no different for children—especially those with emotional challenges.

Example 8-15: Limit Setting

A recreational baseball team establishes that teasing other players is against the rules. Hence, a "no teasing" limit is established. Michael laughed out loud when Josh struck out. Consciously, or unconsciously, Michael had tested the limit.

Staff response 1: None of the coaches addressed Michael's laughter. One heard him laugh, but figured ignoring it was the best response. Soon other students decided to join in. By the end of the game, several players were laughing and booing their teammates after they struck out. The coach addressed the team after the game and reviewed the rules. During the next several games, coaches "nagged" at Michael to stop him from teasing. Michael responded by arguing with the coaches. He yelled back, "If you were any good you could teach these scrubs how to hit!" After the third game, Michael was thrown off the team.

Staff Response 2: The first time Michael laughed, Mr. Will spoke with Michael away from his teammates in private. "Michael, we do not laugh at people who strike out on this team. Laughing is teasing, and it hurts people's feelings. Players that tease sit on the bench. You are one of our best players, we want you on the field, not on the bench." Michael told Mr. Will that he understood. Mr. Will informed Michael that this was "strike one." The consequence for "strike two teasing" was one inning on the bench. The consequence for "strike three teasing" was removal from the game to go home with his parents. The limit was communicated as, "Michael, you can play positively or you can sit on the bench." Michael will likely test Mr. Will's limits by teasing a second and or third time. Once he understands that the rule will be enforced consistently and fairly, he is more likely to follow it.

Consider the implications if law enforcement had the ability to monitor each vehicle's speed accurately and consistently—with radar and photography. This is a reality for the limit of "running red lights." When a person receives a photograph of their vehicle travelling through a red light, and the accompanying citation in the mail, the net result is increased compliance with the law.

Re-Direction

Re-direction is a strategy for avoiding power-struggles and arguments. Typically, students will avoid accepting responsibility if they can engage the staff member in a verbal battle of wits. The first challenge is to recognize that the student is manipulating the situation. The second challenge is to remain calm, and speak "matter of factly." The re-direction intervention is like a verbal road-block. It is designed to accomplish two objectives: (A) to communicate to the student that his or her comments have no effect on the staff personally (B) to provide a direction for the student to follow to get back on task.

Once the student is back on task, he or she is praised and reinforced for choosing to be positive.

Example 8-16: Re-Direction

Michael, in example 8-15, may have responded differently to Mr. Will after his laughter was addressed the first time. Consider the following scenario in which Michael challenges Mr. Will's observation. Michael protests, "I did not laugh. Chris laughed and you thought it was me! You always pick on me, even when I didn't do anything wrong! Chris is your pet player anyway...you never yell at him!" If Mr. Will responds to Michael's comments rationally, Michael will likely keep the dialogue going to divert the focus of the discussion away from his personal accountability. Mr. Will, however, recognizes the ploy as an attempted power struggle and provides a re-direction statement. "Michael, we are not talking about anyone but you right now. This is strike one for you. Be a positive player or you will sit out for an inning." Any further attempt to argue should result in a repeat of the re-direction statement, "Your direction is to return to the game and be a positive player." If Michael escalates emotionally, or refuses to return to the game, the coach should be clear that Michael is in control of his choices. The choice to return to the game can keep "a small thing small." The choice to continue arguing might result in strike two—and removal from the game for an inning.

Note that re-direction is very effective, except when the student believes he or she was treated unfairly. For example, if there was a chance that Chris was at fault, and Michael was blamed, the coach would likely experience much more resistance from Michael. These situations commonly end with the student resisting until the most severe consequence is issued. The key is for staff to issue re-directives when they are certain that the student was responsible. If there is a reasonable doubt, students should not receive punitive consequences. Instead, the staff should communicate concern, and alert the student that staff will be aware and observant for future inappropriate behaviors.

Therapeutic Time-Out

Time-out is called many different things and defined in many different ways. It is defined for our purposes as a three-step therapeutic procedure.

1. Staff communicate which behavior was inappropriate and direct the student to "take a minute" in a designated space away from his or her peers.
2. The involved staff person meets with the student to "process." Processing involves student recognition and acceptance of responsibility of an inappropriate behavior. The staff person also communicates the positive outcomes of making good choices (to stop the inappropriate behavior) and the consequences for making bad choices (continue the inappropriate behavior).
3. The student then verbally agrees to follow staff directions and make good choices. The staff person welcomes the student back into the activity in a positive manner.

Time-out as we have defined it works. It works because it is presented in a positive way. Students do not feel punished when taking a minute. Oftentimes, they need the minute to re-group and "get back on track." Most importantly, they are not embarrassed in the presence of their peers. Attempting to set limits in front of peers can be risky in that students often feel the need to "save face" and challenge the limits.

Staff who use this process as a demonstration of "power" over the students are destined for difficulties. The student needs to feel empowered to make choices. The staff simply need to be prepared to intervene and follow through with the consequences of the limits if "bad" choices are made. Students who feel "empowered" will be more likely to make appropriate choices.

Restriction and Removal

Removal of a student from an activity should be the last-resort intervention. Students will sometimes push limits to the last consequence to see what happens when the behavior system is tested. Removal does not mean "permanent" removal from the program or activity. Removal occurs at different levels, depending on the severity of the inappropriate behavior and the frequency of occurrence.

A. Intra-Activity Removal (penalty box concept)-A student is removed for a part of the activity or game, but allowed to re-enter. Example: Michael is "benched" for one inning.
B. Activity Restriction-The student is allowed to remain on site, but restricted in terms of participation, privilege, and/or activity level. Example: Michael loses the privilege of sitting on the bench, and is required to sit with his father during at-bats.
C. Temporary Removal (suspension concept)-The student is suspended for a designated period in which at least one game is missed. Example: Michael is suspended for the second game, but may participate in the third game of the season.
D. Seasonal Removal (expulsion concept)-The student is expelled from all activities during a cyclical period or season. Example: Michael is removed for the season, but may participate next spring.

Non-Violent Physical Crisis Intervention

Students who demonstrate behaviors that risk injury to themselves or others require "hands-on intervention." This should be executed by staff who are trained in safe hands-on practices. Staff that restrain or "hold" students put themselves at risk of being sued. Organizations that provide training in non-violent physical crisis intervention will usually provide documentation and testimony verifying the efficacy of the techniques and practices, given they were employed according to the program guidelines.

Example 8-17: Non-Violent Physical Crisis Intervention

Michael's coaches met with his parents before the season began, and discussed his history of behavior problems on sports teams. Michael's parents agreed to sign a document that allowed his coaches to physically restrain Michael if he displayed dangerous behavior. Four of Michael's coaches attended an eight-hour Crisis Prevention Institute (CPI) training session. During the third game of the season, Michael became angry at an umpire for calling the third strike. Michael argued, and his coaches attempted to re-direct him. The umpire, a 19-year old-volunteer, argued back at Michael. Michael continued to escalate until he charged at the umpire swinging a bat. The coaches held onto Michael's arms, and escorted him off the field. Michael was allowed to vent his anger away from the crowd, until he could talk calmly and rationally. Mr. Will suspended Michael for the fourth game, and invited him to return for the fifth game of the season. Michael understood that he earned strike one assault. Strike two assault resulted in a two-game suspension, and strike three assault meant expulsion for the season.

Chapter 9

When Help is Needed: Resources and Materials

Carol Ann Baglin

Buzz Williams

Intervening with children requires supports, resources, and the everyday bag of tricks. Sometimes a phone call to a specialized organization is enough, other times a game is needed. The trained professional occasionally needs a specialized instrument for assessment or a text to provide a new idea. While varied, the resources below are only a small sample of what is available. A search of the internet can provide a wider range of materials and information on special topics.

Associations

- **Access Limited**
  570 Hance RD
  Binghamton, NY 13903
  800-849-2143
  www.accessinlimited.com
  Provides information and consultation on the use of personal computers for children with disabilities to overall barriers.
- **Adaptive Sports Center**
  PO Box 1639
  Crested Butte, CO 81224
  www.adaptivesports.org
- **American Academy of Pediatrics**
  141 NW Point Blvd
  Elk GroveVillage, IL 60007
  847-228-5005
  www.aap.org
  Pediatric information and referrals for children and adolescents related to health and treatment issues.
- **American Association of Music Therapy**
  8455 Colesville RD
  Suite 1000
  Silver Spring, MD 20910
  301-589-3300
  www.musictherapy.org
- **American Association of People with Disabilities**
  1819 H Street
  Suite 330
  Washington, D.C. 20006
  800-840-8844
  www.aapd-dc.org

- **American Camping Association**
  5000 Satae RD 67N
  Martinsville, IN 46151
  800-653-1409
  www.acacamps.org
- **American Counseling Association**
  5999 Stevenson Avenue
  Alexandria, VA 22209
  800-347-6647
  www.counseling.org
- **American Society for Adolescent Psychiatry (ASAP)**
  PO Box 28218
  Dallas, TX 75228
  972-686-6166
- **Arts in Psychotherapy**
  PO Box 945
  New York, NY 10159-0945
  212-633-3730
- **Bazelton Center for Mental Health Law**
  1101 15th Street NW, Suite 1212
  Washington, D.C. 20005
  202-265-6363
  www.bazelton.org
- **Behavior Therapy and Research Society**
  Temple University Medical School
  Philadelphia, PA 19129
  352-344-2212
- **Federation of Families for Children's Mental Health**
  1021 Prince Street
  Alexandria, VA 22313
  703-684-7722
- **ERIC Clearinghouse on Disabilities and Special Education**
  1110 Glebe Road
  Arlington, VA 22201
  800-328-0272
  www.ericec.org
- **Family Resource Center on Disabilities**
  20 E. Jackson
  Suite 300
  Chicago, IL 60604
  800-952-4199
- **Mental Illness Foundation**
  772 W. 168th Street
  New York, NY 10032
  212-682-4699
- **National Information Center for Children and Youth with Disabilities (NICHCY)**
  PO Box 1492
  Washington, D.C. 20013
  800-695-0285
  www.nichcy.org

- **National Mental Health Association**
  1021 Prince Street
  Alexandria, VA 22314
  800-969-NMHA
  www.nmha.org

Internet Web Sites

www.accessible.org.uk Accessible Games Book.
www.specialolympics.org Special Olympics.
www.ymca.net YMCA. A comprehensive resource for community sport and recreation.
www.policeathleticleague.org Police Athletic League (PAL) recreation centers.
www.outwardbound.org Outdoor adventure activities.
www.optionsforspecialkids.com Nationwide consultation service.
www.aahperd.org American Alliance for Health, Physical Education and Recreation.
www.acacamps.org American Camping Association.
www.palaestra.com Resource Magazine for parents of students with special needs.

Parent Support and Information

- Toys "R" US Guide for Differently-Abled Kids (2001), Geofrey, Inc.
  http://www.toysrus.com/
- Stein, S. B. (1974). *About handicaps: An open family book for parents and children together.* New York: Walker & Co.
- Special Olympics
- Exceptional Parent: Magazine for parents and professionals to assist in the care of children with special needs. http://www.eparent.com

Games

- Behavior Skills Game: Learning How People Should Act
  (Game Board and Supplies Published by PCI Educational Publishing)
  This game helps individuals learn what behavior is acceptable, stressing responsibility for actions and encourages self-control.
  > Source: Idyll Arbor, Inc
  > > 25119 SE 262nd Street
  > > PO Box 720
  > > Ravensdale, WA 98051

- Social Skills Game: Learning to Get Along wit People
  (Game Board and Supplies Published by PCI Educational Publishing)
  This game focuses on socialization skills which are appropriate to everyday life situations.
  > Source: Idyll Arbor, Inc
  > > 25119 SE 262nd Street
  > > PO Box 720
  > > Ravensdale, WA 98051

Books

American Psychiatric Association. (1994). *Diagnostic and Statistical Manual of Mental Disorders* (4th ed.). Washington D.C.

Charles, C.M. (1996). *Building Classroom Discipline* (5th ed.). Longman Publishers USA: San Diego State University.

Hartwig, E. P., & Ruesch, G. M. (2001). *Discipline in the School.* Horsham, PA: LRP Publications.

Kohn, A. (1993). *Punished by Rewards: The Trouble with Gold Stars, Incentive Plans, A's, Praise, and Other Bribes.* Boston: Houghton Mifflin Company

Muss, R.E. (1988). *Theories of Adolescence.* (5th ed.). New York: McGraw Hill.

Muss, R. E., & Porton, H. D. (1998). *Adolescent Behavior and Society: A Book of Readings* (5th ed.). McGraw-Hill College: Boston.

Wunderlich, K.C. (1988). *The Teacher's Guide to Behavioral Interventions.* Hawthorne Educational Services: Columbia, Missouri.

Assessment Measures

- General Recreation Screening Tool (GRST)
  Manual and Score Sheets: Written for individuals with MR/DD to measure the general developmental level in 18 areas related to leisure. 15 minutes to administer.
    Source: Idyll Arbor, Inc
           25119 SE 262nd Street
           PO Box 720
           Ravensdale, WA 98051

- Leisure Competence Measure (LCM)
  The LCM is a testing tool to be used by recreational therapists to measure outcomes in recreational therapy, including leisure awareness, leisure attitude, leisure skills, cultural/social behaviors, interpersonal skills, community integration skills, social contact and community participation.
  Published by LCM Data Systems
    Source: Idyll Arbor, Inc
           25119 SE 262nd Street
           PO Box 720
           Ravensdale, WA 98051

- Therapeutic Recreation Activity Assessment (TRAA)
  The TRAA measures fine and gross motor, social behaviors, expressive and receptive communication, and cognitive skills. Can be administered to four individuals in 30 minutes and includes three activities to assess functional abilities.
    Source: Idyll Arbor, Inc
           25119 SE 262nd Street
           PO Box 720
           Ravensdale, WA 98051

- *Systematic Screening for Behavior Disorders (SSBD): Identify Students at Risk of Developing Behavior Disorders*
  The SSBD provides a systematic screening of students who may be at risk for developing behavior disorders. SSBS consists of three manuals and training tapes.
    Source: Council for Exceptional Children
           1-888-CEC-SPED

- *Early Screening Project (ESP): A Proven Child-Find Process*
Three-stage screening process provides for early intervention by identifying three-to five-year-olds experiencing preschool adjustment problems.
Source: Council for Exceptional Children
1-888-CEC-SPED

Professional Resources

Council of Exceptional Children 1-888-CECSPED

- *Strategies and Procedures in Designing Proactive Interventions with a Culturally Diverse Population of Students with Emotional or Behavioral Disorders and Their Families/Caregivers*
By Gloria D. Campbell-Whatley and Ralph Gardner, IIII
2002, 27 pp.

- *Dealing with Behaviors Perceived as Unacceptable in Schools: The Interim Alternative Educational Setting Solution*
By Reece L. Peterson and Carl R. Smith
2002, 34 pp

- *Culturally and Linguistically Diverse Learners with Behavioral Disorders*
Gwendolyn Cartledge and Kai Yung (Brian) Ram, Editors
2002, 74 pp

- *Applying a Systems Approach to School-Wide Discipline in Secondary Schools: What We Are Learning and Need to Learn*
Teri Levis-Palmer, Brigid Flannery, George Sugai, and Lucille Eber
2002, 59 pp.

- *Developing School and Community Partnerships to Meet the Needs of Students with Challenging Behaviors*
Don Somerville & Shirley McDonald
2002, 45 pp

- *Back Off, Cool Down, Try Again: Teaching Students How to Control Aggressive Behavior*
Sylvia Rockwell
1995, 144 pp

- *Beyond Time Out: A Practical Guide to Understanding and Serving Students with Behavioral Impairments in the Public Schools, Second Edition*
John Stewart
2002, 195 pp

- *Developing Positive Behavioral Support for Students with Challenging Behaviors*
George Sugai and Timothy J. Lewis
1999, 57 pp

- *First Step to Success: An Early Intervention Program for Antisocial Kindergartners*
  Hill M. Walker
  Kit designed to divert antisocial kindergartners from problems in the school and community. It teaches the at-risk child behavior patterns that promote school success and the development of friendships.

- *Positive Academic and Behavioral Supports: Creating Safe, Effective and Nurturing Schools for All Students*
  Lyndal M. Bullock and Robert A. Gable
  2000, 56 pp

- *Behavior Intervention Planning: Using the Functional Behavioral Assessment Data*
  Terry M. Scott, Carol J. Liaupsin, & C. Michael Nelson
  Interactive CD designed to include a six-step process.

- *Interim Alternative Educational Settings for Children With Disabilities*
  George Bear, Mary Magee Quinn, & Susan Burkholder
  National Association of School Psychologists
  2001, 54 pp

Other Sources

- *Functional Assessment and Program Development for Problem Behavior: A Practical Handbook*
  Robert E. O'Neill, Robert H. Horner, Richard W. Albin, Jeffrey R. Sprague, Keith Storey, & J. Stephen Newton
  1997, 122 pp
  Brooks/Cole Publishing Company
  511 Forest Lodge RD
  Pacific Grove, CA 93950-9968

- *Teacher Smart! 125 Tested Techniques for Classroom Management & Control*
  George Watson
  1996, 228 pp
  The Center for Applied Research in Education
  http://www.phdirect.com

- *Special Kids Problem Solver: Ready-to-Use Interventions for Helping All Students with Academic, Behavioral & Physical Problems*
  Kenneth Shore
  1998, 366 pp
  Prentice-Hall
  http://www.phdirect.com

- *Providing Special Education Services to Students with Behavioral-Emotional Disabilities: Teacher's Guide*
  Public Schools of North Carolina
  State Board of Education
  Department of Public Instruction

- *Up to PAR: Designing Positive Learning Environments for All Students: A Team-Based Inclusive Support Model for Preventing, Acting Upon, and Resolving Troubling Behaviors*
  Michael Rosenberg & Lori A. Jackman
  Johns Hopkins University

- *Points for Good Behavior: Cost-Effective Strategies to Prevent Disruptive Behavior in Schools*
  July, 2000
  Advocates for Children and Youth
  www.acy.org

Catalogs
- Childswork Childsplay. A catalog addressing the social and emotional needs of children and adolescents. 1-800-962-1141

- Oriental Trading Company. (A catalog for ordering reward novelties and toys). 1-800-228-2269

- Hawthorne Educational Services Catalog. (A catalog for ordering resources for professionals working with children and adolescents with social and emotional disabilities). 1-800-442-9509

Magazines/Journals
- *Beyond Behavior.* A magazine exploring behavior in our schools.
  Council for Children with Behavioral Disorders
  1-703-620-3660

- *Preventing School Failure*
  Heldref Publications
  1-202-296-6227

Organizations
- National Crisis Prevention Institute, Inc. (An organization providing certification training for staff members working with children and adolescents with social and emotional disabilities). 1-800-558-8976

Index

disturbed neurotics, 21

E

eating disorders, 17

edible reinforcers, 139

Education for All Handicapped Children Act, 105

Education of the Handicapped Act, 104, 105

Elementary and Secondary Education Act (ESEA), 104

emotional disturbance, definition of, 2–3

F

Functional Behavioral Assessments (FBAs). *see also* Behavioral Assessment and Intervention (Maryland State Department of Education)
    definition and purpose of, 36, 38
    definitions of terms used in, 37
    identifying the functions of student behavior, 36
    process of, 36–39
    using a collaborative team approach, 38–39

G

games, 173

goal defending sports, strategies for adapting, 79–80

guidance counselors, as service providers, 111

H

Handicapped Children's Early Education Program (HCEEP), 104

harassment and teasing, 159–60

Head Start, 104

hockey, strategies for adapting, 79–80

homicidal, self-injurious, and suicidal behaviors, 19–20

I

identifying children with emotional and behavior problems, 25–28

Individual, Preparatory, Inclusive (IPI) instructional model, 135–36

Individuals with Disabilities Education Act (IDEA), 4, 9, 35–36

Interim Alternative Educational Settings (IAES), 35

Internet web sites, 173

intimidation, 158–59

I statements, 142–43

K

"Katie Beckett" Waiver, 107

L

lacrosse, strategies for adapting, 79–80

learning disabilities, and disorders/challenging behaviors, 23

leisure activities, adapting. *see* sport, recreation, and leisure

leisure goals and dynamics. *see* sport, recreation, and leisure

limit setting, 167

M

mandala drawing, 94–96

Manic-Depressive Disorder, 19

manipulation, 155

medication, and disorders/challenging behaviors, 22–23

Mills v. Board of Education, 105

misbehavior, vs. behavior, 24

mood disorders, 19

movement therapists, as service providers, 112

music therapists, as service providers, 111

N

negative reinforcement, 139

neglect and abuse, behaviors resulting from, 20–21

nurse/practitioners, as service providers, 112

nurses, as service providers, 112

O

Obsessive/Compulsive Disorder (OCD), 16

Oppositional/Defiant Disorder (ODD), 15–16

P

panic, 161

paraverbal communication, 142

Authors

- Carol Ann Baglin, Ed. D.
  Assistant State Superintendent
  Division of Special Education/Early Intervention Services
  Maryland State Department of Education

- M. E. B. Lewis, Ed. D.
  Principal, Lower School
  Kennedy Krieger Institute
  Baltimore, Maryland

- Dwayne (Buzz) Williams, M. S.
  Director of Physical Education
  Kennedy Krieger Institute
  Baltimore, Maryland

- Valerie Smitheman-Brown
  Recreation Therapist
  Kennedy Krieger Institute
  Baltimore, Maryland

Chapter Co-authors:

- Donna Riley
  Policy and Resource Specialist
  Division of Special Education/Early Intervention Services
  Maryland State Department of Education

- Timothy McCormick, J. D.
  Consultant
  Maryland State Department of Education

- Stephen Bender
  Summer Intern
  Teacher
  Baltimore County Public Schools